Political Participation in Communist China

By James R. Townsend

Political Participation in Communist China offers the first systematic study of a phenomenon that is central to an understanding of political development in contemporary China—the political mobilization of the people in support of government objectives. As the book proceeds, the reader gains insight into the roles of workers, peasants, and housewives in the Communist political process, and into the significance of their participation for political change in modern China.

Mr. Townsend's analysis explores two major themes: the role of popular participation in the political system of Communist China, and the place of contemporary patterns of political participation in relation to modern Chinese history.

He begins with a consideration of the Chinese Communist style of political participation, discussing the influence of the pre-Communist political setting, Soviet Marxism and the historical experience of the Chinese Com-

THE CENTER FOR CHINESE STUDIES

at the University of California, Berkeley, supported by the
Ford Foundation, the Institute of International Studies
(University of California, Berkeley), and the State of
California, is the unifying organization for social science
and interdisciplinary research on contemporary China.

Publications

Schurmann, Franz. *Ideology and Organization in Communist China.*

Wakeman, Frederic, Jr. *Strangers at the Gate: Social Disorder in South China, 1839–1861.*

POLITICAL PARTICIPATION IN COMMUNIST CHINA

Political Participation

in Communist China

JAMES R. TOWNSEND

University of California Press
Berkeley and Los Angeles · 1967

University of California Press
Berkeley and Los Angeles, California
Cambridge University Press
London, England
Copyright © 1967, by
The Regents of the University of California
Library of Congress Catalog Card Number: 67–11422
Printed in the United States of America

To my Parents

PREFACE

Any study of political participation unavoidably raises questions about popular political attitudes and responses. In the case of Communist China, the student cannot answer such questions with certainty, yet he cannot ignore them in his analysis. I have tried, therefore, to focus my attention on the more formal aspects of the subject that are most open to analysis from a distance, while keeping my judgments about popular response to a minimum. As for the "objectivity" of these judgments, I can only say that I have weighed a variety of dissimilar and frequently conflicting evidence in arriving at my admittedly impressionistic conclusions about how the Chinese people have responded to Communist rule. The passage of time and the more systematic acquisition of data from documents, observers, and refugees will permit more confident judgments on this question, which surely lies at the heart of an understanding of political change in modern China. For the present, I hope that my largely institutional approach to the study of political participation in China will help to explain the scope and significance of the subject and to suggest some of the directions that future analysis ought to take.

As this manuscript goes to press in the summer of 1966, a massive campaign is sweeping across China. The "great proletarian cultural revolution," as the movement is known, is in part a direct extension and culmination of the campaigns of 1963–1965, all of which featured ideological indoctrination in the revolutionary Maoist style as a defense against the rise of "bourgeois" and "revisionist" influences both within and without the People's Republic. The "cultural revolution" goes beyond its predecessors in two important respects, however. First, it has attacked not only the vague specter of revisionism, but also a large number of specific individuals, some of them of the highest rank. Second, it has relied heavily on the militant and sometimes violent activities of the "red guards," a new mass organization of young students which has become the chief vehicle for carrying the "cultural revolution" to the people.

Initially, the campaign and purge of 1966 has elevated Lin Piao to the position of Mao Tse-tung's likely successor and has produced in

China an atmosphere of revolutionary struggle that is more genuine than at any time since the early 1950's. It would be premature to assess these changes here, or even to imply that they are permanent. Nonetheless, it is relevant to observe that the current movement demonstrates the Chinese leadership's determination to maintain the revolutionary style of mass mobilization described in this book. The "red guards" are an excellent example of the use of direct mass action to carry out the wishes of the leadership, even when this action bypasses or disrupts established political institutions. Even more important, however, is evidence of increasing resistance to, and tension within, the Chinese Communist pattern of popular political participation. The Mao-Lin leadership has reaffirmed its revolutionary style, but only at the cost of an extensive purge within the Communist Party and some physical resistance to the "red guards" from various strata of Chinese society. It has never been more evident that the attempt to perpetuate the revolution makes it increasingly difficult for the Communist Party to mobilize unified popular support behind its program.

Many people have assisted me in the execution of this book by offering their criticism and suggestions. I owe a particular debt to Robert Scalapino, who has for many years lent his encouragement and support to my studies of Communist China; his reading of the manuscript has been responsible for many improvements in it. My special thanks go to John Schaar and Franz Schurmann, who read the manuscript at various stages of completion and from whose ideas I have profited greatly. The suggestions of others whom I shall not name individually are also gratefully acknowledged. Much of the research on this study was made possible by the generous financial assistance of a Ford Foundation Foreign Area Training Fellowship during 1961–1963. Financial support from the Center for Chinese Studies at the University of California, Berkeley, and from Rockefeller funds administered by the Department of Political Science at Berkeley, also contributed to the progress and completion of the manuscript. My research was greatly facilitated by the assistance of the staff of the Union Research Institute in Hong Kong, to whom I express my gratitude.

Although it is a pleasure to acknowledge my debt to these individuals and institutions, they are not necessarily in agreement with the views expressed in this study. Responsibility for the content of the book rests with me alone.

                                                                              J.R.T.

CONTENTS

KEY TO ABBREVIATIONS

APC	Agricultural Producers' Cooperative
CB	*Current Background*
CCP	Chinese Communist Party
CPPCC	Chinese People's Political Consultative Conference
CPR	Chinese People's Republic
FLP	Foreign Languages Press
JMJP	*Jen-min Jih-pao*
KMJP	*Kuang-ming Jih-pao*
KMT	Kuomintang
NCNA	New China News Agency (*Hsin Hua She*)
NPC	National People's Congress
PLA	People's Liberation Army
PPC	People's Political Council
SCMP	*Survey of China Mainland Press*
SMM	*Selections from China Mainland Magazines*. Also refers to *Extracts from China Mainland Magazines*.

ONE

Introduction

The changing political life of the masses is a recurrent and powerful theme in the Chinese revolution. Many who have studied or witnessed this revolution, in either its past or present phases, have called attention to the rising political consciousness and activity of the Chinese people. Today, this trend has apparently reached a peak in the political system established by the Chinese Communist Party (CCP) in 1949. Commentators on the growing politicization of the Chinese people have affirmed, albeit from diverse points of view, the critical importance of this phenomenon. In so doing, they have suggested two major considerations that are the primary foci of this book. One is the place of contemporary patterns of participation in the political history of modern China; the other is the role of popular participation in the political system of Communist China.

Although these considerations do not require the introduction of materials drawn from other countries and cultures, there is nonetheless a significant comparative interest in analysis of political participation in China. Most obviously, this interest lies in the study of political development and the related concepts of nation-building and political modernization. Leonard Binder has stated that "political development" is a further specification of the more general term "political change" when political change in any historical period has a particular direction.[1] The conviction that political change in the modern era is in fact moving in a particular direction is widespread. Literature in this field consistently refers to broadly similar political changes that derive from global trends toward industrialization, urbanization, and the spread of organization and technology; it cites increasing specialization in governmental structure and performance, the rational recruitment and placement of political actors, the growth of power and effectiveness of central governments, and the drive for nation-state status with an integrated and nationally conscious citizenry as among the main political characteristics of "devel-

[1] Leonard Binder, "National Integration and Political Development," *American Political Science Review*, 58:3 (September, 1964), p. 622.

opment" or "modernization." To be sure, there is throughout this literature persistent and profound disagreement on the specifics of the terminal point and the subtleties of the process. At the same time, there is broad agreement that political development does include increasing popular participation in politics and increasing contact between state and citizen.[2] As a recent book has observed, one of the clear aspects of the emerging "world culture" is what might be called the "participation explosion"—the near universality of the belief that the ordinary man should be an involved participant in the political system.[3] It is equally clear that, in this case, action follows closely on belief, for the growth of popular political action among peoples long isolated from politics is a fact of recent history. The "participation explosion" that China is now experiencing is not, therefore, an isolated or unique event. Whatever the unique features of China's past and present politics might be, the political awakening of the Chinese people is comparable to similar trends elsewhere, whether recently begun or long established, and is directly relevant to a general understanding of political development.

The fact that China now shares with many other states the experience of the common man's entrance into politics does not necessarily mean that political participation in China is identical to, or even moving toward, varieties of political participation that exist elsewhere. There are, of course, strong similarities between the political process in China and in some other "developing" states that have organized a single-party system with a mass political base. But when we speak of political development it is not sufficient to note similarities among societies at roughly comparable "stages of development." We must also compare societies at different "stages" in an effort to understand the dimensions and dynamics of the "particular direction" that gives political development its meaning. In the specific context of political participation, one of the most critical questions is whether or not the Western democratic style of participation defines the direction that participation in other societies will ultimately take.

One need not be culture-bound to assert that Western experience has a dominant place in any discussion of political participation. In both

[2] For a dissenting view, see Samuel P. Huntington, "Political Development and Political Decay," *World Politics*, 17:3 (April, 1965), pp. 386–430. Huntington argues that most characteristics identified with political development, including popular mobilization, are actually associated with "modernization" rather than "development." Development in his view implies stability and institutionalization, characteristics that may actually suffer during modernization and particularly from the effects of mass mobilization. However, Huntington agrees (p. 388) that mobilization or participation is the most frequently emphasized characteristic of political development in the literature, his own views notwithstanding.

[3] Gabriel L. Almond and Sydney Verba, *The Civic Culture* (Princeton, 1963), p. 4.

theory and practice, the Western political tradition has a uniquely long and intense concern with the citizen's role in politics. To a great extent, it is the diffusion of this tradition, primarily through the intellectual exchange that accompanied Western imperialism, that has been the catalyst in the "participation explosion" elsewhere in the world. The history of modern China attests to this as well as most examples. Still the question remains as to whether or not the Western democratic tradition's role as the source of the "participation explosion" thereby ensures that it will determine the results of the explosion. The answer is hidden in the future, but contemporary political patterns suggest a negative one. In China, at least, there has emerged a style of participation that differs sharply from patterns of participation in the modern democratic state and yet seems certain to endure for a long time to come. A general statement of these differences, anticipating the major points to come, will be useful here.

The Chinese Communist and Western democratic styles of political participation have in common a claim to provide representation of popular interests and a demand for extensive popular participation in political life, but the differences between them far outweigh these common characteristics. First, and most important, perhaps, the Chinese style defines the major function of participation as execution of Party policies, whereas the democratic style defines it as exerting popular influence on political decisions. Second, the Chinese style emphasizes direct contact between cadres and masses as the surest means of eliciting popular participation and keeping political leaders in touch with popular demands. The democratic style relies mainly on representative institutions to transmit popular demands to political leaders and to serve as the arena for political action. Third, the Chinese style insists that popular political action support a supreme, unified national interest as defined solely by the Communist Party; it concedes that partial or temporary interests may conflict with the "true" national interest, and it theoretically allows such interests political expression, but it insists that they must be subordinated to, and ultimately submerged in, the national interest. The democratic style recognizes the existence of a national interest, but sees it as a fluid combination of diverse interests that may legitimately compete, so long as they observe the law, both before and after decisions are made. Fourth, the Chinese style emphasizes the quality and morality of political leaders, rather than legal and institutionalized popular controls, as the guarantee of good government. The democratic style exalts its legal and institutional framework and aims at "a government of laws and not of men." Finally, the Chinese style recognizes no theoretical limits to the extension of demands for political activity and no private obligations that can take precedence over public ones. The democratic style values participation highly but insists that the inviolability of private life places limits, however vaguely defined, on public obligations and permits the individual to abstain from political action if he chooses.

While the foregoing statement is a gross simplification open to many qualifications, it demonstrates that the terms of popular political action in China are quite different from those in the Western democracies. The point bears emphasis here to avoid future misunderstanding: our discussion of political participation in China never implies that the Chinese style of participation is now, or in the future must be, identical to that in the West. An analogy to the diversity that may prevail in the emergence of popular political activity is found in Reinhard Bendix's study of nation-building in several different national settings.[4] Bendix observes a common element—the "orderly exercise of a nationwide, public authority"—in the emergence of nation-states, but he finds that the differing historical and cultural backgrounds of his examples produce major differences in the structure of "nationwide public authority" in each case. A similar conclusion is justified in the study of the development of political participation. Political development may demand a "participation explosion," but it does not demand that participation everywhere develop in the same pattern. As Leonard Binder has suggested, it is precisely this potential for a variety of outcomes that makes the study of development interesting.[5]

Acceptance of diversity does not remove the need for careful identification of the common elements that justify the use of the concept of political development. The focus here, of course, is only on the element of increasing political participation, a term that has not yet been defined with sufficient depth. In our view, political participation includes all those activities through which the individual consciously becomes involved in attempts to give a particular direction to the conduct of public affairs, excluding activities of an occupational or compulsory nature. Several explanatory comments are in order, beginning with the "occupational and compulsory" exclusion. Activities such as state employment, compliance with legal restraints and demands (payment of taxes), or compulsory service to the state (forced labor or military service) are clearly not in themselves forms of political participation; they do not, however, preclude individuals engaged in them from participating in politics in ways independent of the normal content of these activities. Next the definition limits political participation to activities related to "public affairs," that is, affairs that are seen to have an impact on the

[4] Reinhard Bendix, *Nation-Building and Citizenship: Studies of Our Changing Social Order* (New York, 1964).

[5] Binder, *op. cit.*, p. 623.

entire community even when they deal specifically with only a part of it; for the most part, public affairs are those that are, or by community standards ought to be, within the province of government. Participation in the internal affairs of various associations and groups within the community is not political participation unless it somehow involves the participant in affairs relating to the community as a whole.[6] Finally, the definition extends political participation to include participation in the execution of some political decisions, rather than limiting it to participation in decision-making or the selection of decision-makers. The fine line of distinction between "political" and "apolitical" execution of policy is the degree of controversy that surrounds the policy in question. Political struggle (which is essentially what is meant by "attempts to give a particular direction to the conduct of public affairs") does not necessarily end with the authoritative public agency's decision. It may end there if the decision is accepted without controversy and can be realized through routine administration; it does not end there if additional pressures and efforts beyond routine channels of administration are needed to translate the decision into reality. The individual who becomes involved in the execution of a policy with the understanding that he is thereby committing himself to one political viewpoint in opposition to another is engaged in political participation, even though he may have had no part in the original decision.

The most difficult aspect of a definition of political participation is the role of voluntarism. The preceding comments imply that some element of voluntarism must be present, but it is one thing to exclude compulsory acts that are not normally regarded as political and quite another when one must judge the degree of voluntarism or compulsion in the performance of acts that lie at the heart of the citizen's role in politics. The most obvious example of the difficulty is the fact that some democratic governments have made the act of voting a legal obligation, but the discussion moves easily into the realm of social pressure to vote or to support a particular policy and the role of unconscious or irrational factors in various acts that are uniformly regarded as political. There is no universal rule for solving this difficulty, but one point is clear: political participation need not be spontaneous, and even the insistence on voluntarism cannot be too rigid, although it must remain one of the

[6] Many political scientists apply political terminology and analysis to the internal workings of associations and groups on the grounds that they exercise government over their members and that participation in their affairs is just as "political," in its policy conflicts and meaning for the individual, as is participation in "public" government. It is not necessary to belabor the issue, as the distinction loses much of its force in Communist China. For a reaffirmation of the view that "political" properly refers only to public government see Sheldon S. Wolin, *Politics and Vision* (Boston, 1960), pp. 431–434.

categories by which political participation is analyzed. Perhaps the critical factor in voluntary participation is a willingness to perform certain acts that are perceived to have political significance even when performance is required by law or other pressures.

The suggestion that conscious though possibly guided involvement in the implementation of political decisions is a meaningful form of political participation runs counter to the traditional democratic concept of participation. It is worth noting, however, that the democratic ideal of an informed citizenry acting rationally to defend its interests through the representative process is at best a loose approximation of the political process in a modern democratic state. The struggle between liberty and equality, defined so eloquently by Alexis de Tocqueville, and the question of how an individualistic political theory can accommodate the growth of state power and "mass society" have called attention to significant departures in practice from the democratic ideal. Several decades of uneasy appraisal of Western democracy have now produced ample evidence that the extensive use of propaganda to mobilize the population, the manipulation of political organizations by their elites, the inability of citizens to exert effective influence on decision-makers, and the lack of significant electoral choice—all characteristic features of Chinese political life—are by no means absent in democratic politics. Equally noteworthy is that some theorists within the democratic tradition have argued that the individualization, atomization, and pursuit of self-interest associated with the liberal state are not the true expression of democracy. Their antidotes frequently take the form of a submersion of individual will in group purpose, with hostility toward "ballot box democracy" and the assertion of individual interest that merely formalize the expression of competing interests, and with emphasis on creation of group unanimity through discussion, persuasion, and face-to-face contact between leaders and citizens. Such themes are similar to the CCP's concern for social consciousness, small-group discussion, and universal acceptance of allegedly common goals. These considerations should not obscure the fundamental differences between the Chinese and democratic styles of participation, but they underline the need for caution in evaluating those forms of political participation that do not conform to traditional democratic ideals.

It is the contention of this study that the form which popular political participation takes in Communist China has a profound importance in Chinese political development and the operation of the Chinese political system. The fact that Chinese claims about the representative and influential functions of their institutions for popular participation are not substantiated is, of course, very relevant to our analysis; we shall try to examine these claims carefully, taking note of their inadequacies and of the stultifying impact of Party controls throughout the political system. At the same time, however, we must recognize that the absence of effective political influence and representation does not exhaust the political significance of our subject. The political meaning of actions is not determined solely by the nature of the actions themselves or the institutions that provide their setting, but involves as well the psychological motivations and interpretations that surround them; that is, it is the way in which actions are rationalized that gives them a public, or political, character. To illustrate this point, Harold Lasswell observes that a man who kills a king because the king has insulted his sister has not committed a political act; it is when he rationalizes the act as in the public interest that it becomes political.[7] In a similar line of thought, another noted political scientist has called attention to the enormous importance of public symbols and rituals (flags, songs, monuments, parades, celebrations, etc.) which, though frequently denigrated as lacking substantive political content, nonetheless hold great political meaning for at least some participants.[8] Without this perspective, which has been incorporated into the definition of political participation offered above, one cannot appreciate the scope of political participation in Communist China. It is the CCP's attempt to attach real meaning to ritualistic political performances and to invest apparently "private" acts with political significance that accounts for the extraordinary politicization of life in contemporary China. Granted the Party may extend the idea to ludicrous limits, as in arguing that observance of high standards of personal hygiene is "political" because it contributes to the success of a state-sponsored public health campaign; in such cases, we may conclude that the "political" attribution fails because too few people truly accept it. On the other hand, the Party's persistent stress on the political importance of increased production, as an indication of individual political activism and as a contribution toward supremely important national goals, cannot be dismissed so easily. Merriam says that the performance of daily work is, "in a sense, a perpetual plebiscite in which the votes are not formally cast but in which the signs and symbols of assent and dissent are clearly understood by skilled observers."[9] In China, the fact that work performance is a "plebiscite" is openly proclaimed and thoroughly understood, and productive activity does become to some degree political.

We must also take note of multiplicity of function in various types of social behavior. In his discussion of "manifest" and "latent" function,

[7] Harold D. Lasswell, *Psychopathology and Politics* (new ed., New York, 1960), p. 76.
[8] Charles E. Merriam, *Systematic Politics* (Chicago, 1945), pp. 81–93.
[9] *Ibid.*, p. 103.

Robert Merton points out that the unintended and even unrecognized consequences of some actions may perform significant social functions. For example, an Indian rain ceremony may perform the "latent" function of reinforcing group identity, and the American political "machine" may perform the "latent" functions of assisting the needy, dispensing political privileges to business, and providing channels of social mobility.[10] With specific reference to political participation, it is now widely recognized that democratic political practices, though "manifestly" devoted to exerting influence on decisions or decision-makers, are "latently" powerful agents for the creation of consensus, the cementing of individual loyalties to the community, and the gratification of individual psychic needs. Clearly, the "manifest" function of the Chinese style of participation—popular execution of Party policies—does not exhaust the full meaning of the actions involved. Whether the other functions of these actions are "latent" in Merton's sense of producing unintended or unrecognized consequences is open to question. It might be more accurate to refer to primary and secondary functions of participation in China, with the understanding that some of the secondary functions may be "latent" from the Party's point of view. For example, to return to the major themes of this study as stated in the opening paragraph, it is obvious that the political mobilization of the Chinese masses during the first half of the twentieth century contributed heavily to a Communist victory in 1949, even though this was not the intended result in many cases. It is not so obvious, perhaps, that the mass participation which the CCP organizes for the implementation of its policies may also be accelerating the construction of a national political community in China, a trend which clearly antedates the Communist revolution and which has no necessary attachment to communism as such. Fuller discussion of these issues is left to later sections, but they illustrate the importance of identifying multiple functions and distinguishing between intended and unintended results.

The purpose of this introduction has been to outline some of the definitional and analytical considerations that help to understand political participation in China. There remains the job of citing additional limitations on this study. The emphasis falls on post-1949 China, except for such background as is necessary for comment on general patterns of political participation in modern China. Emphasis is further directed toward "mass" rather than "elite" participation, which requires certain categorical exclusions. There is no systematic discussion of political life in the armed forces, within the Party, and among the intellectuals, although references to these areas will occasionally be

[10] Robert K. Merton, *Social Theory and Social Structure* (rev. and enl. ed.; Glencoe, 1957), pp. 51, 60–82.

necessary, as all represent special cases; the minority nationality areas are also excluded. To put it more positively, this is a study of how the workers, peasants, and housewives of Communist China participate in politics, and what significance their participation has for the functioning of the Communist political system and for political change in modern China.

TWO

Participation in Pre-Communist China

The degree to which Communist rule has preserved, modified, and revolutionized the Chinese political tradition is a complex and fascinating question. Judging from the wide divergence in answers to this question, its complexity often overpowers its fascination. The difficulty in assessing elements of continuity and change in Communist China rests only partly on an inability to understand fully the political character of a new and relatively isolated Communist state; it rests also on ambiguities and uncertainties within the political tradition that the CCP inherited. Although the relative stability and longevity of the Chinese political tradition are well known, the Chinese Communists have not imposed their rule on a system that can be identified simply as "traditional." The tradition has never been totally static and it was undergoing major changes in the nineteenth century when the Western impact began its fateful disruptions of Chinese society. Many aspects of the system against which the radicals of the late nineteenth and early twentieth centuries revolted—the purchase of governmental office, the concentration of land ownership, the power of military and bandit elements in rural areas, the incompetence of the central government, and, above all, the diffuse effects of the Western presence itself—were symptoms of change rather than characteristics of the traditional order. Chinese communism, in this sense, is a revolt against a mutant tradition rather than the tradition rightly understood.

The dangers of generalization notwithstanding, simple distinctions are still useful. In this discussion, "traditional" China refers generally to China of the Ch'ing dynasty (1644–1911), with the understanding that the "traditionality" of some of the characteristics included is questionable. "Transitional" China refers to the period of changes, beginning in the latter half of the nineteenth century and accelerated after the First World War, in which the erosion of the old and the adoption of the new produced a system that was manifestly different from that of imperial China. Nevertheless, both traditional and transitional elements were present in the political system that preceded the Communists' rise to power. Traditional attitudes toward government were most enduring at the local level, in some cases remaining virtually unchanged down to 1949. Among the leaders and intellectuals, the progress of change was more rapid, and by the turn of the century concepts and programs that deviated substantially from the traditional had emerged. Finally, in the two decades before Communist victory, the Kuomintang (KMT) established a government based on a shaky balance of traditional and transitional forces. These are some of the subjects that must be considered, along with the traditional political order itself, in a discussion of political participation in pre-Communist China.

THE TRADITIONAL POLITICAL ORDER

The traditional Chinese state was a monarchy in which the emperor theoretically held absolute power over a highly centralized empire. In practice, neither absolutism nor centralization was as strong as the theory held. The power of individual emperors varied with their energies and abilities, but the bureaucracy and key Court officials normally controlled most political affairs. Centralization, too, was qualified by tendencies, sometimes quite pronounced, toward provincial and *hsien* (county) autonomy in spite of central powers of appointment over all officials. The boundaries of the empire fluctuated with the political and military effectiveness of the ruling dynasty. Even in theory, however, these boundaries were vague because of the Chinese belief that the emperor's heavenly mandate to rule extended over all mankind. Although the emperor did not try to exert his global authority by force, the concept inhibited the emergence of national political consciousness such as developed in Western Europe.

The legitimacy of the emperor's "mandate" to rule theoretically rested on his right conduct, which was tested by his ability to maintain harmony in nature and society. Military force was necessary in seizing and retaining political power, but the Chinese tradition insisted that virtue and morality were the final legitimizers of political authority. Moreover, just as the emperor's authority was morally based, his governing of the people was to be by moral example. There was a conflicting theme in the tradition that advocated the necessity of legal restraints for effective rule. Generally, however, the legalist doctrine was a pragmatic corollary, while the ideal of rule by moral example and instruction remained the primary principle of good government.

The cement that held this system together was the Confucian ethic, which provided the standards by which the bureaucracy was recruited and by which the ruling elites from the emperor down to the *hsien* magistrate sought to guide their actions. The fact that these moral precepts were not always observed did not alter the pervasive influence of the prevailing orthodoxy. Confucian philosophy was primarily the domain of the superior man of learning and virtue, but the system could not have endured without broad popular acceptance of the Confucian ideal of good government. During the Ch'ing dynasty the government recognized this fact by attempts to indoctrinate the population in the fundamentals of the official morality.[1]

These general observations make a point of fundamental importance for the nature of political life in traditional China. The idea that correct adherence to a universally accepted and moralistic philosophy is the foundation of good government necessarily reduces the importance of legal and institutional responsibilities for political actors. Institutionalized education and indoctrination may be necessary to produce the good men, but once produced their qualification for office is precisely the primacy of their obligation to act in accordance with moral principles. The public official in imperial China was by no means free from prescribed rituals and bureaucratic controls from above, but his basic guidance in governing came from his own perception of right conduct. Thus, the traditional Chinese political system was frankly elitist in its theory of who should govern and basically hostile toward the kinds of institutional restraints on elites that encouraged the growth of popular participation in the West. Moreover, to the extent that the ideology of the ruling elite sets the political tone of a society, the "amateur ideal" of the Confucian scholar-official tended to devalue political commitment in general. The scholar-official's loyalties were more to Chinese culture than to the Chinese state, and although he recognized his obligation to serve society, he did not believe that public office was the highest form of service to society. On the personal level, he found his greatest rewards outside public life in the intellectual pursuits for which his studies prepared him.[2]

It is not surprising, therefore, that there was no popular involvement in national politics in imperial China. Public service was the prerogative of an educated elite who perhaps felt responsible *for* the people but certainly not *to* them. Even among this elite, the concept of national political loyalty was blurred by a cultural and philosophical commitment that transcended the fortunes of any particular government. For the peasants, the imperial government was remote from daily life; its authority was felt only indirectly through collection of taxes and occasional mobilization for defense or construction tasks, and these were relation-

[1] Hsiao Kung-chuan, *Rural China: Imperial Control in the Nineteenth Century* (Seattle, 1961), pp. 184–205.

[2] Joseph R. Levenson, *Confucian China and Its Modern Fate: The Problem of Intellectual Continuity* (Berkeley and Los Angeles, 1958). See especially chap. 2.

ships that the peasants feared and avoided. As one scholar has put it, there was an "ideological vacuum" in the countryside; most of the population paid little attention to anything beyond the circumstances of their daily lives and were neither positively loyal nor opposed to the existing regime.[3]

It has sometimes been suggested that the presence or absence of rebellions gave a rough measure of the degree of popular satisfaction with government and that the institution of rebellion, which was justified in classical Chinese theory as a legitimate weapon against bad government, gave the Chinese system a democratic flavor.[4] There is a superficial validity in such statements, but they say little about the people's ability to understand or control even the broadest of policies. There is little evidence to suggest that this "institution" actually translated popular wishes to central political authorities; whether approved in principle or not, rebellion by itself is not a reliable or efficient form of participation in government. A more serious proposition is that the theoretically open selection of officials on the basis of merit, coupled with persistent ties of officials to their clans and localities, produced a form of popular political representation. Officials did protect the interests of their immediate families, but the number of people protected in this way was small. Generally speaking, the lower levels of Chinese society might partake of the prestige of a kinsman who attained a position of political responsibility, but they could not necessarily capitalize on his influence.[5] Others have argued that the ability of local leaders to ignore governmental orders gave them a voice in national policy, as the central government would change policies which the local gentry refused to enforce.[6] This may have happened in some cases, but if so it was the interests of the gentry rather than the local population that were defended. In any case, it is doubtful that the local gentry had any consistent influence on central policy; the central government's failure to enforce some of its policies at the local level is, in fact, more indicative of the gulf that separated central and local levels of government than of institutionalized checks on central power.[7] Therefore, neither popular rebellion nor the undeniable power of local officials and gentry alters the general statement that the masses in traditional China had virtually no interest or involvement in national politics.

[3] Hsiao, op. cit., pp. 253–254.

[4] Hsieh Pao-chao, The Government of China (1644-1911) (Baltimore, 1925), pp. 6, 11.

[5] Maurice Freedman, Lineage Organization in Southeastern China (London, 1958), pp. 53–62.

[6] Fei Hsiao-tung, China's Gentry (Chicago, 1953), pp. 79–84.

[7] See Daniel Harrison Kulp, Country Life in South China: The Sociology of Familism (New York, 1925), p. 133.

Popular isolation from politics in traditional China has had immense significance. It has been a critical problem for all Chinese governments in the modern era, an era in which some form of popular support is necessary for international prestige and domestic power. However, it has not been the only element of the traditional system that has influenced the effort to rouse the Chinese people to political consciousness. National patterns never tell the full story of the political life of a society, particularly when one is interested in potentialities. A brief discussion of local government and associational activities in traditional China will fill in impressions gleaned from the preceding analysis.

Under the traditional Chinese system, the central government's administration stopped at the *hsien* level. Although the *hsien* magistrate was responsible for the collection of taxes and the maintenance of law and order in his district, in practice these responsibilities were normally executed by various agents in the villages, subject to the magistrate's general supervision. Virtually all other matters of village administration were in the hands of village government and associations. The fact that the Chinese village performed a variety of political functions, and did this essentially without interference from higher authorities, has led to such exuberant statements as ". . . the real China is . . . a great aggregate of democratic communities." [8] But self-government for the autonomous community does not mean that the form of community government must be democratic, and a more careful appraisal shows that the villagers in traditional China had little voice in community decisions.

The characteristic pattern was one in which a few leaders, owing their position to age, wealth, family status, or learning, or a combination of these, assumed responsibility for all major community decisions.[9] The process by which these men gained and exercised their power varied in different localities. In some cases, village leaders were "elected" at a meeting of family heads, but though there might be discussion, there was no formal voting and the results were largely predetermined. In other cases, the influential members of the community would simply select the main village officers. Frequently in South China, where clan organization tended to be coterminous with the village, the oldest effective males of the lineage would be the recognized leaders. Generally, it is possible to

---

[8] L. T. Hobhouse in his preface to Y. K. Leong and L. K. Tao, *Village and Town Life in China* (London, 1915), p. ix.

[9] This discussion is based on two general studies of local government in imperial China: Ch'ü T'ung-tsu, *Local Government in China Under the Ch'ing* (Cambridge, Mass., 1962), and Hsiao, *op. cit.;* and on relevant materials in several village studies including the following: Fei Hsiao-tung, *Peasant Life in China* (London, 1939); Freedman, *op. cit.;* Sidney D. Gamble, *Ting Hsien: A North China Rural Community* (New York, 1954); Kulp, *op. cit.;* Arthur H. Smith, *Village Life in China* (New York, 1899); and Martin C. Yang. *A Chinese Village: Taitou, Shantung Province* (New York, 1945).

distinguish two main groups of village leadership. One was the official leadership, the men who held specific positions of authority in the community and were formally responsible for overseeing village affairs. These men would usually be of relatively advanced age and hold at least some local prestige, but they were not necessarily the most respected and powerful members of the community. The true elite was the unofficial leadership, the local gentry who played a major role in selecting and advising official village leaders and in administering and negotiating village relationships with the *hsien* magistrate. The gentry were few in number and owed their authority primarily to their education and to the wealth and official connections normally associated with their scholarly status; typically, they would be degree-holding scholars who had not attained official positions through the central government, or officials who had retired from public service to their native locality.

The point is not that villagers were subjected to elite control against their wishes, but simply that there was little actual participation by villagers in the selection of leaders or the making of decisions. Generally, the people accepted the system of decision-making and the criteria which determined leadership. Normally, there were few restraints on wider participation, or at least few restrictions on speech or assembly that prevented the villagers from expressing their opinions if they wished to do so. The leaders might support their decisions with extensive consultation and even put some matters to a formal vote. Nevertheless, there was little general participation in most decisions and there was little chance of the influential members of the community being overridden if a conflict should arise. Popular participation, where it occurred, was usually a response to solicitation of support by village leaders who had every reason to expect that support would be forthcoming in view of their standing in the community.

The role of the head of the *pao-chia* system, in those areas where this old system of rural organization was still practiced, is of some interest. This leader, referred to as the *ti-pao* or *pao-chang*, was an intermediate official between the magistrate and the people and potentially an important figure in local government. Hsieh Pao-chao asserts that the *ti-pao*, whom he calls the "cornerstone of local government," was elected and performed numerous governmental functions.[10] However, other evidence indicates that the *ti-pao*, whether he was elected or not, was merely a petty administrative official who served as a constable and informer for the magistrate rather than as a responsible leader of the village.[11] This leads to an important point: the extent of responsibility

[10] Hsieh, *op. cit.*, pp. 309–310.

[11] Ch'ü, *op. cit.*, pp. 3–4; Freedman, *op. cit.*, pp. 64–66; Hsiao, *op. cit.*, chaps. 2–3; Leong and Tao, *op. cit.*, p. 64. On the *pao-chia* system itself, see Ch'ü, *op. cit.*, chap. 9, and Hsiao, *loc. cit.*

for carrying out decisions and administering orders was much wider than the extent of participation in making these decisions. The making of decisions that affected the local community was the prerogative of the magistrate and a handful of local leaders, while the enforcement of these decisions was the responsibility of family heads, lineage heads, the *ti-pao* (where he existed), and various village officials who were locally recruited or elected. Thus, popular political activity, to the extent that it existed at all, was essentially enforcement or ritualistic approval of decisions made by leaders who owed their position to factors other than popular selection. The gentry were, in fact, free to use their local authority for their own economic advantage, and did so in many cases; in the last analysis, even the gentry's influence was subordinate to the legally superior power of a *hsien* magistrate who wished to override it.[12] The idea that the traditional Chinese village enjoyed local democracy is "another of the old China's official myths." [13]

The associative and cooperative aspects of Chinese society provide further insights into the nature of the traditional political order. In traditional China, the most important associations were kinship groupings, which formed the basic social units and also provided the fundamental standards by which all social relationships, obligations, and values were determined. The basic hierarchical pattern which characterized most Chinese associations was set by the family (*chia*). In this pattern, the eldest male (within generational lines) served as family head with full authority over the members, while the lower members in the family hierarchy owed obedience upward but could not hold their superiors responsible for their actions.[14] There was no form of association in imperial China, including the state itself, that failed to show the influence of the benevolent authoritarianism and subordination of individual interest that characterized family life.

The lineage or clan (*tsu*), though still an involuntary kinship grouping, stands as an important association in its own right. It was an organization of considerable size and varied activities which sometimes served as the principal political organization of the village (if one clan dominated the village) and always occupied an important place among village associations.[15] The result was that almost every family in traditional China had the theoretical right to participate in at least one major association, but whether this right was fully exercised or not is a different question. Clan organization was usually egalitarian in theory, but in

[12] Ch'ü, *op. cit.,* pp. 185–190, 197–199.

[13] John King Fairbank, *The United States and China* (rev. and enl.; Cambridge, Mass., 1958), pp. 186–187.

[14] Marion J. Levy, Jr., *The Family Revolution in Modern China* (Cambridge, Mass., 1949), *passim,* and especially pp. 159–161, 234–235.

[15] Freedman, *op. cit.,* pp. 1–2.

practice an elite of influential and wealthy members actually controlled clan affairs.[16] Of course, lack of widespread participation in clan decisions did not destroy the value of that association; it may have been a source of irritation, especially when the economic activities of the clan were extensive, but members were still grateful for the protection afforded to them by the clan and gave it unified support when necessary. Further, members of the lineage found satisfaction in clan prestige and in the various social and ceremonial activities which symbolized the unity and purpose of the clan.

In addition to kinship organization, the Chinese village normally supported several voluntary associations. Some of these, such as loan associations, crop protection groups, and recreational associations, were common throughout China, while others were organized on the basis of the particular interests and economic activities of the locality. One of the best analyses of these associations is found in Kulp's study of a village in Kwangtung. His observations include the following points: the associations were formed to meet a clearly recognized need, in most cases a need to advance economic status or security; there was an element of sociability in most meetings and an opportunity for self-expression in some of them, but the motive of personal recognition was of relatively low importance; the associations were usually dissolved as soon as the immediate need which had nourished them was satisfied.[17] Broadly speaking, voluntary associations were oriented toward direct action rather than toward advancing their purposes through influence on government or through the acquisition of political power; they were not, therefore, intermediate links between state and citizen. Moreover, they fulfilled many functions that might otherwise have been performed by formal levels of government, thereby contributing to the relatively low significance of the political community. To the degree that they cut across kinship groupings they may have introduced the individual to a broader type of social participation, but their specific purposes and limited scope did little to change the particularism which characterized traditional Chinese life.

The Chinese guilds were another form of associational life. They differed from the voluntary associations in that they were based on a common characteristic of their members, primarily occupation but sometimes religion or native locality, rather than on a limited common purpose. As a result, they tended to be larger and more enduring than the voluntary associations, and they played a more pervasive role in the lives of their members. Guilds were found throughout traditional

[16] Freedman, *op. cit.*, p. 69; C. K. Yang, *A Chinese Village in Early Communist Transition,* (Cambridge, Mass., 1959), pp. 93–96.

[17] Kulp. *op. cit.*, chap. 7. See also Hsiao, *op. cit.*, p. 321.

China, although mainly confined to the cities and towns; their organization was usually local, seldom extending to the provincial level and
almost never to the national level.[18] In some cases a limited degree of
democracy may have appeared, but paternalistic controls by the dominant elders and an atmosphere of authoritarian solidarity that subordinated members to associational discipline were more common features
of guild organization.[19]

As membership was in fact, though not necessarily in principle,
compulsory for all those engaged in the respective occupation, the guilds
held great economic power. If this is taken with the high degree of
solidarity and discipline that the guilds enforced, it is natural to specu-
late on the political pressure they might have exerted. However, they
made little attempt to achieve their goals through local government.
The guilds were technically illegal and could not afford the risks of a
demonstration of political power. The government tolerated them because of their ability to control and care for their membership and might
even negotiate with them on occasion; the guilds, in turn, were sensitive
to the advantages of connections with officials. Nevertheless, the guilds
were essentially autonomous.[20] So far as possible, they devoted themselves to their own affairs, avoiding either assistance or interference from
political authority.

The secret societies were the largest of traditional Chinese associations. Although their illegal and violent activities can scarcely be regarded as institutionalized forms of political participation, the fact remains that some secret societies were more explicitly patriotic and
politically oriented than any other associations in traditional China.
The Hung Society, which was the most powerful of the secret societies
during the Ch'ing period, was specifically committed to the overthrow of
the Manchus.[21] The secret society could also become a vehicle through
which the underprivileged classes could express their opposition to
government and their desire for social and economic change; this development brought with it a democratization of the society's membership.[22] However, while the secret societies may have been movements

---

[18] John Stewart Burgess, *The Guilds of Peking* (New York, 1928), pp. 29–30;
Sidney D. Gamble and John Stewart Burgess, *Peking: A Social Survey* (New
York, 1921), p. 168.

[19] Burgess, *op. cit.*, especially chaps. 5–7, and p. 213. See also Hosea Ballou
Morse, *The Gilds of China* (London, 1909).

[20] Burgess, *op. cit.*, p. 35; Morse, *op. cit., passim.* There were exceptions as some
guilds, especially merchant guilds, were actually agencies of the government.

[21] See the oaths and prohibitions of the Hung Society, quoted in *Sources of
Chinese Tradition*, comp. by Wm. Theodore de Bary, Wing-tsit Chan, and Burton
Watson (New York, 1960), pp. 652–658.

[22] B. Favre, *Les Sociétés Secrètes en Chine* (Paris, 1933), chap. 12, and
Freedman, *op. cit.*, pp. 118–124. Note also the egalitarian quality of many of the
oaths of the Hung Society.

of incipient social protest in some areas, they more commonly served as protective organizations for families of wealth and influence.[23] Whatever the case might be, the secret societies are further evidence of the Chinese capacity for, and dependence on, associational rather than governmental activity. Note, too, that the most political of Chinese associations were forced to rely on illegal and violent methods to achieve their goals. It is no accident that the Chinese nationalist movement in the last two decades of the Ch'ing not only relied upon the secret societies for support but also copied many of their characteristic features.

Two conclusions emerge from this discussion of village government and associations. First, with few exceptions, the local units and associations of which the common people of China were members had elitist patterns of leadership in which a few men made the major decisions and demanded cooperation and submission from the other members. Leaders relied on group opinion and widely accepted values to support their authority, but in the last analysis they were not responsible to their subordinates and could act arbitrarily if they wished. The vast majority of Chinese had no real influence in their village governments and associations, although they were expected to give active support to the goals of these units.

Second, virtually every Chinese was thoroughly experienced in the benefits, problems, and adjustments of cooperative and associational life as a result of membership in small-scale social units. These units lay between the individual and the state, but they served as a wall rather than a bridge in their effect on the individual's relationship to the state. From the central government's point of view, they were the basic social units; from the individual's point of view, they were the primary governing bodies. The Chinese citizen found his social identity, his security, and his hopes for advancement in his local associations and not in the wider political community. Local associations were either ends in themselves (the family, the village, the guild) or were temporary organizations for achieving specific goals by direct action (crop protection and loan associations). They did not seek to influence the actions of the state in a positive way but only to establish the minimal connections necessary to avoid the harmful effects of state power.

Thus, Chinese associational life did not broaden the individual's horizon and involve him in ever-widening communities. Instead, it restricted him to, and reinforced his preoccupation with, his own particular affairs and interests. Throughout the literature that deals with the villages and associations of traditional China is the theme of general indifference to matters beyond one's own affairs or occupation, an

[23] Fairbank, *op. cit.*, pp. 187–188. The economic protection afforded by the secret society is also evident in the oaths of the Hung Society.

attitude that one observer found summed up in the Chinese saying "scholars talk of books—butchers of pigs." So strong was this particularism that it weakened the individual's loyalties even to those associations outside the family. In this sense, there was a kind of "individualism" in traditional China that asserted the interests of oneself and one's family above all others, and it helps to explain why the Chinese, for all of their associational tendencies and talents, seldom developed secondary associations that commanded the full loyalties of their members. When Sun Yat-sen described China as a "sheet of loose sand," he was attacking the "individualism" that encouraged the formation of a multitude of associations but denied most of them the ability to expand their scale and purposes without loss of loyalty and discipline. It was this restricted and particularistic outlook that made meaningful political participation virtually nonexistent in traditional China.

When one turns to the question of why this pattern persisted, the attitude of the imperial government assumes great importance. On the one hand, lacking the resources and incentive to extend its authority directly into the villages throughout a vast empire, the central government encouraged village government and associations to assume local control and welfare functions; for integrative purposes, it contented itself with a loose and rather ineffectual program of ideological indoctrination that emphasized morality and social conservatism rather than political loyalty. On the other hand, the central government was determined to maintain its ultimate control, its ability to suppress any actual or potential political competition. Consequently, it discouraged full autonomy or any sense of active community service and participation at the local level. So long as the local gentry, the clans, or the guilds helped control the population, their autonomy was tacitly accepted. But when their power began to expand or to challenge the local imperial authorities, they were broken up or suppressed.[24] So long, also, as the central government retained its power, this blend of official indifference and control endured. But when imperial power declined, as it did throughout the nineteenth and early twentieth centuries, the way opened for the growth of uncontrolled authority and ultimately for the establishment of a new central government that sought to change for all time the absence of grass-roots loyalty to the national political community.

EROSION OF TRADITIONAL PATTERNS

To a great extent, the patterns described above were a product of Confucian values that tried to mold all social relationships on an ideal

[24] See Hsiao, *op. cit., passim,* but especially pp. 256, 320–322, 348–357.

model of the family. It followed, therefore, that any challenge to traditional values would make itself felt throughout the social structure. Such a challenge arose in China in the latter part of the nineteenth century, and during the first four decades of the twentieth century there was increasing evidence of the erosion of traditional patterns. The changes of this period are too complex for detailed analysis, but some indication of their effect on popular political life is necessary.

The challenge stemmed from a combination of dynastic decline and Western intrusions that gave rise to the conviction that something must be done to strengthen and revitalize the Chinese empire. Initially, this conviction produced a reaffirmation of traditional values, best represented in the "T'ung Chih Restoration" (1862–1874) that reestablished central authority in the wake of the Taiping Rebellion. As it grew, however, it revealed two new tendencies: first, a reexamination of Confucian teachings that became, increasingly, an open attack on traditional Chinese institutions; second, an emerging nationalism that devoted more and more emphasis to the independence and unification of the national government. The origins of these tendencies lay in the Chinese response to Western ideas, technology, and political encroachment, but their development was accelerated by internal reform and revolution. That is to say, the spread of ideas that were subversive of traditional patterns was facilitated and reinforced by the changing conditions of Chinese life. The elimination of the old examination system, the growth of modern schools, the improvements in communication and transportation, the process of industrialization and urbanization—all of these contributed to the erosion of traditional patterns. Furthermore, as the Chinese revolution gathered momentum and old systems of authority were swept aside, a period of disorder and civil war ensued in which new governments sought to establish their authority and traditional arrangements for security and protection became inadequate. A few illustrations will give a more concrete image of the effect of these changes.

The process of transition was readily apparent in the weakening fabric of traditional associations. In the family, transition resulted mainly in a negativistic revolt against familial authority, but it was also marked by some more or less conscious efforts to give a greater voice to women and youth, to place greater emphasis on ability and less on age, to replace responsibility toward the ancestral family with responsibility toward the state or individual family members, and to devote increasing attention to the interest of the individual.[25] Some voluntary associations were losing their restricted outlook and were becoming long-range community projects for reform or even paramilitary centers of local power.[26] In the

[25] Levy, *op. cit.,* pp. 335–338.
[26] Gamble, *op. cit.,* pp. 133–142, 152–164; C. K. Yang, *op. cit.,* pp. 109–110.

cities, the guilds were declining, owing to a weakening of religious ties, the loss of prestige of old leaders, and an inability to enforce rules or monopoly of power; interference from government and the growth of labor unions and chambers of commerce cut into their former autonomy and influence. The guilds could no longer avoid greater cooperation among themselves and with municipal government, while the new unions and commercial associations displayed increasing interest in civic and national affairs.[27]

Changes were also in progress in local government. As economic and social changes eroded the position of traditional leaders and as new ideas and values spread out from the cities, there was more and more opportunity for those who had previously been excluded from positions of influence to assume leadership. For example, Kulp noted the emergence of the "natural leader" or "practical politician"—a significant phase—who owed his position to personal success achieved by force of personality and cleverness rather than to conventional determinants of leadership; Kulp saw in this development the portent of "mob rule" democracy replacing familism as the people exercised greater freedom in the selection of leaders.[28] Equally pronounced was the increasing impact of external government on village affairs. In one sense, this impact was negative, as internal struggles destroyed the central government's ability to control large areas of China. The result was to force localities to defend themselves from constant exploitation by lower governments and warlords and to create stronger demands for national unity and stability. External government also had a positive impact, however, in those areas where its control was relatively secure. Here the influence of the central government began to grow through active efforts to propagandize among the people and to establish programs in which the people could be educated in the ideals sought by the government.[29] As particularism declined and governmental action became more prominent, there was a growth of nationalism, a more evident concern with public issues, and a desire to express one's views on public matters while converting others to these views.[30]

These trends can easily be exaggerated. Old institutions and attitudes remained strong in many areas, preventing the growth of political consciousness among the population as a whole. Nevertheless, the changes

[27] Burgess, op. cit., chap. 13.
[28] Kulp, op. cit., pp. 114–117. The changes in rural leadership in transitional China are discussed in Fei Hsiao-tung's China's Gentry, chap. 7, and are graphically demonstrated in the six life-histories of local leaders which accompany that volume.
[29] See Gamble, op. cit., chaps. 6–7; Gamble and Burgess, op. cit., pp. 147–151; Kulp, op. cit., pp. 323–324; Martin Yang, op. cit., p. 186.
[30] Levy, op. cit., pp. 346–357.

that were taking place, especially between the end of the First World War and the beginning of large-scale hostilities with Japan in 1937, were deep and widespread. Traditional patterns of local government and association were beginning to disintegrate; popular participation in government was not a reality but it was becoming a possibility. The question that remained was whether or not the political potential of the masses was to be encouraged and, if so, what role mass political activity was to play in the government of China. The ideas and needs that shaped the Nationalist Revolution provided a temporary answer to this question.

POLITICAL CONCEPTS IN TRANSITIONAL CHINA

It was probably inevitable that the first advocates of democratic institutions in China would be intellectuals, that their interpretation and advocacy of these institutions would be shaped by the Chinese setting, and that the first attempts to establish a constitutional government would end in failure. The first of these assertions needs only brief explanation. The extent of illiteracy and political apathy in traditional China precluded the possibility that ideas about Western political institutions could develop anywhere except among the educated classes. With all due respect to the CCP's insistence on the "creativeness of the masses," the advancement of political proposals and the leadership of political movements, from the 1890's down to the present, has remained essentially the responsibility of the intellectuals. However, the other references to the Chinese interpretation of democratic institutions and to the failure of early constitutionalism require additional comment.

The Chinese intellectual who urged the adoption of Western political institutions had no real basis, in Chinese tradition, for argument or understanding. The earlier discussion of village government and associational life has made it quite clear that democracy and individualism, in the meaning they hold as the foundations of Western democratic government, did not exist in traditional China.[31] Chinese political philosophy was equally unrewarding, even though it was not lacking in democratic ideals in the sense of government in the interests of the people. As Liang Ch'i-ch'ao once said:

. . . [The Chinese philosophers] believe thoroughly in the principles that the country is the common possession of the people, and that politics exist solely for the sake of their common advantage. But they neither studied the method nor even seem to have accepted the theory that government must be "by the

[31] For a short but informative discussion of democracy and individualism in China, in which a variety of viewpoints are presented, see Derk Bodde, *China's Cultural Tradition* (New York, 1957), pp. 64–68, 76–77, 83–85.

people." . . . There is no point in speaking of the people as the foundation of the country, and then denying them all powers of participation in politics.[32]

The closest approach which the Confucian tradition could make to government by the people was through reforms such as those advocated by Huang Tsung-hsi in the seventeenth century. Huang proposed that the schools become centers for the expression of opinion and the discussion of policy; but, though he would have expanded public education and removed the schools from central supervision, he did not suggest any institutions through which the people could control the schools or have a voice in government.[33] Huang also suggested that the bureaucracy be reduced by rotating minor administrative tasks among households, but he still relied on consultation with the wise and virtuous to ascertain the interests of the people rather than on direct expression of popular demands. As De Bary points out, Huang's retention of the Confucian ideal of harmony precluded his acceptance of the idea of competing political forces or interests.[34] It was not until the second half of the nineteenth century, after exposure to Chinese weaknesses and Western strengths, that Chinese scholars began to break out of this tradition.

Between the reforms of 1898 and the establishment of the republic in 1912, many Chinese intellectuals advocated the adoption of some representative institutions of government. In so doing, however, they revealed the influence of a tradition that lacked either the institutional or philosophical foundations of representative government. These early interpretations of Western political institutions displayed two main characteristics: the theoretical understanding of democracy was abstract and naïve; the major emphasis was on the utility of democratic institutions in strengthening the Chinese state, whether it was to be a constitutional

[32] Liang Ch'i-ch'ao, *History of Chinese Political Thought During the Early Tsin Period*, trans. by L. T. Chen (New York, 1930), p. 10.

[33] W. T. de Bary, "Chinese Despotism and the Confucian Ideal: A Seventeenth Century View," in *Chinese Thought and Institutions*, ed. by John K. Fairbank (Chicago, 1957), pp. 178–193. The students in China have been the only group, outside of government officials themselves, with a tradition of political activity; see Chow Tse-tsung, *The May Fourth Movement* (Cambridge, Mass., 1960), pp. 11–12, and Kiang Wen-han, *The Chinese Student Movement* (New York, 1948), pp. 1–3. De Bary observes (*op. cit.,* p. 194) that the imperial government was so successful in limiting the economic and social bases of potential political opposition that only popular revolt or scholarly criticism could seriously challenge the regime. Since the schools were indispensable in the traditional system, they survived as the only source of articulate opposition.

[34] De Bary, *op. cit.,* pp. 184–186, 196–197. As we have seen, the idea of involving the people in implementation of policy was common in traditional associations and village government, and is similar in principle to that type of political participation emphasized by the CCP.

monarchy or a republic. Those who addressed themselves to the theoretical justification of democratic institutions fell back on romantic concepts that showed little understanding of the actual workings of democracy. For example, T'an Ssu-t'ung, a republican reformer who died a martyr in the Hundred Days of Reform, argued that at the beginning of history there were only common people, that the people had chosen princes to govern them, and that princes and ministers were therefore secondary to the people and subject to their control.[35] Another defender of "people's rights" and popular participation in a constitutional monarchy said that the people would elect only the superior and the wise, and that their decisions and elections would be carefully considered.[36] Hu Han-min, in his interpretation of the T'ung-meng hui's revolutionary program, defended a republican form of government simply by claiming that it was acknowledged to be the appropriate system for a modern civilization. He then observed that the greatest difficulty in establishing a constitutional government is the popular struggle against monarchy and nobility; since China would have no such nobility once the Manchus were overthrown, he concluded that constitutional government would be easier to establish in China than in other countries.[37] It is not surprising that the Chinese conservatives attacked such views as both foreign and ignorant.

The most successful justification for some popular role in government was that of national strength and solidarity. Like the advocates of "self-strengthening" in the 1870's and 1880's who had noted the utility of Western technology, the constitutional reformers of 1898–1911 came to believe that selective adoption of Western political institutions would strengthen the nation and unify the people under the emperor's rule. In Wang K'ang-nien's words: ". . . when the people have no power, they do not realize that the nation belongs to all the people, and they keep at a distance from the emperor. When the people have some power, then they will realize that the nation is their own concern, and they will be drawn close to the emperor. . . . [When] the power of the empire comes from one person, it is weak. When it comes from millions of people, it is strong." [38]

Both of the two great competitors for leadership of the nationalist movement in the first decade of the twentieth century, Sun Yat-sen and Liang Ch'i-ch'ao, subordinated their views on democratic institutions

[35] *Sources of Chinese Tradition*, pp. 750–752.
[36] Teng Ssu-yu and John King Fairbank, *China's Response to the West* (Cambridge, Mass., 1954), pp. 161–164.
[37] *Sources of Chinese Tradition*, p. 764.
[38] Teng and Fairbank, *op. cit.*, p. 163. See also the arguments for political participation offered by a Chinese mission which had studied Western constitutions in 1905 (*ibid.*, pp. 207–208).

to more general demands for national unity and regeneration. Sun included a republican form of government in his program, but he was far more concerned with the development of nationalist sentiment and the overthrow of the Manchus. Liang's great lament was that there was no one "who looks on national affairs as if they were his own"; he urged a "renovation" of the people so that they would serve the public interest.[39]

Constitutional experimentation actually began in the closing years of Manchu rule and continued under the republic that was established after the revolution of 1911. However, the rapid disintegration of the republic demonstrated that neither the people nor their leaders were adequately prepared for constitutional government. The revolution took place without any significant mass activity and there was no political organization with roots among the people to give even a semblance of popular participation to the government that followed. Thus, the first attempt to establish governmental institutions of Western origin revealed two points that were significant for the future of political participation in China: first, there was as yet no real urge for popular political participation, nor was there likely to be any until the intellectuals provided the leadership by developing and clarifying their ideas on this point; second, the desire for national strength and unity was a more powerful motive for political change than were democratic principles.

Within a remarkably short period of time, some of the conditions that inhibited wider participation in politics began to change. In the years between 1915 and 1919 there was a great spread of Western political ideas. For the first time, Chinese intellectuals began to think in more serious terms of liberalism, political democracy, and free expression of individual opinion. The truly articulate supporters of these ideas were not numerous, but democratic ideals were spreading throughout the intellectual community. In 1919, even Ch'en Tu-hsiu, who within two years was to be a founder of the CCP, was urging that China should follow the Anglo-American democratic model with emphasis on local self-government.[40] To some extent "democracy" was simply a catchword, but even if it was imperfectly understood, it always carried the message of popular participation in government. From this time on, the great majority of Chinese intellectuals accepted the democratic ideal even though they differed in their interpretation of what it meant and how to achieve it.

[39] *Sources of Chinese Tradition*, p. 757. Liang's emphasis on nationalism rather than democracy, and on moral renovation rather than institutional reform, is amply demonstrated in Joseph R. Levenson's *Liang Ch'i-ch'ao and the Mind of Modern China* (Cambridge, Mass., 1953).
[40] Chow, *op. cit.*, pp. 230–232.

Under the stimulus of intellectual ferment, the possibility of mass political activity, which had appeared so remote as late as 1912, was becoming a reality. The Peking student riots of May 4, 1919, and subsequent demonstrations throughout the country, were vivid indications of growing political activism among the students and other urban strata. The power and spontaneity of the May Fourth Movement stemmed from a coincidence of causes, including the example of the Russian Revolution and dissatisfaction over the Treaty of Versailles as well as intellectual ferment in general, but the following years proved that this manifestation of political interest was far more than a passing incident. Even though an outburst of comparable magnitude did not recur until 1925, there was continuing evidence of rising political consciousness, particularly in the cities where the students and growing numbers of industrial workers were concentrated. Finally, the events of 1925–1927 conclusively demonstrated that popular political activity could be organized, in urban and rural areas alike, and that it could play a significant role in national politics.

To be sure, the rising tide of political activity did not mean that the masses were ready for democratic government. Only a small proportion of those involved in the great movements of 1919–1927 were truly aware of the national issues and objectives that were at stake. The action itself was direct, sporadic, violent, and frequently negativistic in character—hardly the image of an institutionalized and supposedly responsible style of political participation. Moreover, the success of these movements was partly due to the growing influence of Marxism–Leninism as seen in the establishment of the CCP in 1921 and the KMT–Comintern alliance in 1923. Nevertheless, the fact remained that the leaders of these movement were able to organize increasing numbers of people in support of their objectives. As a result, the potential value of mass political activity had been brought home to men who were shaping the future of China. By 1923, when he was reorganizing the KMT under Soviet guidance, Sun Yat-sen stated: ". . . the sole purpose of the present reorganization of the Party is to enable us to avoid relying exclusively on armed force, and to rely on the power of the Party itself. By 'the power of the Party itself' I mean the mind and strength of the people. Henceforth our Party should regard the mind and strength of the people as that of our Party and it should use the mind and strength of the people in its struggles." [41]

The crucial point here is that the new awareness of the people's role in politics was coupled with the idea of "using the mind and strength of the people." Why was it that this idea, so suggestive of the responses of

[41] Teng and Fairbank, *op. cit.,* p. 264.

the earlier reformers, should have been reasserted? If the situation had really changed, if the absence of democratic theory and popular political activity which had thwarted the efforts of 1898–1912 had been rectified, why should Sun regard the people as the servant of his party, the KMT? It is true that in the intellectual ferment preceding the May Fourth Incident Western democratic values had been widely accepted, but, for several reasons, these values had little effect on the development of political participation after 1919. First, there has always been a current in modern Chinese political thought which held that the "form" of democratic institutions was not enough. Many intellectuals, including Liang Ch'i-ch'ao, argued during the last years of the Manchus that new institutions would solve nothing unless accompanied by a rebirth of Chinese spirit. The rapid deterioration of the republican government in Peking after 1912 seemed to be dramatic confirmation of this view. Moreover, in the years after 1919 there was a reappraisal of, and even reaction to, the earlier and less cautious acceptance of Western values. Chinese intellectuals found much to criticize in the materialism, imperialism, and developing economic difficulties that they saw in the West.[42]

Above all, China's leaders had to select their political objectives and techniques in the hard light of Chinese reality. In the aftermath of the First World War, problems of national unity, reconstruction, and independence from foreign control took precedence over all others. Western democracy was hardly relevant in this situation, especially since the Western powers were themselves the targets of Chinese nationalist agitation. Soviet communism, on the other hand, provided a model that was much closer to Chinese experience, and a theory of imperialism that claimed to explain China's predicament. Most important of all, Soviet Russia offered a strategy of mass revolution and the arms and advisers to help carry it out.

For these reasons, the influence of liberalism was declining while that of nationalism and communism was on the rise. Both nationalists and leftists gave primary attention to national liberation and reconstruction and, ideological differences notwithstanding, were able to unite in 1923 on a program of action to attain these goals. The acceptance of democratic values was not as fundamental as it had appeared in 1919; for a time, these values stood as a symbol or perhaps a key to modernization, but they were not in themselves the immediate objective. The main purpose of the May Fourth Movement was national independence, the same goal that had inspired the earlier reforms and revolutions in

[42] See the discussions of this point in Chow, *op. cit.*, pp. 327–332, and Kiang, *op. cit.*, pp. 40–45. The leading critics of the West were conservatives, such as Liang Ch'i-ch'ao and Liang Sou-ming, who did not really represent the intellectual community. Nevertheless, the ideas they espoused were widely debated and served to ensure a critical attitude toward the West.

modern China.[43] Moreover, it was the representatives of nationalist and Marxist views who recognized the political potential of the May Fourth demonstrations and consciously set out to organize the masses in support of their own objectives. As a result, popular political activity emerged largely under the control of the KMT and the CCP, both of which were Leninist-style parties with little tolerance for political democracy. The liberals, on the other hand, tended to withdraw from politics while emphasizing the need for educational and cultural reform.[44]

Democracy remained a principal slogan of Sun Yat-sen's movement, but it had little liberalizing effect on it. In brief, Sun made nationalism the paramount objective of the revolution and admitted that democracy was justified on grounds of expediency—it was part of an irresistible "world current" and it was necessary to make the revolution strong and effective.[45] China was a "sheet of loose sand," suffering from an excess of individual liberty: ". . . on no account must we give more liberty to the individual; let us secure liberty instead for the nation. . . . When the nation can act freely, then China may be called strong. To make the nation free, we must each sacrifice his personal freedom." [46] Sun asserted that his democracy was different from, and superior to, the Western model because it would allow the people to control without impairing the ability of the government to act; but it was clear that popular "control" would be carried out under supervision from above: "We know a way now to make use of democracy and we know how to change the attitude of people towards government, but yet the majority of the people are without vision. We who have prevision must lead them and guide them into the right way if we want to escape the confusions of Western democracy and not follow in the tracks of the West." [47] For all the intellectual discussion of democratic theory, it was never put into practice. The political strength of the masses was needed for other purposes.

POLITICAL PARTICIPATION UNDER THE KUOMINTANG

By 1928 the Nationalist Revolution had succeeded and the KMT was in command of the government of China. Although the KMT was

[43] Chow, op. cit., p. 359.

[44] Ibid., pp. 222–228, 239–253. The Chinese "liberals" were not necessarily mistaken in their views on this matter. If the goal was attainment of democracy, it was probably true that educational and cultural reform would have to be the first step. The problem was that democracy was not the overriding objective at that time.

[45] Sun Yat-sen, San Min Chu I, trans. by Frank W. Price (Shanghai, 1928), pp. 178–181.

[46] Ibid., p. 213.

[47] Ibid., p. 318.

weakened by factionalism, and its direct control of the country was incomplete, it now faced the problem of adjusting its political philosophy and programs to a new position of authority. Direct political action by the masses had assisted the KMT in its rise to power, but the time for revolutionary action had passed; the KMT had to define the proper sphere of popular participation in an established government. Broadly speaking, the KMT's efforts in this direction fell into two categories: attempts to give the people a formal voice in political decisions; continuing efforts to secure mass support for Party objectives.

Formal institutions of democracy under the Nationalist government suffered from the nature of the KMT rule and the acceptance of Sun's theory on the stages of the national revolution. The KMT government established in Canton in 1925 had been a Soviet-style system under the control of the Central Executive Committee of the KMT; it was a Party dictatorship which allowed no room for political democracy.[48] In essence, Party control of the central government was never relinquished, but there was a substantial change in the theoretical nature of Party rule after 1928. Sun Yat-sen had divided China's revolution into three stages: revolution, political tutelage, and constitutional government. In 1928, the KMT announced that the revolutionary stage had ended and that the period of political tutelage had begun. In accordance with Sun's prescriptions, a "Five-Power" government designed to "tutor" the people in preparation for their later constitutional government was established in 1928. The tutelary system secured a firmer basis with the promulgation of the Provisional Constitution of 1931, which was to remain in effect until 1946.[49] The fundamental principle of the period of tutelage was that the KMT would educate the people in political democracy without allowing them any control of the central government. Tutelage was to be carried out by initiating local self-government throughout China, with constitutional government granted only when the establishment of local self-government was complete.

Thus, the theory of tutelage precluded any popular participation in the central government, but it also imposed an obligation to encourage political participation at the local level. The KMT program for local self-government appeared in 1928 in a law that provided for local advisory councils elected by universal suffrage.[50] Additional laws in the following years laid down the organization of provincial, municipal, and lower levels of government. These regulations provided that all citizens

[48] Arthur N. Holcombe, *The Chinese Revolution* (Cambridge, Mass., 1930), pp. 182–189.

[49] For details on the 1928 and 1931 "Five-Power" governments, see *ibid.*, pp. 263–269, and Paul M. A. Linebarger, *The China of Chiang K'ai-shek* (Boston, 1941), chaps. 1–2.

[50] Holcombe, *op. cit.*, pp. 272–276.

who had taken a loyalty oath to the Republic of China and who had not been denied suffrage for various other reasons had the right to attend general meetings and to take part in elections, recall, initiative, and referendum; such rights were obviously limited in meaning by the fact that provincial and municipal governments were established by the central government and were given supervisory powers over all lower levels.[51]

The most complete expression of the KMT program for local self-government was the "New Hsien System" established in September 1939.[52] Under this system, the *hsien* magistrate was responsible only to higher levels, but there was beneath him an ascending series of representative councils that were theoretically designed to bring the individual citizen into the political process. In practice, the system of selection was so indirect as to remove the individual from any significant voice in government. The lowest organized unit was the *chia,* consisting of six to fifteen households; general meetings of all *chia* residents could be held, but the *chia* council, which elected the *chia* chief, was simply composed of the heads of member households. The next level was the *pao* which consisted of six to fifteen *chia;* the *pao* council was composed of one delegate from each member household, and elected two delegates to the *hsiang* council (or *chen* council in urban areas). Each *hsiang* council was the apex of the popularly based representative system, but it had no real power of control over the *hsien* magistrate and was obviously remote from the citizen at the base of the pyramid.

Local government under the KMT would have made every citizen participate at the lowest organizational level, but in no sense did it give the citizen any real control over local political authorities. Of course, the KMT did not claim that this system would provide self-government from the first, since the period of tutelage was primarily designed to educate the people in the ways of democracy.[53] But even this limited objective failed, as the system was never effectively put into practice. Official sources claimed that it was working in a majority of *hsien,* but most evidence indicates that it did not produce significant changes in local patterns of government.[54]

[51] Chinese Ministry of Information, *China Handbook, 1937–45,* rev. and enl. with 1946 supplement (New York, 1947), pp. 106–108.

[52] *Ibid.,* pp. 115–116, 122–126.

[53] Actually, the KMT's main purpose in resurrecting the *pao-chia* system was to strengthen its control over the villages and provide a means of mobilizing the people for local defense and other tasks. The formal aspects of the system have been mentioned here because it was the closest the KMT came to defining the institution of political tutelage.

[54] *The China Handbook, 1937–45,* states (p. 117) that by April, 1944, out of a total of 1,352 *hsien,* 906 had *hsien* councils and 975 had *pao* councils. But whether the forms were partially instituted or not, the intent of the program was not

The KMT made one major effort to provide a representative body at the national level in the form of the People's Political Council (PPC) established in 1938. The PPC was an attempt to promote national unity in the face of Japanese aggression, and it accordingly allowed representation of non-Party groups. However, its functions were only deliberative and advisory. Final decisions on delegates were made by the Central Executive Committee of the KMT, and nominations were made only by provincial and municipal councils (which were themselves appointed by the central government). In its early years the PPC did serve as a forum for debate and expression of non-Party views, but it was in no sense a responsible representative body and in later years it became increasingly lifeless.[55] Finally, national elections, in which all citizens were theoretically eligible to vote, were held in 1936–1937 to select delegates to a National Assembly for the adoption of a permanent constitution. Owing to the conditions in China at that time, this election was never fully completed; in any case, the KMT had dominated the selection of candidates for election.[56]

In sum, the KMT's experiments with elections and representative institutions did little to provide the people with a voice in political decisions or to give them any experience in democratic government. Even where some popular elections did occur, Party control precluded the existence of significant electoral choice. The most that can be said is that these efforts served to spread the conviction that popular participation in government was desirable and that the KMT was not fulfilling its commitments to the principles of tutelage and constitutional government.

The KMT pursued its efforts to mobilize the population behind Party objectives much more vigorously than its program for tutelage and local self-government. As in earlier years, the dominant theme was that the urgent tasks of national reconstruction demanded the fullest possible participation from all citizens. Chiang Kai-shek stated that it was both a privilege and a duty for all citizens to join either the KMT or the *San Min Chu I* Youth Corps, the Party's youth auxiliary.[57] The nation was glorified as the supreme object of loyalty, taking precedence over all

realized. See Ch'ien Tuan-sheng, *The Government and Politics of China* (Cambridge, 1950), p. 133; Fairbank, *op. cit.,* pp. 189–190; Fei Hsiano-tung, *Peasant Life in China*, pp. 109–116; Linebarger, *op. cit.,* pp. 108–111; C. K. Yang, *op. cit.,* pp. 103–107.

[55] Linebarger, *op. cit.,* pp. 69–79; Lawrence K. Rosinger, *China's Wartime Politics, 1937–1944* (Princeton, 1944), pp. 51–53.

[56] Ch'ien, *op. cit.,* pp. 314–315. This National Assembly finally met and adopted a new constitution in 1946, thus ending the period of tutelage. The 1946 constitution was important in postwar politics but it came too late to have much effect on political participation in China.

[57] Chiang Kai-shek, *China's Destiny and Chinese Economic Theory,* with notes and commentary by Philip Jaffe (New York, 1947), p. 216.

partial interests in society. In Chiang's words: "To fulfill the principle of complete loyalty to the state and of filial piety toward the nation; to be altruistic and not seek personal advantage; to place the interests of the state ahead of those of the family; such is the highest standard of loyalty and filial piety.

We must recognize that an individual can survive and make progress only as part of a state and nation." [58]

To realize these principles, the KMT tried to carry out extensive propaganda and organizational activities among the people. The Ministry of Publicity's importance led one observer to state that "no other Asiatic, and few Western, states can boast as alert and effective a system of propaganda." [59] In its efforts to organize the masses from above, the KMT experimented with many techniques later used (with much more effectiveness) by the CCP. Mass movements and organizations carried out a variety of civic and cultural programs under the leadership of high-ranking national and local officials.[60] Membership in labor unions, which were legally under the direction and supervision of government officials, became compulsory. The main function of labor unions was to assist the government in production, recruitment of labor, and stabilization of wages.[61] Within the Party and its auxiliaries, the KMT followed the policy of "democratic centralism" and sought to achieve complete unity and acceptance of policy through the use of guided discussion in small groups (*Hsiao-tsu*).[62]

Although the KMT tried to secure the popular political support that it needed, it was willing to accept mass participation only on its own terms. Movements, parties, youth groups, and unions which did not accept KMT leadership were repressed. In Chiang's own words:

If there were no Three People's Principles, there would be no War of Resistance; if there was no Kuomintang, there would be no Revolution. No political party and no political activity can aid the War of Resistance or

[58] *Ibid.*, p. 165.

[59] Linebarger, *op. cit.*, pp. 13, 138. Ch'ien Tuan-sheng (*op. cit.*, p. 125) offers a different view, claiming that KMT propaganda was ineffectual except in the early years of Nationalist rule; he remarks, perhaps too unkindly, that ". . . little work of a positive nature such as the exposition of the party doctrine or the popularization of the party program was performed. If there was any indoctrination at all, it was largely confined to the glorification of the Party Leader."

[60] This point has been referred to earlier (cf. notes 26 and 29) as evidence of the extension of governmental influence in transitional China. The most prominent national movement was the New Life Movement and its offshoots. A general discussion of KMT efforts in this direction is found in Linebarger, *op. cit.*, pp. 149–158, while many specific examples at the local level are cited in Gamble, *op. cit.*, pp. 127–128, 133–141. Gamble even notes (p. 157) the prophetic appearance of a movement to enlist all residents in antipest work.

[61] *China Handbook, 1937–45*, pp. 381–382.

[62] See the constitution of the *San Min Chu I* Youth Corps and the *Hsiao-Tsu* Training Program, reproduced in Linebarger, *op. cit.*, pp. 331–340, 354–359.

promote the revival of the nation if they differ from the Three People's Principles and from the Kuomintang. This obvious fact ought to be fully recognized by all the people, and particularly by the intellectuals.[63]

For this reason, the development of political participation in China came to depend on the KMT's power, popularity, and effectiveness. If the KMT programs were poorly executed and if large portions of the people were opposed to Party policies, then political participation could only be illegal or simply nonexistent. To a great extent, this is precisely what happened. To analyze the reasons for KMT failure in this respect is too complex a task for this study, but some suggestions can be made. Civil war, intraparty struggles and revolts, and Japanese aggression made thorough and continual control of the country a virtual impossibility and greatly enhanced the power of the military within the KMT. National disruption, coupled with increasing conservatism in the philosophy and personnel of the central government, tended to leave the old socio-economic patterns and authorities in the countryside unchanged. KMT authoritarianism and traditionalism alienated many intellectuals and deprived the Party of its best source of leadership.[64] The combination of ties with traditional rural elites and absence of progressive leaders seriously weakened the grass-roots organization of the KMT and emasculated many of the attempts at political mobilization referred to above. Finally, the KMT's insistence on suppressing all opposition before meeting the Japanese advance incurred widespread opposition on the same nationalist principles that had helped bring it to power.

The Chinese response to full-scale war with Japan in 1937 demonstrated that Chiang had great personal prestige and that the KMT could still rely on some popular support, but this should not conceal the fact that the KMT had failed to establish any permanent patterns of widespread popular participation in government or to realize the full potential of mass political activity. The debate over political tutelage revealed that there were many intellectuals who favored greater political democracy. The debate was largely ineffectual, but it revealed the KMT's suspicion of the people and its remoteness from popular influence.[65] The most powerful popular movement of the 1930's was the "National Salvation" movement of 1935–1937, which started with student demonstrations and developed into a nationwide organization calling for national unity and resistance to Japan; the movement arose in

[63] Chiang, op. cit., pp. 140.

[64] An excellent discussion of authoritarianism and traditionalism in the KMT is found in Fairbank, op. cit., chap. 11. See also Mary C. Wright, "From Revolution to Restoration: the Transformation of Kuomintang Ideology," Far Eastern Quarterly, XIV (1954–1955), pp. 515–532.

[65] For a sampling of the arguments offered in this debate, see Sources of Chinese Tradition, pp. 786–796.

opposition to KMT policy and was carried out in the face of government repression.[66] The resurgence of the CCP in the late 1930's provided a competitor for popular support, and increasing numbers of intellectuals were inclining toward the Communist program. During the years between 1937 and 1945, it was the contrast with the CCP that most fully revealed the KMT's lack of an organized and committed mass following.

The economic and political difficulties of the postwar years were crucial factors in the loss of confidence in the KMT. To a great extent, however, the postwar period merely revealed the weakness of the KMT's political authority. If the Chinese people had felt a strong attachment to the KMT government, if they had felt that their interests were represented by that government and that they had a personal share in its activities, then the KMT might have been more successful in its reconstruction programs and in its campaigns against the Communists. But this attachment did not exist. In his study of a village near Canton, C. K. Yang focused on some problems that are illustrative of those affecting China as a whole. In 1949, as the Communists were moving southward through China, the local government in this village attempted to rouse the populace through the *pao-chia* hierarchy, but failed to stimulate any loyalty to the Nationalist government or to generate popular morale for resistance to communism. The peasants in the village had no real knowledge of affairs outside the village, nor were they interested in them. They were vaguely aware of a higher political authority and the things it was supposed to do, but they did not know how the formal political process worked. They submitted to external political authority but did not identify with it.[67]

In perspective, however, KMT rule had a significant influence on the development of political participation in China. It continued the trend toward increasing awareness of the existence and authority of the national political community. The movement of national troops throughout China, the publicity given to national programs, and the attempts to carry out mass education all contributed to this trend. KMT efforts to bring the people into government and to organize them in support of Party goals demonstrated, through success and failure alike, the potentialities and problems of mass political activity. Twenty years of Nationalist control failed to institutionalize political participation in China but it helped prepare the way for the revolutionary political changes of the Chinese Comumnists.

[66] This movement is described in T. A. Bisson, *Japan in China* (New York, 1938), chap. 4, and Kiang, *op. cit.,* pp. 105–110.
[67] C. K. Yang, *op. cit.,* pp. 105–108.

THREE

The Development of
CCP Doctrine, 1921–1945

The Chinese Communist Party's victory in 1949 brought political unity to the Chinese mainland. The establishment of a government that was the recognized political authority throughout China was the most tangible evidence of this unity. Equally significant, however, was the fact that the Party brought with it a set of political principles that it had tested for several years in rural areas of China under Communist control.

The republican era of 1911–1949 had been marked by confusion and competition among a multitude of ideas and by gross discrepancies between political ideals, as stated in various constitutions, laws, and party programs, and political realities. The CCP itself was not immune to this atmosphere. In the first twenty years of its existence, it, too, experienced internal ideological conflict and frequently misjudged or ignored political moods and realities. By 1949, however, the Party had unified its ranks under Mao Tse-tung's leadership, had developed its theory of what government under CCP control ought to be, and had shown that this theory could be successfully translated into practice. Since 1949, therefore, political unity in China has meant *de facto* control by a single government, plus the existence and conscious application of a single, systematic body of political theory. By the same token, it has meant greater consistency in the theory and practice of politics than ever existed in the republican period, even though CCP doctrine retains its share of myths, unrealized ideals, and unresolved contradictions.

Since the early 1940's, the CCP has held a relatively complete and coherent concept of mass political participation. The fact that the central points in this concept took shape before 1949 and have not been significantly altered since that date reflects the thoroughness with which Party leaders absorbed the lessons of their earlier political environment. These lessons came to the Party from two main sources: Marxism–Leninism and the CCP's own experience in the course of the Chinese Revolution.

THE RESERVOIR OF SOVIET MARXISM

The development of the Sino–Soviet conflict since the middle 1950's has produced a wealth of evidence, in both original documentation and secondary analysis, of the differences between the world's two great Communist states. To explore these differences or to attempt comparisons of the Chinese and Soviet political systems is not the purpose of this study. However, a tracing of the ideas that have guided CCP leaders in their approach to the problem of popular political participation necessarily leads back to Soviet elaborations of Marxism. At a time when Sino–Soviet ideological disagreements are so prominent, it is all the more important to acknowledge the Chinese doctrinal debt to Soviet Marxism.

How is one to explain this doctrinal debt in the light of subsequent divergence? The answer lies in the Chinese use of Marxism–Leninism. For the Chinese Communists, Soviet Marxism has been a guide, an inspiration, to some extent a model. But it has been a model in the sense of defining forms appropriate to a particular socialist society at a given stage of development, not in the sense of dictating Chinese imitation of the Soviet Union. This approach has allowed Chinese Communists to profess their acceptance of the basic dogma and to follow Soviet experience in a great number of cases without accepting the Soviet model uncritically and without relinquishing their freedom to apply the dogma "creatively" in the Chinese context. It has allowed differences to emerge and develop under the cover of an admittedly common source. The Chinese concept of political participation plainly shows the influence of Soviet Marxism. But the application of this concept, while frequently suggested by, and similar to, Soviet practice, was ultimately determined and justified by its appropriateness in the Chinese setting.

The CCP was not always free to engage in "creative application." From its formation under Comintern guidance in 1921 down to 1927, the Chinese Party followed the Soviet line closely. In this period, however, the CCP was so far from power and so immersed in problems of classes, stages, and the practice of revolution, that the question of imitating the administrative and political forms emerging in the Soviet Union did not arise. The CCP later drew heavily on Soviet experience when it began to administer scattered rural areas in the Kiangsi Soviet in the early 1930's, but this episode was still too early and too transitory to have a decisive influence on subsequent Chinese practice. When the Chinese Communists finally reached a point of significant political power and began to govern large portions of China during the war years of 1937–1945, the necessity for direct copying of the Soviet system had passed. The Chinese leaders were now deeply influenced by their own experience, including the dismal results of following Soviet leadership in earlier periods, and were committed to the "creative application" of Marxism–Leninism in the light of Chinese conditions. Their dependence on the Soviet Union had gradually ceased with the retreat of the Communist movement into the relative isolation of the countryside and with the Soviet Union's growing preoccupation with European affairs. As a result, the CCP's style of mass political participation emerged largely as a product of its political environment. Before considering that process, however, we must review briefly some of the well-known elements in Soviet Marxist theory that defined the doctrinal guidelines within which Chinese Communist thinking on the subject developed.

Marx and Engels set forth only the most general ideas about the new socialist society they extolled so highly. No one could truly know how the future society would be organized, they maintained, until the productive forces and relations on which it would be based were also known. Consequently, they limited their observations about it to the assertion that the state itself would ultimately become unnecessary and wither away as a result of the disappearance of classes and the emergence of a new socialist man. However, one aspect of their writings which was to influence all subsequent communist theories about popular political activity was a biting contempt for the institutions of bourgeois democracy. In his *Critique of the Gotha Program,* Marx objected to demands that failed to go beyond "the old democratic litany familiar to all: universal suffrage, direct legislation, popular rights, a people's militia, etc." These "pretty little gewgaws" are appropriate only to a democratic republic, which may be the goal of "vulgar democracy" but certainly not of communism.[1] Marx's aversion to these institutions was based on two points. First, in capitalist society they would inevitably be controlled by the bourgeoisie, and hence would only serve to disguise the reality of capitalist oppression of the proletariat. Second, as indicated above, he feared that these institutions might become ends in themselves and obscure the ultimate goal of communism. Nevertheless, Marx acknowledged one situation in which elections and representative institutions were essential to the proletariat: the transitional period between capitalist and communist society. The necessity for such a transitional period, and the form of state demanded by it, were asserted in his criticism of the Gotha Program when he declared that a "revolutionary dictatorship of the proletariat" was the only appropriate state for the transition to communism.[2]

[1] Karl Marx and Friedrich Engels, *Basic Writings on Politics and Philosophy,* ed. by Lewis S. Feuer (Garden City, New York, 1959), p. 128.
[2] *Ibid.,* p. 127.

The task of applying Marxism to a period of sustained revolutionary activity and to the actual construction of a socialist society fell to Lenin and Stalin. The first point to be noted in this amplification of Marxist theory is Lenin's view of party leadership. Marx had recognized the need for the transmission of scientific knowledge about society to the workers through the medium of the intellectuals. With Lenin, however, the general recognition of the workers' need for guidance became a demand for political leadership by a highly organized party of intellectual elites. This demand was to have a lasting impact on Soviet and Chinese concepts of political participation.

Lenin believed that the workers themselves would never press for social revolution because of their preoccupation with immediate issues. As he stated in *What Is To Be Done?*:

The history of all countries shows that the working class, exclusively by its own effort, is able to develop only trade union consciousness, i.e., it may itself realize the necessity for combining in unions, for fighting against the employers and for striving to compel the government to pass necessary labour legislation, etc. The theory of socialism, however, grew out of the philosophic, historical and economic theories that were elaborated by the educated representatives of the propertied classes, the intellectuals.[3]

Since socialist ideology would not develop spontaneously among the workers it would have to be brought to them from the outside by the conscious efforts of the socialist party, composed primarily of intellectuals. Lacking outside education and leadership, the proletariat would inevitably succumb to bourgeois ideology. Therefore, Lenin asserted that all "subservience to the spontaneity of the labour movement, all belittling of the role of 'the conscious element,' " in fact contributes to the growth of bourgeois ideology. The task of the socialist party is not only to avoid "subservience to spontaneity" but also to "combat *spontaneity, to divert* the labour movement from its spontaneous, trade unionist striving . . . and to bring it under the wing of revolutionary Social-Democracy." [4] The theory that the proletariat could develop a "false" consciousness inconsistent with the objective conditions of its class obviously gave Lenin's party an argument for rejecting proletarian controls over the party and for maintaining that the party alone had the correct interpretation of a given situation.[5]

[3] V. I. Lenin, *Selected Works* (New York, n.d.), II, p. 53.
[4] *Ibid.*, pp. 61–63.
[5] The idea was equally useful in explaining intraparty struggles since it implied that differences were due to the "incorrect" views of dissidents rather than to ambiguities in Marxism itself. Moreover, if differences were due to false consciousness rather than class origins, they could be corrected. Lenin described intraparty disputes as a "sickness" that could be "cured" by careful study of the points in question; *Selected Works*, IX, pp. 28–29. In his report to the Twentieth

To divert the labor movement from its path of spontaneous development onto the road to revolution, Lenin urged the party to carry out constant agitation and propaganda among the workers in order to give them "political education" and raise their "political consciousness." Above all, however, the party had to maintain its own ability to lead, and, to Lenin, this meant centralized organization, ideological unanimity, and a membership made up of dedicated, professional revolutionaries. Nothing less than total adherence to socialism would do, because "to belittle socialist ideology *in any way, to deviate from it in the slightest degree* means strengthening bourgeois ideology." [6]

Lenin tried to shape his party to meet the demands of the times. For the most part, this meant adjusting to problems of clandestine revolutionary activity, of factional strife within the socialist movement, and of strict Tsarist suppression of all known revolutionary organizations in Russia. Lenin himself acknowledged that his writings on party organization and factionalism were based on these circumstances. For example, his primary objection to intraparty democracy was that democracy required open publicity and elections—which would have been open invitations to extinction in Tsarist Russia. After the Bolsheviks seized power in 1917, Lenin was less eager to speak of party leadership in dogmatic terms and more concerned with the practical effectiveness of socialist rule. Nevertheless, he made no attempt to democratize the Communist Party or to lessen the totality of its political control, even though the postrevolutionary situation altered some of the circumstances which had shaped his view of the party's role and organization.

Whatever Lenin's views might have been had he lived longer, Stalin explicitly extended the Leninist idea of party leadership into the stage of proletarian dictatorship. Starting from the premise that the dictatorship of the proletariat was a "historical era" of indefinite duration rather than a "fleeting period of 'superrevolutionary' acts and decrees," Stalin made it clear that the Communist Party, and not the proletariat in general, was to retain full control during the period of dictatorship. He insisted that the Party's leadership would not impose itself on the masses against their will, but he also insisted that only the Party was capable of leading the proletariat's struggle, that all non-Party organizations should be "auxil-

---

Congress of the Soviet Communist Party in 1956, Khrushchev praised Lenin's "therapeutic" approach to misguided party members and attacked Stalin for using "extreme" methods against comrades who had erred but were not true class enemies. Mao Tse-tung had also used the image of "curing the patient" to illustrate the proper handling of deviations within the party; see Mao Tse-tung, *Selected Works* (New York, 1956), IV, pp. 44–45. The general notion that ideological misunderstandings exist but can be corrected by discussion and study is central in Chinese Communist political theory.

[6] *Selected Works,* II, p. 62.

iary bodies" of the Party and "transmission belts" for inducing the masses to accept "voluntarily" the Party's guidance, and that all ideas about the independence and neutrality of non-Party organizations must be dismissed.[7] Under these conditions, exactly what political role was left to the people?

Lenin acknowledged that the dictatorship of the proletariat, like all forms of the state, was an instrument of class suppression, but he insisted that it was a dictatorship with a unique distinction: it would be the first dictatorship of the majority of the people (the exploited classes under capitalism) over the minority (the exploiters in capitalist society).[8] Hence, the dictatorship of the proletariat was "democratic" in a sense that no bourgeois state could ever be. The distinction was important to Lenin because it allowed the Bolsheviks to use the form of some of the same institutions that they ridiculed in capitalist society. The way out of parliamentarism, Lenin said, was not the abolition of elections and representative institutions but their transformation from "talking shops" into "working bodies." In fact, he argued that the dictatorship required "some 'reversion' to 'primitive' democracy" so that the majority could discharge the functions of state; all officials, without exception, should be "elected and subject to recall *at any time,* their salaries reduced to the level of 'workmen's wages.' "[9]

The democratic basis of the new state was to be realized through the soviets, subject to two major limitations. The first was the necessity of maintaining Communist Party control of the state, and the second was the obvious lack of education and experience among the people. These problems were met by construing the mass role in politics as *administration* of state functions and by regarding participation in administration as an educational process. Thus, we find Lenin urging that the masses be drawn into "independent political life" in order to educate them politically by their own experience and to make a start on teaching "the *whole* of the population the art of administration. . . . Our aim is to draw the *whole of the poor* into the practical work of administration. . . . Our aim is to ensure that *every* toiler, after having finished his eight hours' 'lesson' in productive labour, shall perform state duties *gratis.*"[10]

Education through participation in administration meant more than a general rise in cultural levels, although that was admittedly needed in postrevolutionary Russia. It also meant enlisting the strength of the masses in support of the revolution, or, more precisely, in support of

[7] J. Stalin, *Problems of Leninism* (Moscow, 1953), pp. 49, 98, 104.
[8] Lenin, *Selected Works,* VII, p. 41.
[9] *Ibid.,* pp. 42–44.
[10] *Ibid.,* pp. 345–346.

revolutionary objectives as defined by the Communist Party. Although the Russian people had just been freed from the oldest and most durable of fetters, said Lenin, the revolution demanded, in the interests of socialism, that the masses unquestioningly obey the leaders of the labor process; the holding of meetings was a means to this end as it enabled the people to discuss the new tasks and new conditions of life and thereby arrive at "class conscious, voluntary discipline" and an "intelligent appreciation" of the need for proletarian dictatorship and obedience to orders.[11] Thus, popular political participation during the period of the dictatorship of the proletariat was to educate the masses to accept and carry out the revolutionary tasks laid down by the Bolshevik leaders.

The preceding discussion reveals the extraordinary activism implicit in Lenin's view of the revolutionary party. Without this party's constant and conscious intervention in the historical process, the socialist revolution cannot succeed. Stalin extolled the "Russian revolutionary sweep" as a prime characteristic of the "Leninist style in work," describing this "revolutionary sweep" as "an antidote to inertness, routine, conservatism, mental stagnation and slavish submission to ancestral traditions. . . . [It is] the life-giving force which stimulates thought, impels things forward, breaks the past and opens up perspectives." [12] It is important to note, however, that party activism does not remove the necessity for action by the masses as well. Lenin warned that his opposition to following "spontaneous" movements of the people and his insistence on a secret, centralized party organization should in no way lessen mass participation in the revolutionary movement or restrict the growth of non-party activities and organizations that served the revolutionary cause.[13] After 1917, he frequently reminded his followers that the emancipation of the workers must be the work of the workers themselves; that the Communists alone, who were only "drops in the ocean of the people," could not hope to build a Communist society simply by their own efforts. Therefore, activism is required among the people just as it is within the party. Acceptance of party policies by the people must be supplemented by concrete action toward the execution of these policies.

The extent to which Soviet practice has observed the points mentioned in the preceding sketch is beyond the scope of this analysis. What is important here is that Soviet Marxism could serve as a reservoir of ideas on which the Chinese Communists could draw when they began to grapple with the question of the popular role in politics. That they

[11] *Ibid.,* pp. 342–344.
[12] Stalin, *op. cit.,* p. 110.
[13] *Selected Works,* II, pp. 139–141.

did make use of these ideas in the course of applying Marxism–Leninism to the Chinese revolution, albeit with appropriate variations and emphases, will be abundantly clear throughout our discussion of the Chinese concept of political participation.

THE INFLUENCE OF CCP HISTORY, 1921–1934

Political participation is essentially a problem of governments in power. A revolutionary movement may address itself to such matters in its statements on current and future programs, but the problem does not demand resolution until the movement has actually assumed responsibility for governing a particular area and population. In the case of the Chinese Communists, this responsibility arose in the 1930's, first, under confused and temporary circumstances, in the Chinese Soviet Republic of 1931–1934, and later in the areas under Communist control during the Sino–Japanese War. It is not surprising, therefore, that the CCP concept of political participation emerged clearly only in the 1937–1945 period, after the Party had established a relatively permanent government and declared itself on how the people under this government would take part in it. However, just as in the Soviet Union, the earlier history of the Communist Party provided experiences that influenced the Party's subsequent views.

In the first six years of its existence, from 1921 to 1927, the CCP gave only minimal attention to the question of how a communist state in China would be organized. The reasons for this are not hard to find. First, it is questionable if the CCP, in its infancy, was capable of taking a unified stand on this issue or of attacking such thorny matters as Party relations with the masses after the seizure of power. The early membership of the CCP fell far short of the Leninist model of tough and experienced revolutionaries. The leaders were intellectuals, recent converts to Marxism–Leninism who brought with them a wide variety of left-wing and liberal influences.[14] Early reports to the Comintern about the situation in China in 1922 were critical of the CCP's isolation from the masses and extremely pessimistic about the Party's ability to raise the class consciousness of the people.[15]

---

[14] See Benjamin I. Schwartz, *Chinese Communism and the Rise of Mao* (Cambridge, Mass., 1958), pp. 8–27, for an account of the conversion to Marxism–Leninism of Ch'en Tu-hsiu and Li Ta-chao. Robert A. Scalapino and George T. Yu, *The Chinese Anarchist Movement* (Berkeley, 1961), and Conrad Brandt, *The French-Returned Elite in the Chinese Communist Party* (Hong Kong, 1961,) shed light on some of the less known intellectual currents that touched the early leaders of the CCP.

[15] Allen S. Whiting, *Soviet Policies in China, 1917–1924* (New York, 1954), pp. 87–91.

Even more significant was the obvious remoteness of a genuine socialist state in China. Although the Manifesto of the Second National Congress of the CCP in July, 1922, stated that the aim of the Party was a dictatorship of the workers and peasants and urged that the workers prepare for the establishment of soviets, the primary objectives of the Party were the "overthrow of military cliques" and the "removal of oppression by international imperialism." [16] After the CCP was led into an alliance with the KMT by the Comintern in 1923, the emphasis on the immediate tasks of national unification and revolution became even more prominent. In the Sun–Joffe Agreement of January, 1923, that laid the groundwork for the CCP–KMT alliance, the Soviet representative expressly acknowledged that neither communism nor the soviet system could be carried out in China.[17] The alliance with the KMT did not change ultimate Party objectives, but it did preclude open discussion or propagandizing of a communist form of government.

Although the CCP's role in the national revolution prevented it from openly advancing its own political program, the Party was at least able to make a start on overcoming its weakness at the mass level. Alliance with the KMT opened up opportunities for organizational work both within the basic levels of the KMT and among the people at large. Members of the Party and the Socialist Youth Corps took full advantage of this, especially in the great strike of 1925 and the agitation accompanying the Northern Expedition of 1926–1927.[18] These contacts with the reality of organization and revolution at the mass level were soon reflected in Party statements. For example, a Central Committee resolution of October, 1925, pointed out the need for combining organization of the proletariat with political training and education; it also noted that full-blown Marxists could not be found as new Party members and urged that willing prospects should be recruited first and trained later.[19] The same Plenum of the Central Committee also emphasized the necessity of making propaganda intelligible to the masses in both language and content by using only the popular style of writing and by basing propaganda on concrete facts of immediate concern to the peasants and workers.[20] The progress in techniques of agitation is evident in the

[16] Conrad Brandt, Benjamin Schwartz, and John K. Fairbank, *A Documentary History of Chinese Communism* (Cambridge, Mass., 1952), pp. 63–65. Hereafter cited as *Doc. Hist.*

[17] *Ibid.*, p. 70.

[18] See Conrad Brandt, *Stalin's Failure in China* (Cambridge, Mass., 1958), pp. 43–54.

[19] C. Martin Wilbur and Julie Lien-ying How, eds., *Documents on Communism, Nationalism, and Soviet Advisers in China, 1918–1927* (New York, 1956), pp. 100–103.

[20] *Ibid.*, p. 122.

"Resolutions on the Peasant Movement" adopted at the Enlarged Plenum of the Central Committee in July, 1926.[21] These resolutions told Party members to adopt the peasants' style of speech, action, living conditions, and dress, and to avoid active opposition to the superstitions and clan relationships of the village; Party propaganda could be presented through pictorial papers, magazines, slogans, folk songs, slides, and stories, and by adapting village fairy tales and legends to Party work; Party organization was urged to enlist village personnel in its ranks, particularly the primary-school teachers. In all of this organizational work, the alliance with the KMT forced the Party to downplay its distinctive objectives and ideology, but the CCP was gaining experience in the art and prospects of mass mobilization in China.

Chiang Kai-shek's supression of the Communists in 1927 destroyed nearly all the early organizational gains of the CCP, but the abortive revolution of 1925–1927 was to have a permanent impact on CCP thinking about the political potential of the Chinese people. The most significant record of this impact came from the pen of Mao Tse-tung, who was a first-hand witness to peasant rebellion in Hunan in January and February, 1927. Mao was in no sense a sudden convert to an interest in mass action. The experiences of his childhood had given him a strong feeling for peasant discontent. Although he grew away from his rural sympathies during his youth, he nevertheless expressed in 1919, even before he was a Marxist, a passionate populism that clearly coincides with his later faith in the strength of the masses.[22] However, it is in the "Report of an Investigation into the Peasant Movement in Hunan," written in February, 1927, that we see the best statement of Mao's awakening to and respect for the power of mass action. Comments that the peasant movement is a force that no power can suppress and that it has accomplished in a few months what Sun Yat-sen failed to do in forty years reveal Mao's almost mystical faith in the invincibility of mass movements and their potential as revolutionary weapons.[23] Mao was impressed, too, by the way in which the peasant associations had taken power into their own hands, even though some Party members were disturbed by the "excesses" of such spontaneity. These ideas were later to become essential elements in the Party's mass line.

After the rupture of the CCP–KMT alliance in 1927, the CCP became an illegal party devoted to the violent seizure of power in its own name. Since this raised the possibility of the emergence of Communist-

[21] *Ibid.*, pp. 298–302.

[22] See Stuart R. Schram's excellent analysis of Mao's writings, *The Political Thought of Mao Tse-tung* (New York, 1963), pp. 18–20. Extracts from the 1919 article "The Great Union of the Popular Masses" appear on pp. 105–106 and 170–171.

[23] Mao Tse-tung, *Selected Works* (New York, 1954), I, pp. 22–25.

controlled areas, the CCP shifted its policy to approval of the establishment of soviets. The Sixth Congress of the CCP, held in Moscow from July to September, 1928, laid down the guidelines for the organization of the first Chinese soviets. As might be expected, the soviets envisaged were frankly modeled on the pattern that had emerged in the Soviet Union after 1917. The soviets were defined as directly elected organs of the workers and poor people that would provide the masses with political education and bring them into the administration of the state; the Party was to assume a leading role at all times and places, but was not to replace the soviets as the organs of power.[24]

This policy gave official recognition and approval to the existence of isolated Communist regimes, but it had little practical significance. At this time it was impossible for the Communists in China to establish and maintain Soviet-style governments. When Communist regimes sprang up, they were either short-lived, as in the case of the Canton Commune of December, 1927, or the Hai-lu-feng Soviet in Kwangtung from October, 1927, to February, 1928, or they survived only because of their isolation and mobile guerrilla tactics, as in the case of the Hunan–Kiangsi border area under the leadership of Mao and Chu Teh. The Hunan–Kiangsi regime tried to establish local governmental organs, but, by Mao's own admission, these organs were generally ineffectual and the Party organization had to handle many matters directly.[25]

A Communist government of even minimal stability did not appear until November 7, 1931, when the First All-China Congress of Soviets met at Juichin, Kiangsi, and established the Chinese Soviet Republic. This Communist state lasted until October, 1934, when KMT military pressure forced the CCP to withdraw from Kiangsi and begin the "Long March" to China's Northwest. The Soviet Republic consisted of six scattered areas in the south central provinces and varied constantly in extent and population. The key area within the republic was a block of about seventeen *hsien* on the Kiangsi–Fukien border with a population, according to one cautious estimate, of approximately three million peo-

---

[24] "Su-wei-ai Wen-t'i Chieh-shih Shu" (Explanation of the Soviet Question), in *Chung-kuo Kung-ch'an-tang Ti-liu Tz'u Ch'üan-kuo Ta-hui I-chüeh-an* (Resolutions of the Sixth Congress of the Chinese Communist Party) (n.p., n.d.). Initially, representatives in the soviets in Russia were not confined solely to Bolsheviks. In the first few years after the October Revolution, the Bolsheviks eliminated all representatives of other parties from positions of power, although some opposition party members continued to hold office in local soviets. By 1921–1922, all opposition parties were suppressed and the soviet system became a one-party dictatorship. See Merle Fainsod, *How Russia Is Ruled* (Cambridge, Mass., 1957), pp. 124–127. The Chinese soviets were to be of the post-1921 variety; there was no suggestion that any party other than the CCP would be permitted to participate.

[25] "The Struggle in the Chingkang Mountains," *Selected Works*, I, pp. 91–93.

ple.[26] In spite of the limited and variable scope of its authority, the Soviet Republic made a serious effort to establish central and local governments and to enforce its policies throughout the area under its control. The fact that the regime collapsed within three years and that some of its basic laws were either inapplicable in the rural war zones or were carried out with only partial success does not detract from the experience the CCP gained in this experiment. In fact, the effort required to maintain a government and an army under such difficult circumstances had a significant influence on the development of the Party's mass line. The Party's response to such circumstances actually began a few years before the Soviet Republic was set up.

In 1927, Mao Tse-Tung had been deeply impressed by the power of an aroused Chinese peasantry. Less than two years later, as a result of his experiences in the Hunan–Kiangsi border area, he had become equally aware of the difficulties of using the Chinese countryside as a base for a Communist-led revolution. In a report to the CCP Central Committee in November, 1928, Mao summarized the conditions necessary to maintain an independent Red regime as follows: "(1) a sound mass basis, (2) a first-rate Party organisation, (3) a Red Army of adequate strength, (4) a terrain favourable to military operations, and (5) economic strength sufficient for self-support." [27] Since Party and Red Army recruitment and Party utilization of local economic resources were partially dependent on the support and cooperation of the local population, four of the five conditions involved the question of Party relations with the masses. Popular support and cooperation did not come easily, however, for a revolutionary movement that disrupted the traditional order and drew KMT attacks upon the countryside. As Mao observed gloomily, "Wherever the Red Army goes, it finds the masses cold and reserved; only after propaganda and agitation do they slowly rouse themselves." [28] Habitual obedience to authority and lack of democratic experience made it difficult for the peasants to use the political councils set up by the Party; enterprising landlords and rich peasants retained their influence by securing government positions; localism, in the form of village or clan loyalties, created friction among various districts and even pervaded local Party organizations; broader rivalries between the native inhabitants and the "settlers" of recent centuries

[26] Harold R. Isaacs, *The Tragedy of the Chinese Revolution,* 2d rev. ed. (Stanford, 1961), pp. 336–337. In an interview with Edgar Snow in 1936, Mao estimated that the maximum 1934 population of the six areas under the control of the Central Soviet Government was nine million; he also gave three million as the population of the main area in Kiangsi. See Edgar Snow, *Red Star Over China,* (rev. ed., New York, 1939), p. 68.

[27] "The Struggle in the Chingkang Mountains," *op. cit.,* p. 71.

[28] *Ibid.,* p. 99.

sometimes overshadowed or capitalized on the struggle between the Reds and the Whites.[29]

How could a socialist revolution, even in its "democratic stage," be built on a base such as this that seemed to exhibit nearly all of the weaknesses that Marxism–Leninism assigned to the rural classes? Mao's answer was to make carefully implanted ideology and enthusiasm substitutes for proper class origin. For example, the Red Army had no choice but to use *lumpen*-proletarians and soldiers who had previously served as mercenaries; however, Mao asserted that their character could be changed by intensive political education once they had joined the Red Army.[30] Democracy in the Army was another "important weapon" for ensuring loyalty to the Communist cause, as it gave the soldiers a sense of "spiritual liberation" that was lacking in the KMT armies.[31] With the establishment of the Chinese Soviet Republic, these principles could be tested on a much wider scale within a more stable governmental framework.

The Chinese Soviet Republic tried to establish a hierarchy of soviets that would maximize popular participation at the lowest level of government.[32] The basic administrative units were the *hsiang* and municipal soviets. Deputies to the soviets were elected directly by the people on the basis of one deputy for every thirteen workers and one deputy for every fifty peasants; for the peasants, the village usually served as the electoral unit. The *hsiang* soviets were to meet every ten days, report to their constituencies once a month, and establish various committees that would enlist the participation of additional activists in government work. General mass meetings could also be called to discuss major problems and policies. All workers, peasants, and Red Army soldiers who were sixteen or over had the right to take part in elections and to be elected. Political rights were denied to "militarists, bureaucrats, landlords, the gentry, village bosses and monks" on the grounds that they were "exploiting and counter-revolutionary elements." Local elections were administered by election committees selected by the Party, the government, and various people's organizations. The election committees performed the following functions: deciding which citizens were

[29] *Ibid.*, pp. 91–95.
[30] *Ibid.*, p. 80.
[31] *Ibid.*, pp. 82–83.
[32] Data on the local soviet system is drawn from the following sources: "Constitution of the Soviet Republic," in *Doc. Hist.*, pp. 220–224; Mao Tse-tung, "Report to the Second All-China Soviet Congress" (Extract), in *ibid.*, pp. 226–239; Ho Ching-jen, "Ti-erh Tz'u Kuo-nei Ke-ming Chan-cheng Shih-ch'i Ke-ming Ken-chü-ti ti Chi-ts'eng Cheng-ch'üan Chien-she" (Basic Level Political Construction in the Revolutionary Bases During the Second Revolutionary Civil War), *Kuang-ming Jih-pao* (Bright Daily) (Peking), June 27, 1953.

eligible to vote; propagandizing the significance of, and pertinent facts about, the elections through speeches, posters, plays, and small traveling propaganda groups; drawing up candidate lists that would ensure appropriate representation for workers, peasants, and women; turning candidate lists over to popular organizations for discussion and additional nominations; convening election meetings at which the electors would hear and criticize local government reports and then elect their deputies. Regular contact between the government and the people was to be maintained by dividing all the residents of a *hsiang* into groups of thirty to seventy people and assigning one deputy to live with each group. This deputy was responsible for passing on reports to his group and for reflecting its opinions back to the soviet council.

The system outlined above was by no means fully observed throughout the Soviet Republic, but it illustrates one of the ways in which the CCP hoped to transform peasant apathy into active support for the Communist regime. Two general aspects of the system deserve special emphasis. First, the CCP maintained firm control of the local soviets not only by central direction but also by barring potential opposition elements and by supervising elections through the election committees. Second, by keeping electoral units small, assigning deputies to work with specified groups of villagers, and encouraging frequent mass meetings, the Party made political activity a village matter that could be carried out almost entirely by person-to-person contact; this lessened the obstacles of illiteracy and localism that tended to keep villagers ignorant of central government policies. In short, "Soviet democracy" was well designed to produce the "spiritual liberation" that Mao had noted in Red Army democracy, while prohibiting the emergence of any serious internal opposition to the Party.

CCP efforts to secure mass support for the revolution were not limited to the "democratization" of local government. In fact, the Soviet Republic's strongest bid for peasant allegiance was its land policy, which called for the confiscation, without compensation, of all land held by the large landowners and exploiting classes for redistribution among poor and middle peasants, hired farm hands, coolies, and Red Army soldiers.[33] Yet, given the fluctuations in the military situation and in the extent of the Soviet regime's authority, the central government found it extremely difficult to execute its basic policies, including the land law, at the village level. To meet this problem, the Party urged the people themselves, particularly through mass organizations such as peasant's associations, trade unions, and women's and youth groups, to assist local government organs in the execution of important policies.

---

[33] See "Land Law of the Soviet Republic," in *Doc. Hist.*, pp. 224–226.

For example, peasants' associations and mass meetings of villagers did much of the actual surveying and distribution of land during land reform.[34] In a speech delivered in August, 1933, Mao Tse-tung stated that government officials must mobilize the masses, through their organizations and through village and household meetings, to subscribe to bonds, develop cooperatives, regulate food supplies, consolidate finances, and develop trade.[35] Mobilization, Mao emphasized, must follow methods of a "mass character," avoiding bureaucratism and authoritarianism that would only incur mass displeasure.[36] The Party also organized mass movements designed to rally the people for extra effort in the completion of certain projects. These campaigns involved countless meetings for discussion and criticism, the use of "shock troops" and "model teams" to set an example for others, and competition among different units at team, village, and *hsiang* levels.[37]

The Soviet Republic's land policy and mobilization methods probably helped to prolong the life of the regime, but they were not successful enough to withstand growing economic and military difficulties in the soviet areas. The soviet experiment ended in military defeat, and, to the extent that the Party believed it could overcome military inferiority by securing peasant support, political defeat as well. Nevertheless, the period from 1927 to 1934 saw the appearance, although not the successful application, of nearly all the basic ideas and techniques that later made up the Chinese concept of political participation.

It is also important to note that in January, 1934, Mao Tse-tung revealed the foundations of the Party's mass line with a clarity that has never been surpassed. This statement, reflecting the experience of a movement that relied on popular support for daily survival as well as future success, is worthy of special attention. The central task, said Mao, is to mobilize the masses to participate in the revolutionary war, thereby overthrowing imperialism and the Kuomintang. But mobilizing the masses alone is not sufficient. The Party must also attend to the living conditions of the masses to make them realize that "we represent their interests, that our life and theirs are intimately interwoven." On this basis, the Party should make the masses understand the "tasks of a higher order which we propose, namely, the tasks of the revolutionary war."

[34] Chao Kuo-chün, *Agrarian Policy of the Chinese Communist Party, 1921–1959* (London, 1960), pp. 26–29.
[35] "We Must Attend to Economic Work," *Selected Works*, I, pp. 134–135.
[36] *Ibid.*, p. 135.
[37] For example, see "Kan-tung-pei Sheng Su-wei-ai Kuan-yü Fa-chan Keng-chung Yün-tung ti Chüeh-i" (Resolution of the Northeast Kiangsi Provincial Soviet on the Movement to Develop Farming), in *Su-wei-ai Chung-kuo* (Soviet China) (Moscow, 1933), pp. 164–172.

Do we want to win the support of the masses? Do we want to devote all their efforts to the war front? If we do, we must go among the masses; arouse them to activity; concern ourselves with their weal and woe; and work earnestly and sincerely in their interests and solve their problems of salt, rice, shelter, clothing and childbirth, in short, all their problems. If we do so, the broad masses will certainly give us support and regard the revolution as their very life and their most glorious banner. . . . The masses, the millions upon millions of the masses who sincerely and earnestly support the revolution . . . are a wall of bronze and iron which no force can break down, absolutely none. The counter-revolutionary forces can never break us, but we shall break them. By rallying millions upon millions of the masses round the revolutionary government and by expanding the revolutionary war, we shall be able to wipe out any counter-revolution and take over the whole of China.[38]

THE YENAN PERIOD, 1935–1945

By 1935, the Chinese Communist movement had absorbed three broad lessons that contributed to the development of the CCP concept of political participation: (1) respect for the power of mass movements; (2) dependence on the masses for survival; (3) awareness of the enormous difficulty of mobilizing rural China, with its particularism, ignorance, and indifference to political questions. The CCP had also worked out a variety of leadership techniques designed to solve the problems posed by these lessons. Nevertheless, the Party was on the verge of extinction in 1935 in spite of its considerable effort to build a mass following. The next ten years saw a dramatic reversal of this situation: the CCP emerged from the Sino–Japanese War as a movement sufficiently powerful and popular to capture control of the Chinese mainland by 1949. In the course of this reversal in fortunes, the Party continued and elaborated upon the organizational techniques that it had developed before 1935. Moreover, the CCP line on mass mobilization was infused with a new element that was of decisive importance in Communist success and of lasting impact on political participation in Communist China. This element was nationalism, accompanied by its corollary of lesser importance, the United Front. Before attempting to assess the impact of nationalism on the Party's idea of popular political participation, a brief comment on the area under Yenan's influence is in order.

Strictly speaking, the Yenan period and the circumstances with which we are now concerned did not begin until 1937. CCP forces had arrived in China's Northwest, at the end of the "Long March," in the latter part of 1935, and the CCP had called for a united front against Japan in the

---

[38] "Take Care of the Living Conditions of the Masses and Attend to the Methods of Work," *Selected Works,* I, pp. 147–150.

same year. However, the CCP did not establish its headquarters at Yenan, in Shensi, until December, 1936, and the KMT–CCP United Front did not begin until after the outbreak of the Sino–Japanese War in July, 1937. Under the terms of the United Front, the CCP theoretically abandoned its attempts to overthrow the KMT, abolished its soviet government and placed its military forces under the control of the central government in Nanking.[39] The CCP complied with these promises in name, but in fact both the areas and the armies under CCP control remained independent. Moreover, they expanded greatly during the course of the war. In April, 1945, Mao claimed that the CCP had a membership of 1,210,000, that its armies totaled 910,000 men, and that it ruled areas with a total population of 95,500,000; all these figures represented enormous increases over 1937.[40]

The areas under CCP control, usually referred to as "border regions" and "liberated areas," sprang up in the countryside where KMT forces had withdrawn and resistance to the Japanese armies was high. By the end of the war, there were nineteen such areas, mostly in North China but with some strongholds in other areas, such as the lower Yangtze region. Each of these areas had a government of its own, but all followed the leadership of the CCP and looked to Yenan as the *de facto* capital; there were, however, differences in governmental organization and in the directness of Party control in the various regions.[41] The primary function of government in the liberated areas was to organize the population for the resistance effort being carried out by regular Communist armies, guerrilla forces, and local militia. Even this limited purpose involved a substantial amount of political activity through local and regional political organs and through the mass organizations that the CCP established in all liberated areas. Government in the more stable areas was relatively complex, concerning itself with economic, fiscal, social, and educational problems. Still, in spite of their isolation from each other and differences in size and structure, the liberated areas had a common concern with maintaining guerrilla warfare against the Japanese and a common acceptance of CCP leadership in this struggle.

The key factor in Communist success during the Yenan period was the Japanese invasion of China. By destroying established authority

[39] See *Doc. Hist.*, pp. 245–247.

[40] *Selected Works*, IV, p. 242. The figures cited by Mao are subject to question but the pattern of growth is not. Communist armed forces in 1937 were probably between 50,000 and 90,000 men; see the discussion and citations in Chalmers A. Johnson, *Peasant Nationalism and Communist Power* (Stanford, 1962), p. 73. Party membership in 1937 was about 40,000; the population under CCP control in the Shensi Soviet before the outbreak of war could not have exceeded a few millions.

[41] See Tung Pi-wu, *Memorandum on China's Liberated Areas* (San Francisco, 1945) for a brief description of the liberated areas.

and arousing peasant resistance, the Japanese created a demand for anti-Japanese political leadership. The CCP met this demand by adopting a program of armed resistance that won the allegiance of the population in areas threatened or occupied by Japanese armies.[42] In the process, a new dimension was added to the Party's concept of political participation.

Nationalism was not, of course, a new theme for the CCP. The leaders of the Party had grown up in an intellectual atmosphere that was charged with ideas of national regeneration and unification. Before 1927, as we have seen, the Party's alliance with the KMT aimed at a national revolution to unify China and expel the imperialists. Even during the soviet period, when the ultimate objectives of a socialist society were proclaimed, the Party acknowledged that the revolution had not yet completed the overthrow of feudalism and imperialism. Nevertheless, the nationalistic element in the CCP program had had little concrete significance for the great majority of Chinese. The nationalist movement after the First World War was mainly one of the urban classes—intellectuals, workers, and merchants. The great peasant uprising of 1926-1927 drew its strength from economic and social demands rather than nationalist slogans. In the Chinese Soviet Republic, the Party tried to mobilize the rural masses for participation in the "revolutionary war," a war supposedly aimed at imperialism as well as the KMT. But, in the rural soviets of South and Central China, there was no concrete basis for mobilizing an anti-imperialist movement. The peasants saw the war as a struggle between the CCP and the KMT; they might have preferred one side over the other, but their preference was not based on nationalistic impulses.

After July, 1937, however, Japanese invasion began to awaken large areas of rural China to the appeal of nationalism. As a result, the CCP began to play down its economic and social objectives and give primary emphasis to resistance to Japan. In May, 1937, Mao had announced that the "contradiction" between China and Japan had replaced that between feudalism and the masses of the people as China's primary contradiction; internal Chinese contradictions between classes and political blocs remained, but had become "secondary and subordinate" to the general task of uniting to resist Japan.[43] From this time on, the public pronouncements of the CCP always included emotional and nationalistic appeals for total mobilization against Japan.[44] Mao stressed that resist-

[42] Johnson, *op. cit.*, chap. 1. Johnson gives a detailed account of the impact of Japanese invasion and the resulting growth of Communist influence in chaps. 2-5.

[43] *Selected Works*, I, 258-260.

[44] For example, see "The Ten Great Policies of the CCP for Anti-Japanese Resistance and National Salvation" in *Doc. Hist.*, pp. 242-245, and the manifesto of the CCP Central Committee following the Lukouchiao Incident of July 7, 1937, quoted in Mao, *Selected Works*, II, pp. 57-58.

ance must be "total," that is, that it must include popular action; "partial" resistance by the government alone would end in failure.[45]

The nationalistic orientation of 1937–1945 placed political participation in the service of a cause that transcended group interests and the class struggle. The CCP still insisted that it was a proletarian party leading the exploited classes to victory over the exploiters, but class struggle no longer dominated the political arena. After 1937, the political objectives of the working class merged with those of the nation at large. For example, the Central Committee in June, 1938, declared that "the highest interests of the Chinese working class are identical with the highest interests of the Chinese nation and the Chinese people.[46] In practice, the "highest" interests were actually those of the nation. A New Fourth Army manual for political workers engaged in mass movements asserted: "The basic rule is, 'the interests of the people are superior to anything else, but even they are subordinate to the interests of the Resistance War.'"[47] In terms of more concrete policies, the anti-Japanese war demanded maximum production in the liberated areas to support the war effort. Whenever possible, the Party tried to show that increasing production would also advance the interests of the people.[48] In some cases, however, it was clear that the national interest involved a sacrifice or postponement of working-class interests. When this happened, the Party insisted that "long-term" interests were really the same and that it was only "false" or "narrow" interests that were being sacrificed for the war effort. For example, the Party told cadres and peasants who resisted the moderate land policy of the Yenan period that they could not "limit their view to their own immediate and narrow interests" but must merge their immediate interests with future interests and their local interests with national interests.[49] This subordination of individual and group interests to a supreme national cause became a

[45] Selected Works, II, p. 105.

[46] Doc. Hist., p. 258.

[47] Quoted in Johnson, op. cit., p. 86.

[48] In Feb., 1943, the Central Committee stressed that the main role of the women's movement during the war was to organize women for productive activity. The Central Committee took note of women's demands for social and cultural advancement, but said that economic construction was in the best interests of women, as material progress would hasten social emancipation. See "Chung-kung Chung-Yang Kuan-yü Ko K'ang-jih Ken-chü-ti- Mu-ch'ien Fu-nü Kung-tso Fang-chen ti Chüeh-ting" (Decision of the CCP Central Committee on the Present Direction of Women's Work in the Anti-Japanese Base Areas) in Lo Ch'iung, ed., Fu-nü Yün-tung Wen-hsien (Documents on the Women's Movement), (2d ed. Harbin, 1948), pp. 1–3.

[49] Doc. Hist., p. 281. For a summary statement of CCP policies in 1940, reflecting the dominant concern with maintaining production and demonstrating a great deal of leniency toward "reactionary" classes, see Mao, Selected Works, III, pp. 219–224.

permanent fixture in the CCP concept of political participation, even though the CCP's definition of primary national goals was altered after 1945.

Once the Party had identified its ultimate objectives with the national interest, it began to assert a paternalistic responsibility for the realization of national salvation. As Mao said in 1940, "all the anti-Japanese parties and groups and the people of the whole country are responsible for the survival of the Chinese nation but, as we Communists see it, our responsibility is even heavier." [50] According to Mao, the CCP's special responsibility for uniting the nation and acting as a "vanguard" in the national war stemmed from the "adverse circumstances" of this war.

The lack of national consciousness and national self-respect and self-confidence on the part of the broad masses of the people, the unorganized state of the majority of the people, the insufficient military strength, the backward economy, the undemocratic political system, the presence of degeneration and pessimism, the lack of unity and solidarity within the united front, etc., all combine to create the adverse circumstances. Consequently, Communists have consciously to shoulder the great responsibility of uniting the whole nation in order to put an end to all undesirable phenomena.[51]

In the more specific context of the United Front against Japan, Party "responsibility" was easily and quickly translated into Party leadership.

The wartime United Front was the CCP's political formula for realizing national unity in the face of Japanese invasion and, as such, aimed primarily at securing genuine cooperation between the CCP and the KMT. In terms of this objective, the United Front was a failure. Relations between the parties were never good and, after 1941, degenerated into little more than an armed truce. Nevertheless, the United Front represented a significant alteration in Party theory, as it marked the end of the attempt to establish a "dictatorship of workers and peasants." The form of government envisaged under the United Front was a "democratic republic" that would include "the proletariat, the peasantry, the urban petty bourgeoisie, the bourgeoisie, and all persons in the country who agree to undertake a national and democratic revolution." [52] Under the old formula of the soviet period, political participation had been limited by class to workers, peasants, and soldiers. Under the United Front, political rights would be given to anyone, regardless of class, who was willing to cooperate with the Communists on the basis of broad national objectives. For reasons that will soon be discussed, the new policy had only minor significance in the liberated

[50] *Selected Works,* III, p. 211.

[51] *Selected Works,* II, p. 246. The assumption of responsibility for national salvation compelled Mao to defend patriotism as a proper "application of internationalism in the war of national liberation" (*ibid.,* p. 245).

[52] Mao, *Selected Works,* I, p. 267.

areas. However, it did attract many students and intellectuals to the Communist cause and it remains a part of the CCP concept of political participation, although in a highly attenuated form.

From the CCP's point of view, the key problem of the United Front was how to exert Party leadership without disrupting the coalition of "revolutionary classes." [53] Public statements of the Party usually glossed over this problem, but it was an item of constant concern within the CCP itself. The general line adopted was to avoid numerical dominance by Party members in the political structure of the liberated areas and to carry out Party policies through this structure by influence and example rather than by outright control. The guideline for this policy was the "three-thirds system" (*san-san chih*) by which the CCP tried to limit Party members in all political organs in the liberated areas to one-third. The following quotation from a Central Committee directive of March, 1940, illustrates this policy:

According to the principle of the political power of the Anti-Japanese National United Front, we must observe the following proportion of personnel: Communists, non-party leftist progressives and the middle-of-the-roaders should each constitute one-third.

We must ensure the leadership of the Communists in the organs of political power; therefore the Communists who constitute one-third must possess the best qualities. This condition alone will ensure the Party of its leadership even without a greater representation. By leadership is not meant that we have to shout about it as a slogan from morning till night, nor that we should imperiously force people to obey us, but that we should persuade and educate the people outside our Party through the Party's correct policies and our own exemplary work, so that they willingly accept our proposals.[54]

Another Central Committee resolution on the leadership problem stated that the Party should never force obedience to its orders, but that Party committees at various levels should lead all military, political, and mass organizations by checking on their work and by discussing and approv-

[53] CCP leadership of the United Front existed in fact and could be deduced from the Party's claim to special "responsibility" referred to earlier. However, the Party did not openly proclaim its leadership of the "revolutionary classes" until 1949. Statements about CCP and proletarian leadership that appear in "On New Democracy," Mao's 1940 exposition of the United Front, were inserted only in later editions of his works. See Arthur A. Cohen, *The Communism of Mao Tse-tung* (Chicago, 1964), p. 94n.

[54] Mao, *Selected Works*, III, p. 190. Some descriptions say the "three-thirds system" called for one-third CCP members, one-third KMT members, and one-third non-Party people. In practice, the only uniform meaning of the system was the attempt to limit CCP membership to one-third of the organ in question. Local conditions made it impossible to fulfill a uniform standard for the other two-thirds as there might be a shortage of KMT members or the people available might not fit the classifications "leftist progressives" and "middle-of-the-roaders."

ing the major resolutions, orders, and regulations of these organizations. [55]

In this atmosphere, Party literature on the mass line developed rapidly. As in the soviet period, the CCP was initially concerned with winning the respect and support of the people as a bulwark against anti-Communist attacks. However, Party work among the masses was also an essential ingredient in the United Front formula described above, as the CCP relied on its ability to persuade and educate the masses in order to realize its objectives. Party members were constantly exhorted to get close to the masses, both physically and psychologically, and to listen to all popular opinions and demands.[56] By June 1, 1943, the CCP mass line appeared in a form that has remained virtually unchanged down to the present time. A Central Committee resolution of that date contained the following passage:

In all practical work of our Party, correct leadership can only be developed on the principle of "from the masses, to the masses." This means summing up (i.e. coordinating and systematising after careful study) the views of the masses (i.e. views scattered and unsystematic), then taking the resulting ideas back to the masses, explaining and popularising them until the masses embrace the ideas as their own, stand up for them and translate them into action by way of testing their correctness. Then it is necessary once more to sum up the views of the masses, and once again take the resulting ideas back to the masses so that the masses give them their wholehearted support. . . . And so on, over and over again, so that each time these ideas emerge with greater correctness and become more vital and meaningful.[57]

To summarize the discussion thus far, the Yenan period recorded three major advances in the development of CCP ideas about political participation: the injection of nationalistic appeals and goals into the Party program, the acceptance of a united front of several classes as the appropriate formula for China's "new democratic" revolution,[58] and the theoretical crystallization of the Party's mass line. The final point that

[55] *Mao's China: Party Reform Documents, 1942–1944,* trans. and intro. by Boyd Compton (Seattle, 1952), pp. 161–175.

[56] The tendency of some Party members to look down on or ignore non-Party elements was severely criticized by Mao during the Cheng-feng (rectification) campaign of 1942 as a form of "sectarianism"; he pointed out that the Communists were only a tiny fraction of the total Chinese population and that cooperation with non-Party people was essential. See Mao, "Rectify the Party's Style in Work," *Selected Works,* IV, pp. 42–43.

[57] *Ibid.,* p. 113.

[58] The KMT–CCP alliance of 1923–1927 was a united front of several classes during the national democratic revolution, but it differed from the United Front policy adopted in 1937. The earlier policy allowed Communists to join the KMT as individuals and recognized KMT leadership of that stage of the revolution. The later policy maintained the autonomy of all participating parties, at least in theory, and extended the United Front into the stage of socialist revolution.

should be made about this period is that the practical application of Party principles of political participation was far more successful than in the Soviet period. The Shen-Kan-Ning Border Region will serve as an example of political practice during the war years. This Border Region, with a population of about one and a half million people in the three provinces (Shensi, Kansu, and Ninghsia), was by no means a typical example of the liberated areas. As the original Northwest base of the CCP and the area in which the Party Center was located, it was actually a "model" area of CCP control. However, precisely because of its well-established Party presence and its relative security from Japanese attack, the Shen-Kan-Ning Border Region set the pattern of government for all of the liberated areas. Generally speaking, the measures adopted in this region were eventually carried out in the other liberated areas when the military situation permitted.[59]

The distinctive feature of the Shen-Kan-Ning Border Region representative structure was the direct election of representative assemblies at the three principal levels of government, namely, the *hsiang,* the *hsien,* and the Border Region levels.[60] General elections in the Border Region were held in 1937, 1941, and 1945. The Border Region Assembly met only four times in these years (in 1939, 1941, 1944, and 1946), but the *hsiang* and *hsien* assemblies met relatively frequently. Assembly meetings were of short duration. Their major functions were to elect the government at their respective levels and to discuss and criticize the

[59] Local political organizations and activities were quickly organized in all liberated areas when Communist troops or political workers arrived, but the establishment of regional organs of government might be delayed for several years. For example, the Chin-Ch'a-Chi Border Region in Shansi, Chahar, and Hopei provinces was established in 1938 and held local elections in 1938 and 1940; however, the structure of "democratic government" was not completed until the formation of a Border Region Assembly in January 1943. See *K'ang-Jih Chan-cheng Shih-ch'i Chieh-fang-ch'ü Kai-k'uang* (The General Situation in the Liberated Areas During the Anti-Japanese War), (Peking, 1953), p. 32.

[60] This summary of Border Region governmental structure is based on the following sources: "Shen-Kan-Ning Pien-ch'ü Hsüan-chü T'iao-li" (Election Regulations of the Shen-Kan-Ning Border Region), adopted by the First Border Region Assembly in January, 1939, in *Shen-Kan-Ning Pien-ch'ü Ts'an-i-hui Wen-hsien Hui-chi* (Collected Documents of the Shen-Kan-Ning Border Region Assembly), ed. by Chung-kuo K'o-hsüeh-yüan Li-shih Yen-chiu-so Ti-san So (Third Office of the Institute of History of the Chinese Academy of Science) (Peking, 1958), pp. 53–55; "Shen-Kan-Ning Pien-ch'ü Ko-chi Ts'an-i-hui Tsu-chih T'iao-li" (Organizational Regulations for Various Level Assemblies of the Shen-Kan-Ning Border Region), adopted at the First Border Region Assembly in January, 1939, in *ibid.,* pp. 55–58; "Regulations Governing the Election of the Various Grades of People's Councils in the Shensi–Kansu–Ninghsia Border Region," adopted at the Second Border Region Assembly in November, 1941, in *Laws and Regulations of the Shensi–Kansu–Ninghsia Border Region,* (n.p. [Yenan?], 1945); Hsu Yung Ying, *A Survey of the Shensi–Kiangsu [Kansu]–Ninghsia Border Region,* Part I, Geography and Politics (New York, 1945), pp. 47–71.

work of the government. At the village level popular control was greater because the village head as well as a village council were directly elected by the villagers.

All Border Region citizens of eighteen or over had the right to vote and be elected regardless of class, party, sex, religion, race, property, or cultural level. There were exceptions, however, as "traitors, those deprived of civic rights by civil or martial courts and the mentally unsound" were denied political rights. Mao expressed this more simply by saying that "only collaborators and anti-Communist elements" would be denied political office, while all who "favored democracy and resistance to Japan" would have political rights.[61] Electoral regulations in the Border Region changed three times between 1937 and 1945, the purpose being to reduce the number of deputies per population and to lengthen the terms of office of assemblymen. The changes were made in the interests of efficiency as it was difficult to hold assembly meetings and elections frequently; moreover, the high ratio of deputies to population, as well as excessive staff and committee assignments, was removing too many able-bodied people from productive work. In spite of these changes, however, the Border Region population was well represented in terms of numbers of deputies. For example, the election law adopted at the Second Border Region Assembly in November, 1941, provided that each "residents' group" of 20–60 people would have one deputy in the *hsiang* assembly, and each 8,000 people would have one deputy in the Border Region Assembly. The "residents' groups" in the *hsiang* were based on natural living conditions and ensured that each *hsiang* deputy would have contact with and responsibility for a known group of his neighbors. Certain other groups, such as the safety-preservation corps, the anti-Japanese garrison forces, universities and technical schools, and factories employing over a hundred workers, could serve as independent electoral units.

The Border Region assemblies did not exercise final control over the governments at their respective levels. In the Shen-Kan-Ning Border Region, higher levels of government could suspend or correct "inappropriate" resolutions of lower bodies, and lower-level governments were responsible to higher-level governments as well as to their own assemblies; moreover, the Border Region Government had to endorse the election of all *hsien* magistrates, members of the *hsien* government, and *hsiang* chiefs, and could remove or transfer *hsien* magistrates and *hsiang* chiefs.[62] The Border Region assemblies' main function was to

---

[61] *Selected Works,* III, pp. 200–201.
[62] See Hsu Yung Ying, *op. cit.,* pp. 51–52, and "General Regulations Governing Discipline in the Administration of the Shensi–Kansu–Ninghsia Border Region," in *Laws and Regulations of the Shensi–Kansu–Ninghsia Border Region.*

inculcate a sense of civic responsibility in the population by involving as many people as possible in the administration of local affairs. Hsieh Chüeh-tsai, vice-chairman of the Border Region Assembly, stated this purpose in the following way: "Democracy is not made sufficient by discussion or by doing things well; it requires that the people truly do things themselves. The people feeling that the government is good and the people themselves managing the government are two completely different matters. In the latter case the people not only know they have power, they further know they have responsibility." [63]

To give a concrete illustration, *hsiang* assemblies were surrounded by many fixed or temporary committees that enlisted the participation of activists and other capable people, thereby giving training to the participants and making more people "promoters of government work." [64] Model rules laid down for assembly meetings indicate that little spontaneous action was allowed but that as many deputies and residents as possible were exposed to the work of the assembly. Each meeting concentrated on one central problem for which proposals had been prepared in advance. These proposals were given to deputies before the meeting so that each deputy could go over them with his residents' group; if this preparation was not carried out, it was warned, there would be "nothing to do or say" at the meeting and attendance would decline. The meeting itself was short, a half-day to a little over a day. Deputies with prepared speeches could talk for 10–20 minutes, but the general rule was "no one should speak too long, everyone should say his piece." Meetings were to be attended by all assembly deputies, all village heads who were not deputies, government officials concerned with the topic under discussion, various officials from higher levels of government, and primary-school teachers. The higher-level officials were needed to guide the work, while primary-school teachers were needed to do the writing (and officials were urged to respect and use their knowledge). [65]

The CCP made a serious effort to put the three-thirds system into practice in the Border Region assemblies and governments, but its success was limited. The CCP held such power and respect in the villages that most local representatives supported the Party regardless of the system. [66] Before the system was proposed, poor and middle peasants held 80–90 percent of elected positions at the *hsien* level and below,

[63] "San-san Chih ti Li-lun yü Shih-chi" (The Theory and Reality of the Three-Thirds System), in *Shen-Kan-Ning Pien-ch'ü Ts'an-i-hui Wen-hsien Hui-chi*, p. 202.

[64] Hsieh Chüeh-tsai, "Hsiang-shih Ts'an-i-hui Tsen-yang Kung-tso" (How the *Hsiang* and Municipal Assemblies Work), in *ibid.*, p. 181.

[65] *Ibid.*, pp. 183–184.

[66] See Johnson, *op. cit.*, pp. 13–14, and Chao Kuo-chün, *op. cit.*, pp. 65–66.

while rich peasants, landlords, merchants, and intellectuals together held only 6–7 percent of the positions.[67] Thus, at local levels, the Party had to compel resignations of some of its supporters and to support the election of KMT or upper-class candidates. This practice probably accounts for the high percentage of new officeholders that emerged after the 1941 and 1945 elections. Even so, the three-thirds system was only partially carried out. After the 1941 elections, it was announced that Party membership had been reduced to one-third or below in some government organs but by no means in all. The system was closest to realization in newly occupied areas, but far from realization where the CCP was long established. It was closer to realization at the *hsiang* level than at the *hsien* level, while the Border Region Assembly had 56 percent CCP members.[68] The three-thirds system and the existence of popularly elected assemblies certainly softened the harshness of CCP control but did not materially lessen the effectiveness of that control. Given the absence of organized opposition and the widespread approval of the Party's wartime policies, it is likely that the CCP could have maintained its leading position with even fewer Party members in key posts.

CCP influence was further strengthened by its work in the mass organizations. In 1939, Lin Po-ch'ü, the chairman of the Border Region Government, stated that every citizen in the Border Region belonged to at least one organization and that many took part in two or more. All these organizations, including unions, peasant associations, national salvation associations, and various resistance, relief, and cultural organizations, were organized on the basis of democratic centralism; that is, they had a broad mass base, but lower levels submitted to orders from higher levels and the individual submitted to organizational discipline. Lin added that these mass organizations were devoted to mobilizing the masses for assisting the government in national resistance and construction. In recognition of this service, the government assisted the organizations financially and by providing them with buildings, meeting places, and equipment.[69] The CCP was in firm control of these organizations, most of which its political workers had initially organized.[70]

[67] Lin Po-ch'ü, "Shen-Kan-Ning Pien-ch'ü Cheng-fu Tui Ti-i Chieh Ts'an-i-hui ti Kung-tso Pao-kao" (Work Report of the Shen-Kan-Ning Border Region Government to the First Assembly), in *Shen-Kan-Ning Pien-chü Ts'an-i-hui Wen-hsien Hui-chi,* pp. 17–18.

[68] Hsieh Chüeh-tsai, "San-san Chih ti Li-lun yü Shih-chi," *op. cit.,* pp. 198–207. The three-thirds system approached realization only after the elections of October, 1945.

[69] Lin Po-ch'ü, *op. cit.,* pp. 19–20.

[70] See Johnson, *op. cit.,* pp. 84–91.

A report on the 1941 election, prepared by the Civil Affairs Bureau of the Border Region Government, illustrates both the process and problems of mass participation during the Yenan period.[71] A Border Region Election Committee, established by the Civil Affairs Bureau, exercised overall control of the election, which was called to implement the three-thirds system adopted after the first Border Region election in 1937. The election movement began with the training of election cadres in January, 1941, moved through mobilization, nominations, and elections at lower levels, and ended with the convocation of the new Border Region Assembly in November. The Civil Affairs Bureau regarded the general situation as favorable, owing to previous electoral experience in 1937 and the relatively high political consciousness stemming from the wartime atmosphere. It also noted several obstacles, however. One item of concern was that each *hsiang* consisted of 20–30 villages that had little contact with each other, making it difficult to call meetings and exchange opinions within the *hsiang*. Another problem was that 85 percent of the village population was illiterate, and hence unable to read propaganda or write ballots. There were also "political shortcomings" that the bureau expected the election movement to correct. Anti-Communists, who were said to be few in number but who sometimes put up verbal or even armed resistance, had to be removed from positions, of influence; peasant distrust of landlords and capitalists had to be overcome to implement the three-thirds system; cadre defects, such as corruption in office, aloofness from the people, or neglect of the democratic system, were to be rectified. In short, the election campaign was a multifunctional tool for filling offices, strengthening the United Front, educating the masses, subduing Party enemies, and reforming Party and government officials.

The movement began with the training of core cadres, mostly students and *hsien* officials chosen by the Border Region government, who then fanned out to organize local election committees. These committees, too, were carefully chosen from Party, army, school, and other organizations, but they were predominantly lower-class in composition. Election work teams, composed mainly of students and operating at a ratio of almost one team per village, then initiated propaganda and registration at the village level. In addition to propagandizing through slogans, rustic songs, village meetings, and home visits, the work teams tried to overcome fears about registration (some peasants believed it would lead to military service), advised and assisted "ignorant, illiterate, or forgetful" village officials in the preparation of work reports, and sought out "activists" among the population to question officials when their reports

[71] *Shen-Kan-Ning Pien-ch'ü Hsiang-hsüan Tsung-chieh* (A Summary of Village Elections in the Shen-Kan-Ning Border Region) ([Yenan], 1941).

were publicly presented. Nominations for office came mostly from various organizations, including the government, but special efforts were made to solicit nominations from village small groups and to seek out women candidates. The Civil Affairs Bureau acknowledged that many villagers resisted nomination of themselves, or even of a neighbor for fear they would have to work his fields if elected. Finally, the work teams called for proposals from the people to guide the successful candidates. As might be expected, activists and the mass organizations submitted most of the proposals; election workers assisted by writing down proposals or simply by turning in comments that they overheard.

The election itself was something of an anticlimax, although no efforts were spared to secure high attendance at election meetings. Meetings were open for debate, but most candidates were embarrassed to talk about themselves, and only CCP candidates had platforms to discuss. After the elections, in which a variety of voting techniques were used, local officials arranged ceremonial convocations of the new *hsiang* assemblies, complete with welcoming songs and banners from school children and the mass organizations. The Civil Affairs Bureau did not try to conceal the frustrations and errors that appeared during the election, but it felt that the movement was successful, particularly in securing the participation of people who had previously been divorced from political life. The bureau concluded that the only way to strengthen the *hsiang's* foundation was to organize the masses for political participation.

The bureau's report is a candid revelation of the CCP's ability to guide the masses into political activity without entrusting to them significant political power. What is significant in this is not the intent but the fact that it was done so well, for even a brief discussion of political activities in the Shen-Kan-Ning Border Region shows that the Party had come a long way from its frustrating attempts to establish a stable mass following in the 1920's and early 1930's. Of course, the population of rural China still resisted political mobilization; the constant supervision and prodding by cadres bears testimony to the presence of illiteracy, peasant apathy, and even some outright hostility toward the Chinese Communists. The important point, however, is that during the period 1937–1945 the Party was able to cope with these problems within the framework of a relatively stable government that did, in fact, rely heavily on popular support. As noted earlier, the Japanese invasion created the necessary conditions for the emergence of Communist-dominated governments in the liberated areas. But it is also a fact that the CCP capitalized on this opportunity by the successful use of organizational techniques that directed popular political activities toward the realization of Party goals.

The Yenan period was well suited to a unification of Communist political theory with the realities of the Chinese revolution. On the one hand, it gave Party leaders the opportunity to study Marxist–Leninist theory in greater depth, a study that was reflected in increased citations of Communist classics as well as in an increased flow of dogmatic writings from the Chinese themselves, particularly Mao Tse-tung. On the other hand, the nationalistic atmosphere of the Yenan period produced a conscious summing up of Chinese experience and a demand that all theory be tested in the practice of the Chinese revolution.[72] As a result, the Chinese concept of political participation that emerged at the end of the war was broadly modeled on Soviet theory, particularly in its emphasis on Party leadership independent of popular controls, its use of all forms of social organization as agencies for carrying out Party objectives, and its attempt to educate the masses politically through participation. At the same time, it was unmistakably stamped by the CCP's experience in rural revolution and national war. The mystical reliance on the masses, the simple yet thorough techniques of mass mobilization that depended primarily on face-to-face discussion, the broad appeal for a coalition of classes to struggle for national salvation, and the deliberate attempts to play down CCP leadership by such devices as the three-thirds system were all consequences of this experience. Not all of the political practices of the Yenan period survived after the end of the war; the three-thirds system and the direct election of all levels of representatives were two of the more permissive techniques that disappeared after 1945. Nevertheless, the CCP has continued to maintain the fictions of popular control of the representative structure and multiparty participation in government that entered its concept of political participation during the war against Japan.

[72] See the discussion by Boyd Compton in his introduction to *Mao's China: Party Reform Documents, 1942–1944.*

FOUR

The CCP Concept of Political Participation 1945–1965

The desire of Communist theoreticians to maintain the continuity of their doctrine and to protect themselves against future shifts in policy gives their theory an aura of consistency that is frequently misleading. Whatever the trend of a particular period might be, one is almost certain to find qualifying remarks that tie in with the previous line or warn against carrying the current line to extremes. The CCP concept of mass political participation is a case in point. In terms of Party theory, it appears to have been fully developed by 1945 and to have changed very little since that time; in application, however, it has changed frequently during the years between 1945 and the present. Therefore, analysis of the Chinese Communist concept of popular political participation requires not only a review of its relatively constant elements, but also a survey of the major changes that have occurred since 1945 in the Party's attitude toward mass political activity.

The CCP does not express its ideas about political participation in a simple or summary way. There are, of course, many brief references to the ultimate political power vested in the people or to political rights guaranteed to the people, but these references are meaningless unless amplified by other aspects of Chinese political life. The problem in defining the CCP's position on this matter is that it involves principles which are taken for granted by Party spokesmen and frequently left unsaid. Nevertheless, there is nothing obscure about the ideas that determine the theoretical character of politics in Communist China, and the essence of the CCP's concept of mass political participation can be found within them. The relevant principles are the following: the dictatorship of the proletariat; the supremacy of the collective interest; Party leadership; the mass line; activism and political consciousness; socialist democracy.

THE DICTATORSHIP OF THE PROLETARIAT

The Communist state established in Peking in 1949 was, strictly speaking, defined as a "people's democratic dictatorship" rather than a "dictatorship of the proletariat." The former term emphasized the multi-class composition of the new state, but it did not signify any departure from the role to be performed by the proletarian dictatorship in the Marxist–Leninist formula described in the previous chapter. In fact, the CCP has now accepted "dictatorship of the proletariat" as a proper definition of the Chinese People's Republic (CPR). In his "Political Report" to the Eighth National Party Congress in 1956, Liu Shao-ch'i said that the people's democratic dictatorship was "in essence a form of the dictatorship of the proletariat." [1]

In Party theory, the formation of a "people's democratic dictatorship" signified that China had embarked on the road leading to the abolition of classes, political parties, and the state itself. [2] Theoretically speaking, therefore, all political rights and activities in China are temporary arrangements to help bring about the harmonious and stateless communist society. The ultimate objective of the proletarian dictatorship also imposes certain conditions on it. First, the dictatorship must be strong and highly centralized because it is undertaking "the greatest and most difficult tasks." At the same time, since its goal is the "material and spiritual emancipation of the people" and "harmony and equality among mankind," it must do its utmost to "bring into full play the initiative and positive role of the masses." [3] The extinction of state, classes, and political parties obviously has little practical meaning for China at present and, in fact, the CCP rarely raises the subject at all. [4] Nevertheless, the idea that the dictatorship of the proletariat will realize its mission only when it achieves the stateless society and the material and spiritual liberation of man compels the CCP to regard political activity as a process

[1] Eighth National Congress of the Communist Party of China, I, Documents (Peking, 1956), p. 68.

[2] Mao Tse-tung, "On the People's Democratic Dictatorship," Selected Works of Mao Tse-tung, IV (Peking, 1961), p. 411.

[3] "On the Historical Experience of the Dictatorship of the Proletariat," Jen-min Jih-pao (People's Daily) (Peking) (hereafter cited as JMJP), editorial, April 5, 1956, in The Historical Experience of the Dictatorship of the Proletariat (Peking, 1959), pp. 4–5.

[4] Two important exceptions can be noted. In 1958, during the first flush of enthusiasm over the people's communes, some references were made to the approaching disappearance of the internal functions of the state. More recently, the imminence of communist society has been an item of debate between China and the Soviet Union. The CCP's position now is that communism is not likely to appear anywhere in the world for a very long time. See the letter of the CCP Central Committee to the Central Committee of the Soviet Communist Party in The New York Times, Western Edition, July 5, 1963, pp. 5–6.

that is constantly advancing man's ability to live in social harmony without the need for formal governmental institutions.

The second major impact of the dictatorship of the proletariat on political participation in China is the sharp distinction that it makes between those who are entitled to political rights and those who are not. Since the dictatorship is imposed on reactionary classes for the purpose of achieving socialism, political rights are exercised by all those who support socialism and denied to those who do not. In China, according to Mao's dictum, those who support socialism consist of four classes and are defined as the "people."

Who are the people? At the present stage in China, they are the working class, the peasantry, the urban petty bourgeoisie and the national bourgeoisie. These classes, led by the working class and the Communist Party, unite to form their own state and elect their own government; they enforce their dictatorship over the running dogs of imperialism—the landlord class and bureaucrat-bourgeoisie, as well as the representatives of those classes, the Kuomintang reactionaries and their accomplices. . . . Democracy is practised within the ranks of the people, who enjoy the rights of freedom of speech, assembly, association, and so on. The right to vote belongs only to the people, not to the reactionaries.[5]

Although the dictatorship is led by the proletariat, it must be based on an alliance among all the "people" and secure the broadest participation by the masses in the work of government. Political parties of nonproletarian classes that support socialism are allowed to exist so long as traces of their nonproletarian ideology remain and need representation. The proletarian party (the CCP) accepts alliance with these parties on the basis of "long-term co-existence and mutual supervision" even though they are ultimately destined to disappear.[6] Of course, any members of the classes and parties belonging to the alliance will remove themselves from the ranks of the "people," and thereby lose their political rights, if they oppose socialism.

THE SUPREMACY OF THE COLLECTIVE INTEREST

During the Yenan period, the CCP legitimized its political leadership by taking up the transcendental cause of national unity for resistance to Japan. In a similar way, the CCP asserts that the dictatorship of the proletariat aims at a goal of such importance to the people that it eclipses all other political interests. The CCP does not recognize that the shift in goals represents a shift from national to class interests; that is, the Party continues to insist that its basic objective, now the attainment

---

[5] Mao, "On the People's Democratic Dictatorship," *op. cit.*, pp. 417–418.
[6] Liu Shao-ch'i, "Political Report," *op. cit.*, pp. 69, 72–73.

of socialism, is in the highest national interest just as was resistance to Japan in 1937–1945. Therefore, when the CCP speaks of the collective interest it means not only the total interest of the "people," as defined above, but also the state interest, which represents the people's interest during the dictatorship of the proletariat, and the national interest. Since socialism represents the highest collective interest, patriotism and support for socialism are inseparable. As Lu Ting-yi, director of the Propaganda Department of the CCP Central Committee, has said: "On what basis are we to unite? On the basis of patriotism and socialism. What do we unite for? To build a new, socialist China and combat our enemies both at home and abroad." [7]

Since the identical interests of state, nation, and society are manifestly of the highest order, no individual interests are allowed to compete with them. "We permit no one to impair the interests and freedom of the majority, the public interests of the country and society, for the sake of the interests and freedom of any individual or individuals." [8] According to Party theory, this prohibition does not indicate a lack of concern for individual interests. On the contrary, the state's defense of public interests is said to be a defense of "the very foundation on which the individual interests of the masses of the people can be satisfied." The masses cannot possibly lose personal interests and individual freedom by fulfilling their obligations to society and country because "personal interests are indivisible from the public interests of the country and society; . . . they are one and the same." [9] The most that the CCP concedes is that "partial and temporary interests" of the masses may come into conflict with their "total, long-range interests"; when this happens, the Party states flatly, the former must be subordinated to the latter. [10]

Since the collective interest is not only superior to any partial interest but is also the truest statement of long-run individual interests, the CPR gives great stress to civic duties. Both rights and duties are laid down "for the sake of building and preserving our great fatherland, for guaranteeing a happy life for the people, and for realizing the great cause of socialist construction and socialist reform." [11] The overpowering supe-

[7] Lu Ting-yi, "Let Flowers of Many Kinds Blossom, Diverse Schools of Thought Contend!" (Peking, 1959), pp. 15–16.

[8] Liu Shao-ch'i, "Report on the Draft Constitution of the People's Republic of China," in Documents of the First Session of the First National People's Congress of the People's Republic of China (Peking, 1955), p. 49.

[9] Ibid., p. 50.

[10] Liu Shao-ch'i, On the Party (Peking, 1950), p. 63. This pamphlet is Liu's report on the revision of the Party constitution, delivered at the Seventh Party Congress in May, 1945.

[11] Li Kuang-ts'an, Wo-kuo Kung-min ti Chi-pen Ch'üan-li ho I-wu (The Basic Rights and Duties of our Citizens) (Peking, 1956), p. 6.

riority of the public interest imposes obligations on the citizen that go far beyond simple observance of state laws. "The problem of respecting the law is not merely a legal obligation but a moral obligation as well. Each citizen should not only be a model in his observance of the Constitution and laws; he also ought to struggle resolutely against all illegal manifestations in order to support the interests of the state and the people." [12]

The highest collective interest, of course, is that of the state or the people as a whole. However, collectivism as such is a virtue and the individual is subordinate to the group at every level of Chinese society. For example, middle-school students are urged to follow this rule of conduct: "The class and the school are collective groups and the students are the component members of the groups. Every member should be devoted to the group to which he belongs and heighten his sense of duty toward it. He should strive to protect its reputation, be proud of its good name, resent any act which is not in keeping with its interests and fully develop the spirit of collectivism." [13]

In June 1957, Mao Tse-tung's famous speech, "On the Correct Handling of Contradictions Among the People," was made public. This speech is of interest here because of Mao's admission that "contradictions" can and do exist among the people in Communist China. Specifically, Mao stated that there could be contradictions within and among the classes composing the "people," that is, the workers, the peasantry, the intelligentsia, and the national bourgeoisie. There could also be contradictions between the government and the masses.[14] The question raised here is whether or not this remarkable admission implied any change in the Party's theory of the inseparability of public and individual interests. In the first place, Mao carefully pointed out that contradictions among the people are "non-antagonistic," in contrast to "antagonistic" contradictions between the people and their enemies, and are underlain by "the basic identity of the interests of the people." [15] Mao also stated that contradictions among the people could be resolved,

[12] *Ibid.*, p. 93.

[13] "Explanatory Notes on the Contents of the Rules of Conduct for Middle School Students," *Jen-min Chiao-yü* (People's Education), July 9, 1955, in American Consulate General, Hong Kong, *Extracts from China Mainland Magazines*, No. 3 (August 29, 1955). With issue No. 213 in June, 1960, the title of *Extracts from China Mainland Magazines* was changed to *Selections from China Mainland Magazines;* the two titles are hereafter cited as *SMM*. Most of the literature designed to inculcate the collectivist ideal concentrates on the homespun example drawn from lower-level production units. For example, see the stories in *SMM*, No. 320 (July 3, 1962).

[14] Mao Tse-tung, "On the Correct Handling of Contradictions Among the People," in *Let a Hundred Flowers Bloom*, with intro. and notes by G. F. Hudson (New York, n.d.), pp. 16–17.

[15] *Loc. cit.*

one after another, by the socialist system itself and that socialist society would become more united and consolidated through the correct resolution of contradictions.[16] The meaning of the last statement becomes clearer when we examine the causes of the contradictions in question. According to Mao, contradictions exist in China because of various imperfections and imbalances in the system. For example, the socialist system is relatively new and not fully consolidated, some elements of capitalism remain, bourgeois ideology survives in some quarters, state organs have not completely rid themselves of bureaucratism, some state institutions have flaws, some of the masses are not yet accustomed to the system, government workers need more experience, and so forth.[17] The existence of contradictions is due not to conflicts between socialism and the people's true interests but to departures from correct socialist institutions and behavior.

Contradictions among the people can be solved, Mao stated, by distinguishing between right and wrong.[18] The critical question, obviously, is how people are to know what things are "right" and deserve advocacy and practice, and what things are "wrong" and deserve correction. To answer this, Mao suggested six criteria by which words and actions could be judged "right." Of these, the two most important are "beneficial, not harmful, to socialist transformation and socialist construction" and "tend to strengthen, not to cast off or weaken, the leadership of the Communist Party." [19] Thus, Mao did not alter the fundamental limit of political participation in Communist China—that the only acceptable political demands are those made in the name of the collective interest or socialism. Mao acknowledged that other types of demands exist among the people and urged that they be heard. But such demands are by definition "wrong" and are allowed public expression only so that they can be corrected.

PARTY LEADERSHIP

The principle of Party leadership is the most fundamental fact in the political life of a Communist state.[20] The justification of Party leadership is a dual one, resting first on the fact that the dictatorship of the proletariat must be led by the proletarian party and secondly on the

[16] *Ibid.*, pp. 26–27.
[17] *Ibid.*, pp. 28–30.
[18] *Ibid.*, p. 18.
[19] *Ibid.*, p. 49. The six criteria were probably not in the original form of the speech as delivered on February 27, 1957; see Roderick MacFarquhar, *The Hundred Flowers Campaign and the Chinese Intellectuals* (New York, 1960), pp. 17–25, 262–263. Our interest here is in the public version of June that was incorporated into CCP dogma.
[20] For a thorough analysis of the subject, see John Wilson Lewis, *Leadership in Communist China* (Ithaca, 1963).

assertion that the Communist Party, because of its scientific knowledge and political experience, is superior in leadership abilities to any other political organization.

As we have said before, the cause of socialism in our country cannot do without the dictatorship of the proletariat which is realized through the leadership of the party of the proletariat—the Communist Party. The strength of leadership of the Chinese Communist Party lies in the fact that it is armed ideologically with Marxism–Leninism, is correct in its political and organizational lines, rich in experience in struggle and in work, skilled in crystallizing the wisdom of the whole country and turning that wisdom into a united will and disciplined action. And not only in the past, but in the future, too, the leadership of such a party is essential in order to ensure that our country can deal effectively with complex domestic and international affairs.[21]

In Communist doctrine, the Party is totally altruistic in accepting its leading role; it is motivated solely by its desire to serve the people and bring about their welfare and emancipation.[22] Since the Party's interests are identical with those of the people, all Party policies and state plans are said to represent mass interests. Moreover, there can be no distinction between a Communst's responsibility to the Party and his responsibility to the masses, as it is the same in each case.[23] In this way, the Party adds to its other qualifications for leadership the claim of being the true representative of popular will.

Party leadership does not mean that the CCP should directly command state organs or address itself to purely administrative tasks of state. It does mean that the Party must regularly discuss and decide on major principles, policies, and organizational matters in state affairs. It also means that the Party should exercise constant supervision over the work of state organs, looking into problems and making proposals and revisions. Finally, it means that the Party will assume a leading role in all public affairs, including the work of the various people's organizations. In all of these cases, Party policies and decisions are to be carried out through the medium of Party members within state organs and public bodies. Needless to say, the CCP places extreme emphasis on intraparty unity and discipline to ensure that its members will lead according to the wishes of the Party Central Committee.[24]

[21] Liu Shao-ch'i, "Political Report," *Eighth National Congress of the Communist Party of China,* I, pp. 95–96.

[22] Liu Shao-ch'i, *On the Party,* p. 53.

[23] Tu Ching, "Kung-ch'an-tang-yüan Ying-kai Shih Jen-min Ch'ün-chung ti Chung-shih Tai-piao" (Communists Should be Loyal Representatives of the Masses), *Hung Ch'i* (Red Flag), 1962, No. 6, p. 2.

[24] Teng Hsiao-p'ing, "Report on the Revision of the Constitution of the Communist Party of China," *Eighth National Congress of the Communist Party of China,* I, pp. 201–213, and Articles 34, 50, and 59 of "The Constitution of the Communist Party of China," *ibid.* See also Lewis, *op. cit.,* especially pp. 140–144.

The CCP's leading position, which cannot be interrupted or contested by any other political force, gives the Party the power to make all major political decisions. On the other hand, the Party insists, at least theoretically, that it will not monopolize governmental positions, issue direct commands to state organs, or undertake the execution of the policies that it has decided. This concept has been touched upon in reference to the Party's acceptance of alliance with other parties and classes during the dictatorship of the proletariat, but its full significance is revealed in the mass line.

THE MASS LINE

The mass line, which Liu Shao-ch'i describes as a fundamental political and organizational line of the CCP, permeates virtually every aspect of Party theory and practice.[25] Broadly speaking, it can be viewed as presenting two different, but closely related, propositions to guide Party work: first, a general statement of the Party's dependence on the masses and the need for constant contact with them; second, a more specific statement on the correct method of exercising Party leadership.[26] The first proposition is based on the assertion that history is created by action of the masses. CCP theory constantly stresses that the masses are the motive power in history and the creators of all material and cultural wealth; recognition of this fact is said to distinguish the materialist view of history from the idealist view which sees history as created by particular individuals.[27] From this it follows that the Party cannot achieve its goals by its own actions but must depend on the masses to carry out the steps toward communism. "Every cause led by the Party, be it revolution or construction, is the people's own and must be achieved by the people themselves. Party policies must rely on the people for realization." [28]

In Communist China, the Party's reliance on the masses includes a seemingly mystical reverence for the political and inspirational powers of the masses. Mao's views on the irresistible force of mass movements have already been noted, but CCP dogma also assigns great creative

[25] On the Party, p. 44. For a thorough discussion of the manifold implications of the mass line, see Lewis, op. cit., chap. 3.

[26] See Teng Hsiao-p'ing, op. cit., pp. 176–177, for this distinction.

[27] For examples, see Yang Hsien-chen, "Collective Leadership is the Highest Principle of Party Leadership," Hsüeh-hsi (Study), 1954, No. 3, and Sun Ting-kuo, "The Role of the Masses and the Role of the Individual in History," ibid., 1954, No. 5, in American Consulate General, Hong Kong, Current Background (hereafter cited as CB), No. 384 (April 17, 1956).

[28] Shih Tung-hsiang, "Pan Tang ti Cheng-ts'e Chiao-kei Ch'ün-chung" (Hand Party Policies to the Masses), Hung Ch'i, 1961, No. 2, p. 1.

powers to the collective body of people. "The wisdom of the masses is limitless. The greatest creativity exists only with the masses, the greatest wisdom exists only with the concentration of the wisdom of the masses. In fact, any difficult problem, any matter which we cannot think out for ourselves, can be easily managed and quickly illuminated as soon as it is discussed with the masses." [29] For these reasons, Party members must adopt the mass-line style of work that keeps them in constant contact with the people; they must listen to the masses, actually experience their living and working problems, and never assume an attitude of aloofness or superiority toward them. Failure to do so will result in such evils as "bureaucratism" and render the Party incapable of representing the people. Once it is "isolated from the masses," the Party cannot lead the revolution to a successful conclusion.

The second aspect of the mass line lays down the method by which the CCP policies are executed through a synthesis of Party leadership and mass action. [30] The procedure is summed up as "coming from the masses and going to the masses." This means that the scattered and unsystematic views of the masses are to be collected by Party organizations, carefully studied and coordinated, and then turned into statements of Party policy. Because of this process, the CCP claims that it "learns from the masses" and that all its policies originate with the masses. At the same time, however, the Party insists that its leading role requires it to make the actual decision on the basis of its superior knowledge and experience; it cannot accept "incorrect" mass views that would lead the Party itself into error. The Party is guided in its decisions by the conviction that it alone clearly understands the long-run collective interests of the people.

Once a policy has been decided, it must be taken back to the masses for execution. As conceived by the CCP, "going to the masses" does not mean dictating policies with obedience ensured by force. It is a long, complicated process that uses all available media to inform the

[29] Ch'en Po-ta, "Yu Shih ho Ch'ün-chung Shang-liang" (Discuss Everything with the Masses), in Liu Shao-ch'i, *et al., Lun Ch'ün-chung Lu-hsien* (On the Mass Line) (Hong Kong, 1949), p. 24.

[30] The following description is a summary based on standard Party expositions of the mass line. The first statement of the mass line in its present form was the 1943 Central Committee resolution, "On Methods of Leadership," quoted in chap. Three; it was drafted by Mao and appears in *Selected Works* (New York), IV, pp. 111–117. The first extended exposition of the mass line appeared in Liu Shao-ch'i, *On the Party*, pp. 44–66. Other sources used here are the following: Teng Hsiao-p'ing, *op. cit.,* pp. 175–187; Shih Tung-hsiang, *op. cit.;* Tu Ching, *op. cit.;* Tu Ching and Chang Hsien-ch'ao, "Chien-ch'ih 'Ts'ung Ch'ün-chung Chung Lai, Tao Ch'ün-chung Chung Ch'ü' ti Ling-tao Fang-fa" (Insist on the Leadership Method of "From the Masses, to the Masses"), *Hung Ch'i*, 1961, No. 14; Yen Ling, "What Is the Party's Mass Line? *Cheng-chih Hsüeh-hsi* (Political Study), 1955, No. 6, in *SMM*, No. 11 (October 24, 1955).

masses, raise their level of understanding and consciousness, and ultimately translate Party policies into conscious popular action.

As soon as a policy of the Party is formulated, it can be widely propagandized to the masses in various ways through the government and Party organizations at all levels, through all kinds of mass organizations and by the use of such tools as newspapers, magazines and the radio. The consciousness of the masses may then be heightened so that they will, under the leadership of the Party, take action consciously and voluntarily in the struggle for the realization of this policy.[31]

Since the policy in question has theoretically originated among the masses and been decided by the Party on the basis of the collective interest, there cannot be any significant change in it. However, the CCP recognizes that "low political consciousness" or "backward ideology" may cause some of the masses (even a majority) to resist execution of a policy when it is first presented to them. When this happens, the Party cannot use coercion, but neither can it wait indefinitely for mass action. What it must do is carry out "patient persuasion and education" until the masses are ready for "conscious and voluntary action." The masses are to be roused to action by going over policies "article by article and sentence by sentence," by explaining *why* something is done this way and not that way, by relating policies to actual conditions and personal experiences, and by developing popular discussion to settle doubts and refute "incorrect" opinions.

Three points emerge from the foregoing summary. First, the mass line demands extensive mass participation in the political process, but this participation is designed to produce popular execution of policy rather than popular formulation and control of policy. Second, since the CCP wants the people to accept Party policies as their own, political activities in China are always aimed at changing popular political thinking and producing an ever higher degree of acceptance of Communist policies and ideology. This effort conforms to the general purpose of the dictatorship of the proletariat in preparing the people for a fundamental change in man's social relations. Finally, the mass line blurs the distinction between governmental and nongovernmental activity by using state organs, propaganda media, mass organizations, and direct contacts between cadres and masses for the same purpose of securing popular acceptance and execution of Party objectives. Since the Party demands "conscious and voluntary action," rather than simple obedience, it must reach down to establish direct contact with the masses. In the process, the state structure is sometimes bypassed or reduced to only one of several agencies for transmitting political information and directives to the people.

[31] Tu Ching and Chang Hsien-ch'ao, *op. cit.,* pp. 1–2.

ACTIVISM AND POLITICAL CONSCIOUSNESS

The mass line requires the masses to act whenever a Party policy is presented to them, but this is only the particular instance of the CCP's desire for a generally high degree of activism and political consciousness among the people. The CCP's demands in this respect are an attempt to transfer Party virtues to the people at large. Political action is the very life of a member of the Communist Party. Party theory states that "to know the world is merely our means while to change the world is our end." The Communists' ability to change the world is admittedly limited by objective conditions, but within these limits subjective consciousness can play an important role. In any given situation, the conscious activity of a zealous individual can mean the difference between success and failure.[32] Knowledge itself is held to derive only from social practice and must be tested constantly in the field of action.[33] The CCP regards activity as so important to revolutionary success that it condemns nonactivity as equivalent to opposition. In fact, "lethargic mentality" is an expression of "rightist" political tendencies because it leads to belittling the enemy, remaining indifferent to class struggle, overlooking subversive actions, and weakening the revolutionary ranks.[34]

The CCP does not demand that those outside the party dedicate their lives to revolutionary action, but it does expect that they will participate in the political life of the state as much as possible. This expectation includes not only the exercise of basic political rights but also active efforts to keep the political system functioning smoothly. For example, all citizens are urged to observe labor discipline, which includes coming to work on time, taking care of tools and machinery, conserving materials, and fulfilling production quotas; it also includes knowing all the relevant government, enterprise, and trade union regulations, striving to observe them oneself, and preventing violations of them by others. Citizens should preserve public order, guard state secrets, watch suspicious men and acts, and help suppress all acts (such as arson, robbery, murder, fighting, and riots) that endanger public security. Citizens are also expected to uphold the "new social virtues," such as equal treatment for women, respect for the aged and care for the young, and

[32] Chiang Wei-ch'ing, "Hsüeh-hsi Mao Tse-tung Ssu-hsiang Chung-fen Fa-yang Tzu-chüeh ti Neng-tung-hsing" (Study Mao Tse-tung's Thought and Fully Develop Conscious Activity), *Hung Ch'i,* 1960, No. 2, pp. 7–16.

[33] Lewis, *op. cit.,* pp. 40–43.

[34] "What Is Party Spirit? Why Is Revolutionary Vigilance a Noble Quality? Why Is Lethargic Mentality a Rightist Trend?" *Hsüeh-hsi,* 1955, No. 8, in *SMM,* No. 11 (October 24, 1955).

maintenance of public sanitation.[35] In attending meetings, which forms a major part of everyone's activities, the expression of one's views is not simply a privilege but an obligation to the collective enterprise. Expression of opinion is not a personal matter, since meetings depend on gathering the wisdom of all, and problems can be solved only when mistakes and incorrect views are aired in public.[36]

The CCP insists that political activity must be "conscious" activity. "Political consciousness" is attained when a person understands the political significance of his acts and is motivated by some degree of acceptance of Communist ideology. It is the key to inducing "voluntary" action among the masses, which is essential to the permanence of Communist achievements; "without mass voluntarism, nothing can achieve results, or, if achieving results, cannot be consolidated . . . ."[37] The CCP is under no illusions about the natural emergence of political consciousness. It concedes that the entire process of socialist construction must be one of raising the popular level of socialist and communist ideology. Mass ideological consciousness is a result of long-term political and ideological education among the masses rather than a spontaneous development.[38]

Popular political consciousness is a matter of degree. Judging from Communist statements, it is constantly being raised and yet is never high enough. The Party explains this by reference to the "thousands of years of feudalism" that preceded Communist triumph, and the traditional particularism and peasant capitalism of rural China, that have made it extremely difficult to induce a Communist-style political consciousness among the people. These obstacles are not, however, a cause for relaxation of efforts. It is precisely because of the prevalence of antisocialist ideas among the Chinese people that the effort to rouse them to conscious political activity demands constant and penetrating education. As a leading official of the Communist Youth League has said, revolutionary ideas do not arise spontaneously, but neither will the minds of youth remain a vacuum; "either the red flag of proletarian thinking or the white flag of bourgeois thinking is planted on their minds."[39] Relaxation of political education will concede the ideological field to the "white flag of bourgeois thinking."

[35] Li Kuang-ts'an, op, cit., pp. 101–13.
[36] "Speak Up as Much as You wish," Chung-kuo Ch'ing-nien, (China Youth), 1961, No. 15, in SMM, No. 277 (September 5, 1961).
[37] Tu Ching, op. cit., p. 2.
[38] Chao Hsü-kuang, "Cheng-chih Kua-shuai yü Wu-chih Ku-ch'in Hsiang Chieh-ho" (The Mutual Unity of Politics Takes Command and Material Incentive), Kung-jen Jih-pao (Workers' Daily) (Peking), December 1, 1961.
[39] Hu Yao-pang, "Communist Education for the Chinese Youth," JMJP, October 1, 1959, in CB, No. 600 (October 26, 1959).

SOCIALIST DEMOCRACY

Constitutionally the CPR is a democratic state in which all power belongs to the people and is exercised through a system of national and local people's congresses. The constitution grants citizens an impressive list of political rights including equality before the law; universal suffrage; freedom of speech, press, assembly, association, procession, and demonstration; inviolability of homes and privacy of correspondence; and the right to bring complaints, by verbal or written statement, against state personnel who have transgressed the law or neglected their duty.[40] Moreover, certain non-Communist parties exist and non-Communists are encouraged to hold various state positions. How are provisions such as these to be reconciled with the principles discussed in the preceding sections? There is, to be sure, a good deal of cynicism in Communist democratic pretensions, but generally the CCP does take its "democratic" system seriously. The fact is that socialist democracy, as interpreted by the Chinese Communists, is actually an attempt to incorporate the Party concept of political participation into the state system.

The CCP's first step in the defense of its state system is the rejection of bourgeois democracy and its institutions; socialist democracy is said to be distinct from bourgeois democracy and not to be judged by its standards. This hostility is partly due to the dogmatic belief that democracy in Western Europe and the United States is a decadent and corrupt system for the perpetuation of bourgeois dictatorship.[41] Beyond this, however, the CCP is fundamentally suspicious of the philosophy of liberalism. In a brief document written in 1937, Mao Tse-tung argued that liberalism is decadent, undisciplined, self-seeking, and passive; its prime characteristic is compromise of principle in order to advance personal interests and avoid revolutionary action.[42] Another Party theoretician has made it very clear that alliance with bourgeois parties in no way constitutes an acceptance of their ideology; the ideology of the Chinese bourgeoisie contains nothing progressive and is the very antithesis of revolutionary principles.[43]

Socialist democracy has a specific purpose that forbids any compromise or confusion with bourgeois democracy.

[40] "Constitution of the People's Republic of China," in *Documents of the First Session of the First National People's Congress of the People's Republic of China* (Peking, 1955), especially Articles 1, 2, 85–90, and 97.

[41] For an example of this view, see Chang Yu-yü, "The Farce of Bourgeois Parliamentary Democracy," *Peking Review,* 1962, Nos. 34–35, reprinted and slightly abridged from *Hung Ch'i,* 1962, No. 13.

[42] "Combat Liberalism," *Selected Works,* II, pp. 74–76.

[43] Ai Ssu-ch'i, "Recognize Clearly the Reactionary Nature of the Ideology of the Bourgeois Class," *Hsüeh-hsi.* March 16, 1952, in *CB,* No. 179 (May 6, 1952).

The sole aim of socialist democracy, in the political, economic and cultural fields alike, is to strengthen the socialist cause of the proletariat and all the working people, to give scope to their energy in the building of socialism and in the fight against all anti-socialist forces. If there is a kind of democracy that can be used for anti-socialist purposes and for weakening the cause of socialism, it certainly cannot be called socialist democracy.[44]

The mixed class composition of the government does not detract from this singleness of purpose. On the contrary, the fact that people from many different classes, nationalities, and groups, with many different social, educational, and political experiences, participate in government work makes uniformity of policy and ideology indispensable. Meetings of state organs, as well as other kinds of meetings, discussions, and individual study, are tools for coordinating policies and ideology; the Communist Party, of course, takes the initiative in this task.[45] In China, therefore, democracy and freedom are relative rather than absolute; they are means rather than ends.[46] They are means for the attainment and expression of socialist unity, a goal that the Party believes to be attainable. Since all state organs base their work on the common interests and unity of will of the people, it is possible in all these organs "to arrive at political unanimity of the people based on democracy." [47]

Given these limitations, what is the content of "democratic" activity in China? According to Mao, acceptable democratic methods are discussion, criticism, persuasion, and education, which are brought into play to resolve contradictions among the people.[48] As noted previously, contradictions can never be resolved in any way that lessens Party leadership or departs from socialism. Socialist democracy tolerates ideas and opinions that differ from socialism, so long as they occur "among the people," only in the sense that it corrects them through discussion and persuasion rather than by the use of force. The practice of democracy broadens ideological unity and toughens Marxism–Leninism by forcing it to defend itself against wrong ideas.[49] The persuasive and educative

[44] "More on the Historical Experience of the Proletariat," *JMJP*, editorial, December 29, 1956, in *The Historical Experience of the Dictatorship of the Proletariat*, p. 49.

[45] Li Wei-han, "The Further Strengthening of the United Front Work Within All Government Organs," New China News Agency (hereafter cited as NCNA), June 9, 1951, in *CB*, No. 96 (July 12, 1951).

[46] Mao Tse-tung, "On the Correct Handling of Contradictions Among the People," *op. cit.*, pp. 21–22.

[47] Liu Shao-ch'i, "Report on the Draft Constitution of the People's Republic of China," *op. cit.*, p. 46.

[48] "On the Correct Handling of Contradictions Among the People," *op. cit.*, pp. 22–23. In "On the People's Democratic Dictatorship" (*op. cit.*, p. 419), Mao defined "democratic methods" as "methods of persuasion" and distinguished them from the dictatorial methods used against reactionaries.

[49] Mao, "On the Correct Handling of Contradictions Among the People," *op. cit.*, pp. 25, 47–48.

functions of socialist democracy are also seen in explanations of popular political rights. For example, the objective of developing free speech is "to encourage progressives and educate those who are backward." The desired use of "freedom of publication" is equally clear. "As everyone knows, the publishing enterprises of our people are the collective organizers and propagandizers of Marxist–Leninist ideology and are an exceedingly powerful instrument for carrying on communist education toward the people." [50]

An intriguing question is how democratic methods are to correct errors that occur among the leadership—a possibility, it will be remembered, that Mao has admitted may occur. The answer is that the people must still confine themselves to verbal criticism, even though some of their constitutional rights would seem to be more effective.[51] The question arose during the "hundred flowers" period of 1957 when some people suggested calling parades, demonstrations, and strikes from work or classes in order to force cadres to correct their mistakes. The reasons given for rejecting these suggestions are of particular interest. Parades, demonstrations, and strikes, the answer claimed, do not fit the formula for resolving contradictions among the people, namely, criticism leading to a higher level of unity. On the contrary, their characteristic is the use of pressure and threats, and the inflicting of political and economic losses on the opponent to force concessions, compromises, and acceptance of mass demands from him. Use of these methods was encouraged in the past, against imperialists, Chiang Kai-shek, and the landlords, when acceptance of the people's demands was the highest objective. But these methods cannot be used against other comrades, even though they may lead to the rapid solution of a particular problem, because they "damage democratic centralism" and do not solve problems according to "normal democratic procedure." Parades, demonstrations, and strikes are, "in fact, a direct appeal to the masses" over the heads of the Party and the leadership; they are a manifestation of "petty bourgeois anarchism." The constitution permits parades and demonstrations for use against internal and external enemies; it does not authorize them to be used blindly against the leadership.[52]

Since socialist democracy is primarily a means of carrying on discussion and education, it cannot be confined to infrequent contacts between the citizen and his government. "Democratic life" in China includes not only elections and the work of representative bodies, but a great variety of other activities and associations that involve the people in political

---

[50] Li Kuang-ts'an, *op. cit.*, pp. 32–34.
[51] Chiang Ming, "Cheng-ch'üeh ti Shih-yung Min-chu Fang-fa" (Use Democratic Methods Correctly), *Chung-kuo Ch'ing nien*, 1957, No. 3, pp. 2–4.
[52] *Loc. cit.*

problems. For example, the masses may be organized to discuss laws and state plans that are in the process of being drafted; basic-level productive organizations, such as factories and cooperatives, should form mass-based representative bodies to bring workers into the management of production; the people are urged to visit their deputies and various state organs and regularly to air their opinions through letters to officials, mass organizations, and newspapers; even the mass movements are vehicles for developing democratic life.[53] In all of these aspects—rejection of liberal standards, devotion to the victory of socialism, enhancement of political unity under Party leadership, concern with persuasion and education, and encouragement of mass participation in a wide variety of political activities—the theory of socialist democracy fulfills the elements that make up the CCP concept of political participation.

THE CONCEPT IN THEORY AND PRACTICE

Chinese Communist theory assigns the masses a definite role in the political process. This role is to execute policies decided by the CCP or by state organs under Party leadership. Since the Party asserts that the masses must accept and understand its policies, and then carry them out "consciously and voluntarily," the masses must take part in discussion, propagandization, and ratification of policy. The Party also theoretically encourages the expression of opinions and demands from all sections of the people, exclusive of those elements defined as reactionaries. However, since the Party regards itself as the only group capable of defining the true collective interest, and since that interest is superior to any other interest that might be advanced, popular political participation cannot serve as a means of debating and reconciling competing interests. All political activity of voters, people's congresses, non-Communist parties, mass organizations, and so forth, must ultimately contribute to unified support of Party objectives. There may be debate on some questions, but the result of debate is predetermined. Those holding "incorrect" ideas must be persuaded to accept "correct" ideas and thereby advance unanimity to a higher stage. The Party makes the final decision on what is "correct" and "incorrect."

The most striking feature of this concept of political participation is the frequency and extent of demands for political action by the citi-

---

[53] Chou En-lai, "Cheng-fu Kung-tso Pao-kao" (Report on the Work of the Government), *Chung-hua Jen-min Kung-ho-kuo Ti-i Chieh Ch'üan-kuo Jen-min Tai-piao Ta-hui Ti-ssu Tz'u Hui-i Wen-chien* (Documents of the Fourth Session of the First National People's Congress of the People's Republic of China) (Peking, 1957), pp. 38–39.

zenry. This is partly due to the CCP's desire to secure total mass mobilization, to enlist the active support of every citizen. It is also due, however, to a remarkable broadening of the area of action that the Communists regard as political. In Communist China almost every act has political significance, at least in the eyes of the CCP. When the Communist Party, invoking the name of national interest and collective will, asserts that it is the duty of all citizens to carry out its policies in a certain area of life, then that area has become part of the political arena. To work for the success of the policy is to affirm support for the Party and to demonstrate loyal membership in the community; to ignore the policy is to deny the demands of the collective will. Political consciousness can be exhibited by killing flies, by collecting manure, by fulfilling one's production quota, or in any number of other ways. The following statement may help to demonstrate this point.

If [a revolutionary youth] must have revolutionary ideals, is it not an indication that he has noble revolutionary ideals when he marches to the front line of agriculture as required by socialist construction? If he must serve the people, is it not a full indication of his desire to serve the people when he exerts efforts in agriculture, in which all the 650,000,000 people are interested? If he must have high consciousness, is it not a proof that he has it when he actively carries out the Party's general line and exerts efforts to develop agriculture and build beautiful and happy rural people's communes as required by Party policies? [54]

By investing acts that are not in themselves political with an aura of civic obligation, the CCP opens up a much broader sphere for the display of political activism. The "initiative and creativity" of the masses, which the Party constantly extols and seeks to utilize, can hardly be applied in elections or representative bodies. It can be applied, however, in various aspects of production, law enforcement, and communications that the Party regards as political situations. For this reason, the CCP's emphasis on individual initiative is not as illogical as it would seem from the tightly controlled political system.

To what extent does this theory describe and prescribe the practice of mass political activity in China? Subsequent chapters analyze the question in detail, but two general considerations merit discussion here to place it in better perspective. The first is that the Chinese concept of participation is a complex blending of Soviet Marxism and Chinese experience, reflecting both the Marxist–Leninist inheritance and previous Chinese practice. The theory as it stands today is consistent with the Marxist–Leninist view of the dictatorship of the proletariat, the

[54] Cheng Chih, "The Youths Participation in Agricultural Construction Is a Demand of the Times," *Chung-kuo Ch'ing-nien*, 1960, No. 22, in *SMM*, No. 241 (December 28, 1960).

leading role of the Communist Party, the suppression of all political opposition, and the broad mobilization of the masses for participation in the socialist revolution. At the same time, it is clear that these points became meaningful parts of Chinese theory only when they were proven to be adaptable to the CCP's role in the Chinese revolution.

For example, the idea of the necessity of elite leadership, armed with special knowledge of society and its problems, was not accepted simply because of Lenin's dogmatic strictures or an all-consuming faith in the communist future. The need for leadership was inherent in the depth of China's economic and social problems and in the extent of ignorance and apathy among the population. The Chinese Communists were by no means the only Chinese who were convinced that firm leadership was essential for China's regeneration. Moreover, the Chinese tradition of bureaucratic rule by an educated and enlightened elite made the idea of Party leadership attractive to the students and intellectuals who were to play such an important role in the Chinese Communist movement. And, in spite of Mao's widely quoted assertion that political power grows out of the barrel of a gun, there was a strong traditional appeal for the Chinese intellectuals in a movement that based its claim to political authority on moral as well as historical necessity and that relied on conscientious observance of an orthodox ideology for its political cohesiveness.

During the 1930's and 1940's, the Communists' claim that they alone were capable of leading the revolution successfully, that any concession toward the "bureaucratic capitalists and imperialists" was an invitation to extinction, was at least partly defensible even though not beyond dispute. The KMT supplied ample evidence of its own deficiencies and its determination to destroy the Communists, while Mao's comments about the vacillations and ureliability of the Chinese "national bourgeoisie" and "liberals" were not without some justification. Party dictatorship was not simply an article of faith to the CCP, and in fact some concessions were willingly made in this area during the Sino–Japanese War. But Party leadership could never be relinquished without endangering both the Party and the goals that it sought.

Moreover, there was little novelty in the Chinese Communists' assertion of the supremacy of the collective interest and the need for mobilizing the entire population in the cause of socialist construction. As we have seen, these ideas were accepted by nearly all Chinese political leaders in the twentieth century, assuming only that "national unity and reconstruction" be substituted for "socialist construction." In any case, the CCP itself hardly needed doctrinal support for a principle that it had applied with such success throughout the Sino–Japanese War. The Chinese Communists' belief that the entire population could be mobilized for socialist construction probably owed much more to their own experience in the Yenan period than to Soviet writings on this point.

Finally, more than any other point, the mass line reflects the adaptation of Marxism–Leninism to Chinese realities. The mass line emerged as a means of imparting Communist ideology to a peasant population, of propagandizing Party policies among isolated villages and illiterate peasants, of arousing national loyalties and political consciousness in a traditionally particularistic society, of enlisting mass support in the execution of policies that could not be enforced by Party organization alone, and of correcting bureaucratic tendencies in an organization stocked with intellectuals who abhorred physical labor and frequently adopted a patronizing air toward the masses. All of these points, like the preceding ones, found some degree of doctrinal justification in Marxism–Leninism, but their vitality in CCP theory rests with their pragmatic orgins.

The point is that the Chinese leaders view the dichotomy between theory and practice as a false one. They regard their concept of political participation as their own product, their own application of Marxism–Leninism to the Chinese setting. They believe that it is not simply a doctrinal rationalization for their political behavior but rather a systematic description of it. They may, of course, be wrong, but the fact that their historical experience includes situations in which the theory was tested and practiced lends urgency to their attempts to make current practice conform to it. For example, it appears that the CCP's reliance on popular support and mass mobilization in its rise to power has given Chinese doctrine a much greater emphasis on the "power of the masses" and the importance of popular political action than exists in Soviet doctrine. Both systems extol their popular foundations, but Lenin's mistrust of mass "spontaneity," a reflection of his own revolutionary setting, and the subsequent development of Soviet bureaucratic controls contrast sharply with the populistic and antibureaucratic tendencies of the CCP. Were this only a difference in propaganda or doctrine, it might merit little attention. But it is precisely because the Chinese take this aspect of their theory so seriously that the two systems appear to differ in practice on this point.

The second consideration that enters here is the plain fact that the CCP has seldom reconciled its theory and practice of political participation in the years since 1945, in spite of very serious attempts to do so. The two are not irreconcilable of necessity, but reconciliation depends on very special conditions. The theory assumes that both Party leadership and mass voluntarism can be preserved; low consciousness may delay the desired results, but ultimately persuasive efforts by the Party will bring about voluntary mass action on Party policies. The assumed harmony between Party and people, or the assumption that the Party can create it when it is lacking, grossly simplifies the central problem in the CCP concept of participation. In reality, both Party leadership and mass voluntarism are variables. Party leadership may vary in quality, in the significance assigned to a policy, or in the time allowed for the completion of a project. Mass voluntarism may vary in scope, in intensity, or in speed of development. Once the Party has adopted a policy, it must decide whether execution requires mass mobilization; if so, it must decide how much preparation is needed, how much mass support is necessary, and how long it can wait to secure the desired level of support. At the same time, the Party must decide how it will deal with adverse reactions that arise when a policy is propagated or, more generally, how it will deal with genuinely spontaneous pressures from the people. There are limits to the variations that may occur. On one side, the Party can never give up its leading position or its ability to enforce its will when necessary. On the other side, the people can never avoid giving token support and minimal obedience, unless, of course, they are prepared to revolt. Within these limits, however, is room for substantial differences in the way the mass line is applied and the degree of success it achieves.

The Party came closer to realizing the theoretical ideal of the mass line during the Yenan period than it has at any time since those years. Party leadership of the liberated areas was real enough, but it rested on the foundation of a broad popular consensus that virtually eliminated the need for coercive measures against the population of these areas. Mass support was generally voluntary, while Party control was moderate and circumspect. The reasons for this success were essentially simple. First, there was in fact an identity of interest between the CCP and the population of the liberated areas. The Party was asking for popular support of policies aimed at resisting the Japanese invader; the people were eager to support this objective and accepted the Party's guidance in attaining it. Second, the Party's acceptance of political cooperation from non-Party elements and its reluctance to force its measures on the governments of the liberated areas was, to a large degree, a matter of necessity. The CCP had no real political competitor, but neither did it have the personnel to dominate all of the regional and local governments in the areas that it controlled. As pointed out earlier, the mass line was developed to a high degree in the Yenan period precisely to overcome the problems inherent in maintaining some sort of general direction over a guerrilla war waged from scattered rural bases.

The end of the war brought new situations that altered the natural harmony of CCP relations with the masses and subsequently produced great tension in the attempt to retain both Party leadership and voluntary mass action in support of it. There have been six major stages since 1945 in the development of political participation in China: civil war, 1945–1949; Communist political construction, 1949–1955; liberalization, 1956–1957; the Great Leap Forward, 1957–1960; retrenchment, 1961–1962; political consolidation, 1962–1965. Each of these stages, which are admittedly somewhat arbitrary, will be discussed briefly to demonstrate the general development of the Party's application of its concept of political participation.

Civil war, 1945–1949   In the four transitional years of civil war leading up to the establishment of the CPR in 1949, the CCP attempted to transfer the focus of popular political action from the resistance effort to elimination of the Party's domestic opponents. The Communists tried to obscure this shift by insisting that their postwar program was simply a continuation of the movement for national liberation and construction. Nevertheless, there was a difference as the CCP began to push harder for social and economic reforms and entered into open political and military conflict with the KMT. The Party program no longer rested on a virtually unopposed policy of national salvation. Instead, it advanced demands that met the determined opposition of the KMT and its supporters. Therefore, in spite of its efforts to present itself as the sole defender of the national interest, the CCP engaged in a campaign to recruit mass support as a weapon against internal political enemies.

The shift in character of Communist-controlled mass political activity was evident in the tasks that the CCP assigned to its mass organizations. In March, 1946, when the CCP hoped to avoid or delay civil war by establishment of a coalition government, the women's movement was urged to work for "peaceful and democratic unity." In KMT areas, women were to support the decisions of the Political Consultative Conference and to oppose "fascist forces"; in the liberated areas, they were to take part wholeheartedly in "democratic political construction," that is, in the consolidation of CCP political power.[55] As the postwar political situation degenerated into civil war between the CCP and the KMT, Communist appeals for mass action against the KMT became much more open. The Sixth Congress of the All-China Federation of

[55] "Chung-kuo Fu-nü Chin-hou ti Jen-wu" (The Present and Future Tasks of Chinese Women), *Chieh-fang Jih-pao* (Liberation Daily) (Yenan), editorial, March 7, 1946, in Lo Ch'iung, ed. *Fu-nü Yün-tung Wen-hsien* (Documents on the Women's Movement) (Harbin, 1948), pp. 7–9. The Political Consultative Conference was a multiparty conference convened in January, 1946, to lay down plans for the establishment of a postwar coalition government. The Conference agreed on some compromises that were unacceptable to the KMT and were initially supported by the CCP.

Labor, which met in Harbin in August, 1949, defined the establishment of a "new democratic people's republic" as the prerequisite for improving the circumstances of the working class and the "highest interest and highest task of the working class and other democratic classes of the people." The workers' movement was called on to support the People's Liberation Army in every way, to do battle against the "American imperialists, and the KMT reactionary government," and to "participate actively in the revolutionary activities, organizations, political authority and policies proposed by the CCP." In KMT-controlled areas, workers were to obstruct KMT military movements and preparations, unite with the masses and expand their ranks, strive to improve living conditions, and protect all public and private machinery and equipment in anticipation of "liberation." In those areas already liberated, the situation was quite different. Here, the workers' major tasks were the development of production and political study in preparation for participation in the politics, army, economy, and culture of the "new democracy." [56]

The apparent ease of Communist victory in 1949 has concealed the difficulties posed by this transition. Before the final military collapse of the KMT in 1949, a bitter struggle was waged to rouse the masses against the old political and economic forces that still controlled many villages even after the withdrawal of KMT armies. As the area under CCP control expanded, the Party discovered that popular political action was much more difficult to initiate and maintain than it had been during the period of resistance to Japan. The broad consensus among peasants, landlords, and local officials that had facilitated unified support of the CCP program in 1937–1945 had vanished. Instead, the Party found the peasants fearful of "overturning" the traditional village order, while the old rural leaders proved to be remarkably adept at maintaining their influence even after liberation. Mass mobilization required delays, occasional resort to violence, and some changes in policy.[57]

With the establishment of the CPR in 1949, Party leadership of a long-range drive for socialism became the controlling factor for mass political activities throughout China. The great majority of Chinese

[56] "Kuan-yü Chung-kuo Chih-kung Yün-tung Tang-ch'ien Jen-wu ti Chüeh-i" (Resolution on the Present Tasks of the Chinese Workers' Movement), in Chieh-fang She (Liberation Press), editor, *Chung-kuo Chih-kung Yün-tung ti Tang-ch'ien Jen-wu* (Present Tasks of the Chinese Workers' Movement) (Shanghai, 1949), pp. 39–46.

[57] For graphic description of the difficulties mentioned here, see David and Isabel Crook, *Revolution in a Chinese Village, Ten Mile Inn* (London, 1959), chaps. 7–8, and Jack Belden, *China Shakes the World* (New York, 1949), pp. 174–189, *passim*. Changes in CCP agrarian policy in this period are summarized in Chao Kuo-chün, *Agrarian Policy of the Chinese Communist Party 1921–1949* (London, 1960), chap. 2.

accepted the idea of Party leadership in the new government as the natural result of CCP victory. A lesser, but probably still substantial, proportion was also prepared to support the CCP program as it was presented at that time. Nevertheless, the CCP was far short of holding the nearly unanimous backing that it had enjoyed during the war. The rapid expansion of Communist territory in 1948–1949 had outstripped the Party's efforts, limited as they were by the problems mentioned above, to mobilize the population under its control.

Political construction, 1949–1955   The early years of the CPR saw a strenuous effort to consolidate the regime's mass base. Political construction, as the effort was called, was devoted to two broad objectives: to overcome the most pressing problems facing the new government and to mobilize the masses for political action. In keeping with CCP theory the two objectives were tightly integrated. The Party's struggle against internal and external enemies, its attempt to restore the shattered Chinese economy, and its plans for social reform were expected to win popular support and eliminate potential opposition. At the same time, political organization and indoctrination of the population were expected to place all the energies of the people behind the Party's program. The CCP was well prepared for this effort by its previous experience and its doctrinal outlook. It was aided, too, by the support that it had already gained among some parts of the population, especially in North China. On the other hand, the majority of the people, including those in many of the largest cities, were totally unprepared for the political role assigned to them by the CCP. Political construction was, therefore, a monumental campaign, carried out in an atmosphere of urgency and aimed at revolutionizing the political behavior of the Chinese people.

The heart of the CCP's attempt to win over the masses and mobilize them for the CCP style of political participation was the launching of a series of great mass movements. Land reform had been in progress for several years before 1949 in some areas of China, but it became a national movement after the promulgation of the Agrarian Reform Law in June, 1950. The Marriage Law, designed to modernize the social and economic status of women, also appeared in the spring of 1950 and was followed by a long campaign of enforcement. The outbreak of the Korean War in June, 1950, resulted in the Resist America–Aid Korea Movement that lasted up to and after the Korean Armistice of 1953. The first Suppression of Counterrevolutionaries Movement was carried out in 1951. The Three-Anti Movement, aimed at eliminating corruption, waste, and bureaucracy in government offices, began in December, 1951. Its companion, the Five-Anti Movement, which struck at bribery, tax evasion, theft of state property, cheating on government contracts, and stealing of state economic secrets for private speculation, followed almost immediately. These two last-named movements continued throughout the spring of 1952. Throughout this period, these campaigns swept across China, dominating public and private life and keeping the masses in almost constant political activity.

No brief description can do justice to the impact of these movements. Probably every citizen in China was directly involved in at least two or three and was acquainted through the propaganda media with the others. At a minimum, exposure to a mass movement included a series of meetings to learn about and discuss the official policy or objectives and participation in various kinds of parades and rallies. Depending on the movement, the people might be led to donate money or services to the government, observe public trials, act as witnesses or accusers at trials or public meetings, report on violations of regulations, or serve on committees organized in the course of a movement. Each movement had two aspects. The first was the accomplishment of the primary objective as defined by the Party, that is, redistribution of land, uncovering of corruption, arrest and punishment of the regime's enemies, and so forth. All of the movements aimed at problems of major significance, and the Party genuinely relied on popular efforts to make them a success. The second aspect was the secondary political impact of the movement. Through these campaigns, the people were forced to probe the "why" of CCP policies and to take their stand, at least in their public behavior, for or against the objectives of the regime. From the Party's point of view, understanding of the significance of a movement was a step toward higher political consciousness; active participation in it was a sign of commitment to the new society.

Political construction also included a sweeping reform of governmental institutions. The reform aimed, first, at placing supporters of the CCP in control at every level of the state hierarchy and, second, at instituting a system of direct or indirect election of all governmental bodies. The most difficult and immediate problem was the establishment of sympathetic political organs in the countryside where basic-level administration might be either nonexistent or still controlled by the old rural elite. This problem was met by allowing the peasants' associations to govern the villages and by appointing government personnel at the *hsiang* level from above (the *hsiang,* an administrative unit normally consisting of several villages, was the lowest rural level of the administrative hierarchy). After the central government adopted regulations for the organization of basic-level government in December, 1950, the CCP slowly began to establish popular representative bodies in the rural *hsiang* and the urban *ch'ü,* the principal basic-level units of administration.[58] These "people's representative conferences" (*jen-min tai piao hui-i*), as they soon came to be called, were composed of a variety of elected and appointed delegates from residential units, popular organizations, and government offices. They were given advisory and consultative functions in basic-level government, but the government councils and executives that held decision-making power continued to be appointed by higher levels of government. Ultimately, as the local situation became stable and more and more of the conference delegates were elected, the conferences would begin to elect the government councils at their levels. When this stage was reached, the representative conferences had assumed their full powers and became known as "people's representative congresses" (*jen-min tai-piao ta-hui*).

By September, 1952, "people's governments" and people's representative conferences had been established at all governmental levels in China. The process of political construction was by no means complete, however, as some conferences retained appointed delegates and a substantial proportion of the conferences were not exercising the powers of "congresses" by electing government councils.[59] Only in 1954, after the passage of new regulations on government organization and the national elections of 1953–1954, was political construction basically completed. The length of time required to complete this task reflected the CCP's insistence that people's conferences and congresses serve as instruments to help translate Party policies into action. The CCP had no intention of establishing representative institutions at the basic level until it was sure of its ability to guide their work. A report summarizing model experiences in rural political construction in East China concluded that the establishment of "democratic political power" in the *hsiang* was inseparable from the work of land reform and other mass movements, such as Resist America–Aid Korea and the Suppression of Counterrevolutionaries because the objectives of all these projects were the same. The report stated that political construction could take place only when the old political power was overthrown and the political and economic base of the revolution was consolidated. Generally *hsiang* conferences or congresses could not be called until the following four conditions were met: (1) land reform was basically completed; (2) the masses were mobilized and mass organizations were fully established; (3) the masses had attained "democratic consciousness" and were responsive to the influence of the peasants' representative meetings; (4)

---

[58] See *CB,* No. 144 (December 12, 1951) for the text of these regulations.

[59] Hsieh Chüeh-tsai, "Achievements in Administrative Construction and Civil Affairs," NCNA, September 20, 1952, in *CB,* No. 218 (November 5, 1952).

cadres had a basic knowledge of the national system of representative conferences and congresses and understood the substance and spirit of central government regulations on *hsiang* political organization.[60]

Given the scope of its problems and objectives, the period of political construction was one of great success for the CCP. Its political authority was extended down to the lowest levels of administration throughout China, it overcame the most pressing internal and external problems with which it was faced, and as a result, it laid the foundation for socialist economic construction. There was, of course, opposition from those people who were the objects of the great mass movements; the ruthless suppression of these elements left no doubt about the CCP's willingness to assert its authority forcefully when necessary. Nevertheless, the CCP did secure widespread mass participation in these movements, and it could not have accomplished what it did without popular assistance. The Party's ability to enlist mass support during the period of political construction was due to two main factors. First, Party policies, at least in their stated objectives, were consistent with majority interests. Land reform, resistance to American military action in Korea, economic reconstruction, elimination of corruption, and so forth, were of basic appeal to all save scattered minorities. The second factor was the Party's skill in rousing the people to action through organization and political education and by providing them with opportunities for political expression. The obvious presence of CCP control makes it easy to underestimate the attraction of participation in the early mass movements. It must be remembered that the Party was soliciting political action, however ritualistic it may have been, from people who previously had been almost totally divorced from political life. Land reform alone, which still stands as the most significant mass movement in Communist China, involved every peasant in a process of enormous symbolic and practical political importance, namely, the redistribution of the major source of wealth (and to some extent status) in rural China and the overthrow of the old political authorities. The fact that the CCP initiated this process and guided it at every stage did not destroy its impact on the Chinese peasant.

In spite of impressive achievements, political construction also revealed the basic tension in the Chinese style of political participation. Much of the political activity in this period, even though it contributed to the success of CCP policies, lacked the consciousness and voluntariness that Party theory demands. The political "backwardness' of the masses was one reason for this problem. Many people took part in politics for what the Party regarded as the wrong reasons, such as

[60] *Chieh-fang Jih-pao* (Shanghai), July 25, 1951.

gratitude to the Party or hope for personal gain, or else they participated in a superficial way without displaying genuine understanding of, or enthusiasm for, their actions. A report from the Party Committee of Hsüch'ang *Hsien,* Honan, on the "democratic movement" in one *hsiang* offers an example of this situation. The *hsiang* under consideration, which was said to be the best in its district in carrying out the movement, had raised the proportion of the population with membership in organizations from 17 percent before the movement to 32.9 percent after the movement. Nevertheless, the Party Committee stated that of the 848 members of the *hsiang* peasants' associations and women's organizations, only 148 were active in attendance and speaking out at meetings. It also estimated that 40–50 percent of the *hsiang* population was still "backward." [61] In cases such as this, the Party's organizational work was sufficient to mobilize the masses for action but not deep enough to replace peasant apathy and reserve with the desired political consciousness.

Another major departure from the Party's concept of political participation was the frequent appearance of "commandism" and "bureaucratism," usually manifested in cadres issuing orders to the masses, violating regular democratic procedures, or ignoring mass demands. The militancy and turmoil of the period were partly responsible for this; with so many changes in progress and so many "enemies" to be exposed or struggled against, it is not surprising that cadres sometimes resorted to arbitrary methods in order to complete their assigned tasks. Also involved, however, was a more general problem that has never been fully resolved by the CCP—the difficulty of locating and training a sufficient number of cadres who have the personal qualifications (not to mention the political qualifications) necessary to lead the masses into voluntary acceptance of Party policies. Many examples of the type of complaints lodged against cadres were brought out at a conference of *hsien* magistrates from Shantung in November, 1952. The conference which was called to discuss local political construction in Shantung heard reports of critics of cadres being beaten and of candidates being appointed to office over others who received more votes. After learning of these conditions, the masses were reported to be saying, "Chairman Mao's policy is clear as water but it becomes muddied at lower levels." Meetings of representative conferences were strongly attacked for simply transmitting orders and supervising delegates without even considering mass proposals. As a result, delegates were losing interest and saying, "The conference's good point is that one eats well; its bad point is that no problems are solved." [62] Given the Chinese Communists' emphasis

[61] *Ho-nan Jih-pao* (Honan Daily) (Chengchow), February 27, 1952.
[62] *Kuang-ming Jih-pao* (Bright Daily) (Peking), January 14, 1953.

on self-criticism, some reports of errors and deviations arise in every movement. However, criticism of the type cited here was too widespread to be dismissed as a ritualistic confession of imperfections. The CCP later acknowledged that the intensity of the early mass movements had created undesirable strains in Party relations with the masses.

Liberalization, 1956–1957   "Liberalization" describes the 1956–1957 period only in the most relative sense. With the exception of the outburst of anti-Party criticism in the spring of 1957, probably no single incident in these years would have been totally out of place in other periods of the CPR's existence. Nevertheless, when taken as a whole, the events of these years do convey a sense of political moderation relative to those of earlier or later years. There is always criticism in Communist China, but the criticism raised during 1956–1957 hinted, although only temporarily, at a fundamental change in the character of Chinese Communist politics.

Relaxation in domestic political life was mainly a product of general improvements in China's internal and external situation. The Korean War had ended in 1953 in an armistice easily interpreted as a victory for the Chinese forces. China's rising military prestige was coupled with a moderate diplomatic policy that was beginning to bear fruit, especially among other Asian Countries. Through Chou En-lai's appearances at international conferences and a multitude of official and unofficial contacts with other countries, China appeared to be living up to its declarations about "peaceful coexistence." Internally, the Chinese economy had been restored and the First Five-Year Plan was well under way. A new constitution and state structure, marking the end of political construction, had been adopted in 1954. For all practical purposes, the danger of counterrevolution was over. There were, of course, some potentially dangerous internal problems and recurring indications of the CCP's intolerance of opposition. In 1955, the campaign against counterrevolutionaries was temporarily revived. The notorious Hu Feng case in the same year revealed the CCP's hostility toward any disagreement with official Party line. Cooperativization of agriculture progressed very rapidly in late 1955 and early 1956 but was clearly causing some dissatisfaction among the peasantry. In the balance, however, the Chinese leaders had cause to be optimistic about economic and political progress toward a socialist society.

The Eighth National Congress of the CCP in September, 1956, officially acknowledged that the improved situation demanded a new approach to internal political life. In his "Political Report" to the Congress, Liu Shao-ch'i asserted that the centralization of authority that had been necessary at the time of the founding of the CPR was now leading to bureaucratism and excessive restrictions on local authorities. He called for decentralization of administrative powers, extension of democracy, and a determined war on bureaucratism.[63] Liu also observed that during the revolutionary war and the early period after liberation it had been necessary to draw up "temporary laws in the nature of general principles" as an expedient for destroying the old order, but that more regular procedures were now needed.

During this period, the chief aim of the struggle was to liberate the people from reactionary rule and to free the productive forces of society from the bondage of old relations of production. The principal method of struggle was to lead the masses in direct action. . . . Now, however, the period of revolutionary storm and stress is past, new relations of production have been set up, and the aim of our struggle is changed into one of safeguarding the successful development of the productive forces of society, a corresponding change in the methods of struggle will consequently have to follow, and a complete legal system becomes an absolute necessity.[64]

This point was expanded by Tung Pi-wu, president of the Supreme People's Court and a member of the Political Bureau of the Party Central Committee, into a general appeal for codification of laws and strict observance of existing laws and the system of people's congresses. He conceded that laws had been violated and democratic principles neglected in previous years. Tung observed that since "mass revolutionary movements do not depend entirely on law, they are likely to bring a by-product—encouragement of an indiscriminate disregard for all legal systems." [65]

In this climate of basic criticism of past policies, Lai Jo-yu, chairman of the All-China Federation of Trade Unions, felt emboldened to defend the particular interests of the workers. Lai stated that maintaining close ties with the masses was the primary condition for success in trade union work. To maintain these ties, trade unions must ". . . show a serious concern for the interests of the mass of workers and employees and conscientiously safeguard those interests.

"Some people seem to think that because the working class wields state power, the state as a whole will safeguard the interests of the working class and the trade unions have lost their function as protector of the workers' interests. This view is wrong." [66] Lai said that there is unity

---

[63] *Op. cit.*, pp. 75–78.

[64] *Ibid.*, pp. 81–82.

[65] "Speech by Comrade Tung Pi-wu," in *Eighth National Congress of the Communist Party of China*, II, Speeches, pp. 88–95. In his speech on the "Correct Handling of Contradictions" (*op. cit.*, p. 26), Mao Tse-tung admitted that "good people were sometimes mistaken for bad" during suppression of counterrevolutionaries and that "suitable measures of rehabilitation" should be taken.

[66] "Speech by Comrade Lai Jo-yu," in *Eighth National Congress of the Communist Party of China*, II, p. 238.

between the interests of the state and those of individual workers, but that "the two are often at odds with each other, i.e., there is a certain contradiction between them." [67] While Lai's statements did not propose a new role for the trade unions or conflict with the established Party line on the relationship between particular and collective interests, they nonetheless signified an increased willingness to emphasize the group interest within the Communist presumption of the essential identity of all interests.

The practical effect of the moderate political climate of these years was to encourage people to test the voluntary or spontaneous aspect of the Party's mass line. This aspect had always been present in theory but it had been tightly controlled during the rigorous early years of the CPR. By 1956, there seemed to be grounds for hoping, on the basis of improving conditions and Party statements, that the leadership would be more tolerant of genuine individual or group expression so long as it did not challenge the basic character or ideology of the Communist state. In 1956, this hope was cautiously tested by the intellectuals after the CCP indicated its willingness to improve their position.[68] The Party suggested two general areas of improvement: first, greater tolerance of free discussion and criticism in academic and cultural matters, with an ambiguous hint that political discussion might also be liberalized; second, improvements in the rational use of intellectuals' abilities and in their working conditions. In the intellectuals' response to these overtures were the tentative beginnings of a movement to defend and advance the group interests of the academic and technical professions. The movement was necessarily unorganized and was carefully built around the general vocabulary of socialist construction. It was clear, however, that the intellectuals were demanding fewer political controls, more authority in professional matters, and material gains in such realms as funds for books and research activities.[69]

Political relaxation remained essentially in the realm of theory and hopes until 1957, but in the spring of that year, during the Party rectification movement and the "hundred flowers" campaign, it became a reality.[70] The leadership's motives in initiating the "hundred flowers" experiment were complex. The move was certainly consistent with

[67] *Ibid.,* p. 239.

[68] The two major documents on CCP policy toward the intellectuals in 1956 are Lu Ting-yi, *op. cit.,* and Chou En-lai, *Report on the Question of the Intellectuals* (Peking, 1956).

[69] See the collection of articles in *CB,* No. 379 (February 23, 1956), especially Feng Yu-lan's, "Bring Out the Latent Strength of the Intellectuals." Another revealing article is Tao Shih-lung, "Is Such Criticism of Individualism Appropriate?" *Chung-kuo Ch'ing-nien,* 1956, No. 5, in *SMM,* No. 33 (April 30, 1956).

[70] See Mac Farquhar, *op. cit.,* for documentation and analysis of this period.

some of the previously cited criticism that cropped up at the Eighth Party Congress and with the CCP's desire to mend its fences with non-Party groups, particularly the intellectuals. However, Khrushchev's denunciation of Stalin and the crises in Poland and Hungary undoubtedly influenced the decision and its timing by giving both encouragement and a sense of urgency to respect for popular grievances. What is significant for our purposes is that the Party did encourage free political discussion and criticism and that the response, after some delay and uncertainty, was a flood of complaints and suggestions. It is significant, too, that the greatest part of this outburst fell within a liberal interpretation of the Party's concept of political participation. Except for a few extreme attacks on the CCP and a few unruly demonstrations, little was said or done that openly challenged the CCP's leading position or the general path of socialist construction. Criticism focused on the *exclusiveness* of Party leadership, the methods of leadership, and the mistakes and excesses of the past. Theoretically, such criticism was justified by the Party's call for non-Party participation in the rectification campaign, by the slogan of "mutual supervision" among the classes and parties within the United Front, and by the CCP's proclaimed desire to hear and discuss the opinions of the masses. Therefore, the "hundred flowers" episode forced the CCP to face up to the central problem in its conception of popular political activity. In theory, political criticism and discussion among the people would be beneficial and would be resolved in a higher stage of unity. In practice, the CCP found that this was not the case, or at least that the dangers involved were too great to allow the experiment to be completed.

The "hundred flowers" period ended in June, 1957, a date that must be recognized as the most significant in the history of political participation in Communist China. Before 1957, the CCP had never encountered widespread and serious public criticism. From 1937 to 1956, the combination, in varying degrees, of general popular support and suppression of major opposition groups had placed a moratorium on such criticism. As a result, the CCP had clung, perhaps in genuine ignorance, to its assertions about the possibility and even necessity of free political discussion among the ranks of the people. When this belief was finally tested during the "hundred flowers" period, the Party decided that it could not, in practice, tolerate any significant criticism from outside the Party. Since June, 1957, there has been no doubt that the principle of Party leadership precludes any genuine political spontaneity among the masses.

THE GREAT LEAP FORWARD, 1957–1960 Although the CCP has continued to use the slogan of "blooming and contending," the "hundred flowers" period in its original character was ended on June 8, 1957, by an editorial in *Jen-min Jih-pao*. After this date, the most violent critics of the Party were denounced and attacked as "rightists." The rectification campaign continued, but basic policies and practices were no longer open to discussion; primary emphasis shifted from criticism of the Party to exposure of deviant ideology among the population. During the years between 1957 and 1960, a political mood that was quite different from the one just described became dominant. Because of its apparently reckless energy and optimism, the new mood was aptly represented by the slogan of a "great leap forward."

The period of the Great Leap is perhaps best known for the formation of people's communes in the countryside in 1958 and for the attempt to score sensational advances in all areas of production by the extravagant expenditure of human resources. This was a period in which China proclaimed its ability to catch up with the industrially advanced nations by virtue of human effort and enthusiasm. Hundreds of millions of Chinese were to be organized for a "war against nature." Planning and statistics were forgotten, obstacles were ignored, and everyone, regardless of position, was expected to make some contribution to productive labor. The Great Leap was equally distinctive, however, in its political style, a style that was marked by three major characteristics.

The first characteristic was a tough reminder, directed mainly at the intellectuals and bourgeois elements who had been most critical of the CCP during the "hundred flowers" episode, of the inevitability of socialism. All those who had doubts about the course pursued by the CCP were pointedly warned that they must get in step. Liu Shao-ch'i made this warning unmistakably clear in a speech on November 6, 1957.

At this time, all people, no matter whether they approve or oppose or are willing or unwilling, must sooner or later follow the socialist road. . . . If the exploiters who begrudge giving up their lives of exploitation are not willing to destroy themselves, they also will be compelled to follow this road. It is the trend of events and the direction of public opinion—this road must be followed. The only difference is that most men will take it themselves, while a few will be forced to take it. Some cases where the road is taken sooner or later can be tolerated, but the freedom to not follow it at all does not exist.[71]

Liu added that many people who are following the socialist road are actually "reluctant" and "wavering"; they feel that the socialist system reduces their freedom and that others do not respect their will. Their

[71] "Tsai Pei-ching Ko-chieh Ch'ing-chu Shih-yüeh She-hui Chu-i Ko-ming Ssu-shih Chou-nien Ta-hui Shang ti Chiang-hua" (Speech at a Meeting of Various Circles in Peking Celebrating the Fortieth Anniversary of the October Socialist Revolution), *Hsin-hua Pan-yüeh K'an* (New China Semimonthly), 1957, No. 23, p. 43.

selection of the socialist road lacks "sufficient consciousness" because they do not recognize or respect the "objective laws that cannot be changed by human will." If such people "take the socialist road wholeheartedly and if they consciously change their own ideas, traditions and habits that are not suitable to socialism, then they can become truly free and contented citizens of socialist society." [72]

Finally, Liu admonished the intellectuals to forget their "so-called slogan of 'specialist first and red second' " that could only "serve as a call to escape politics. . . . Our intellectuals must understand that politics is inescapable. Once they have escaped revolutionary politics, then they can move toward reactionary politics. Without a correct political standpoint, they can fall into a reactionary political standpoint." [73] Other classes, too, were warned about putting their own interests against the overall interests of the state. In a speech at the Eighth Trade Union Congress in December, 1957, only fifteen months after he had spoken out for the workers' interests at the Eighth Party Congress, Lai Jo-yu stated that worker wages and welfare benefits had to be considered in the light of overall national interests and the development of production. Lai added that two questions had been common to all great debates on trade union policy since 1949: Should the trade unions accept Party leadership? Should the trade unions regard production as their central task? Needless to say, he answered both affirmatively and said mistakes had arisen when either had been denied.[74]

The second political characteristic of the Great Leap Forward was increased emphasis on CCP leadership. While the Party still insisted that its organization was not to replace the state structure, the concern over codification of law and observance of regular legal and state procedures that had marked the previous period was now missing. In its place was a naked assertion of Party control throughout state and society. The following statement by Liu Lan-t'ao, a member of the CCP Central Committee, illustrates this point.

To ensure the unified leadership of the Party, it is necessary for all revolutionary organizations, including government offices, army units, people's bodies, political and judicial organs like public security bureaux, courts, procuracies, and departments of finance, economy, culture, education, science and public health, to be brought under the unified leadership of the Central Committee and the local committees at all levels (including the Party committees at the basic level) of the Party in their work and in the struggle to implement the general line and the fundamental task of the Party.[75]

[72] *Loc. cit.*
[73] *Ibid.,* p. 45.
[74] NCNA, December 2, 1957, in *CB,* No. 482 (December 13, 1957).
[75] "The Communist Party of China is the High Command of the Chinese People in Building Socialism," *Ten Glorious Years* (Peking, 1960), p. 289.

Liu conceded that this could lead to practical problems within "revolutionary organizations" due to desires for independence and for professional leadership; there might also be those who accepted Party political and ideological leadership but resented Party organizational leadership. Unfortunately, said Liu, there is no alternative since the lines, principles, and policies of the Party cannot be carried out without Party leadership over all revolutionary organizations outside the Party. There can be no "independence" from Party control as this would, in fact, mean submission to bourgeois control.[76]

Finally, the Great Leap involved an unprecedented effort to indoctrinate the entire population with "correct" ideology. This effort reinforced the tendency noted above to move away from regular procedures within the state structure, as it depended essentially on direct mobilization of the masses by cadres at the lowest level. In fact, as Chou En-lai said, it was simply a matter of making the methods of the rectification campaign become a "permanent feature of our political life"; mass meetings, constant discussion and debate and writing of *tatzubao,* which formerly had been used as techniques for mass movements, were to become the very heart of regular political activities.[77] The effort to extend ideological indoctrination and discussion among the masses indicated the CCP's awareness that much acceptance of Party policies in the past had been, from its point of view, too superficial or lacking in consciousness.

In the past, our political and ideological education for the peasants was mainly conducted from above: the *hsien, ch'ü* and *hsiang* cadres . . . propagated the Party principles and policies and told the peasants what they should do and what they should not do. This method of education was useful in that many basic principles could be clearly explained and the peasants could understand the right and wrong and do things according to the Party directives. But this method of education had a certain limit, mainly because negative views of the masses could not be discovered in good time and persuasion and explanations could not be effectively made. . . . By arousing the masses to open public debate, different views, questions, problems and demands can be brought forward and discussed, studied and solved by cadres and the masses together.[78]

The author of this statement admitted that some cadres were not well trained for this kind of work or were worried by the thought of encouraging popular debate. He reassured them by saying that debate would be guided to avoid trouble and that, in any case, "negative" questions

[76] *Ibid.,* pp. 289–291. Administrative decentralization was implicit in the formation of the rural communes, but tighter leadership by the Commune Party Committees precluded the development of local administrative independence.

[77] *Report on the Work of the Government,* delivered at the First Session of the Second National People's Congress on April 18, 1959, (Peking, 1959), p. 45.

[78] Li Shen, "Dispel Misgivings and Lead the Public Debate on Socialism," *Cheng-chih Hsüeh-hsi,* 1957, No. 9 in *SMM,* No. 106 (November 4, 1957).

would be overcome by persuasion and presentation of the facts. Encouraging debate, he concluded, is a "good method of inculcating obedience in the minds of the peasants."

The political characteristics of the Great Leap were unquestionably shaped by the CCP's reaction to the "hundred flowers" period, a fact that was evident in the new suspicion and toughness toward the academicians and technicians as well as in the reassertion of Party control. However, there was also a positive side to these characteristics. The institutionalization of constant political education among the masses, using the methods of a mass movement, reflected the belief that high ideological consciousness was necessary for, and a guarantee of, the rapid economic development of China. While the reliance on mass efforts was indicative of the Party's antagonism toward the professional classes, it was also consistent with the CCP's belief that the road to communism would be marked by a reduction of state activities and an ever increasing element of mass implementation of policies. Party literature during the Great Leap contained more discussion of and emphasis on the mass line than in any previous period. The politics of the period were regarded, therefore, as a progressive step of long duration rather than as a measure to correct the evil manifestations of the "hundred flowers" period. By the same token, the ultimate failure of the Great Leap was a development of profound importance, the significance of which has not yet been fully revealed.

RETRENCHMENT, 1961–1962   The Great Leap Forward was in difficulty almost from the first, although the full extent of its failure did not become apparent to foreign observers until 1962. Retrenchment in the rural communes began soon after their formation in the summer of 1958. Production goals were revised downward in 1959, and economic stagnation became serious in 1960–1961; throughout 1959–1961, the regime was in economic difficulty. After the Ninth Plenum of the Central Committee in January, 1961, an unmistakable policy of retrenchment prevailed as large numbers of people were shifted from the cities to the agricultural front, cultivation of private plots was encouraged, and the production teams—the lowest level of management in the rural communes—became virtually independent in matters of production and distribution. It was apparent, too, that food shortages and other economic difficulties had had a significant impact on public morale. The ultimate effect of these problems on popular political activity is not yet clear, but they resulted in a temporary retreat from the political style of the Great Leap.

The major political change was a relaxation of constant ideological indoctrination and of the insistence that high political consciousness could accomplish all things. This change was dramatized in an August, 1961, speech by Foreign Minister Ch'en Yi in which he stated that not everyone could be both "red and expert." Ch'en's remarks, which were addressed to students in Peking, noted that China desperately needs specialists and that a person should not be criticized for devoting less time to politics if his best contribution to society could be made in specialized studies.[79] During 1962, this policy was applied on a more general basis throughout China with the key point being that meetings and political activities must not interfere with production. The change from the previous period was even more evident in the admission that increased agricultural production was essential for higher political consciousness, rather than the other way around, and that man could only work in harmony with the laws of nature rather than overcome them by sheer effort.[80]

The period of retrenchment was brief and did not alter basic Party theory, but it did weaken the CCP concept of political participation by challenging three assumptions behind the Party's belief that the people can be trained to carry out Party policy on their own conscious initiative. These assumptions are the following: that the masses will accept the superiority of Party leadership without question; that popular ideological consciousness can be significantly raised, even in the face of economic hardship; that basic-level cadres will be able to bridge the gap between Party leadership and mass action. The challenge to the first two assumptions is evident from what has been said. Initially, economic hardship may not have brought loss of faith in Party leadership, but it is unlikely that the CCP could succeed for long in shifting responsibility for such a serious crisis to inclement weather and mistakes of individual cadres. The changes of 1961–1962, welcome as they might have been, certainly cast doubt on the correctness of Party policy in the preceding years. The CCP also lost much of its optimism about its ability to implant collective ideology in the minds of the peasants. In conceding that some material advance is necessary to change the peasants' way of thinking, the Party had to remind itself of the "thousands of years of feudalism" that preceded its victory and admit that "peasant capitalism" was far from dead in the countryside. The challenge to the third assumption is by no means new, as the problem of basic-level cadres has bedeviled the CCP ever since the Yenan period, but the problem was

[79] "Tui Pei-ching-shih Kao-teng Yüan-hsiao Ying-chieh Pi-yeh Hsüeh-sheng ti Chiang-hua" (Speech to Graduating Students of Higher Colleges and Schools in Peking), *Chung-kuo Ch'ing-nien,* 1961, No. 17, pp. 2–5.

[80] Chang Ching, "Pu-wei Nung-shih Shih Ling-tao Nung-yeh Sheng-ch'an ti I-hsiang Chung-yao Cheng-ts'e" (Not Disregarding Agricultural Time Is an Important Policy in Leading Agricultural Production), *Hung Ch'i,* 1962, No. 7, pp. 10–15.

particularly sharp during the difficulties of 1961–1962. The Party makes no secret of its preference for experienced cadres who remain at their posts for long periods of time. In 1961–1962, however, rectification movements, the heavy responsibilities of office, and even the minimal freedom allowed in elections, sometimes combined to cause a rapid turnover in cadre ranks.[81] Many cadres were caught in the dilemma of risking peasant disapproval by adhering strictly to CCP orders or risking Party censure by allowing the masses to violate regulations; either solution was, of course, a compromise of the mass-line principle.[82]

POLITICAL CONSOLIDATION, 1962–1965   Although some of the economic aspects of retrenchment (e.g., emphasis on agricultural production, tolerance of private plots and rural markets, relative independence for the production team) have lingered on, political retrenchment ended with a new offensive launched by the Tenth Plenum of the CCP Central Committee in September, 1962. The Tenth Plenum reaffirmed the goal of a collective economy and forecast a renewal of class struggle and ideological indoctrination.[83] Two years later, in December, 1964, Premier Chou En-lai told the National People's Congress (NPC) that the Tenth Plenum had counterattacked to check the "evil winds and noxious influences" that were then advocating further extension of private plots and free markets, the increase of independent enterprises, "capitulationism in united front work" and "liberalization." [84] The mass movements of 1963–1965, which are strongly reminiscent of the Great Leap period, bear out this assertion. "Socialist education," "learn from Lei Feng," "learn from the People's Liberation Army," and the "cultivation of revolutionary successors" are movements that have reasserted the importance of activism, political consciousness and discipline, socialist ideology, and the Party's desire to mold future generations of Chinese in the image of its present leadership. The primacy of political considerations, a principle that dominated the Great Leap under the slogan "politics takes command," is back in operation again.[85] The Party's response to the uncertainties and problems of 1961–1962 has been renewed emphasis on the mass line as a means of consolidating the

[81] See the report on basic-level cadre problems in *Nan-fang Jih-pao* (Southern Daily) (Canton), June 12, 1962.

[82] Detail on this point, and on all of the basic-level problems discussed in this section, can be found in "Facts about the Basic Levels in Pao-An County," *Union Research Service* (Hong Kong), Vol. 27, Nos. 7–9.

[83] "Communique of the Tenth Plenum of the Eighth Central Committee of the Communist Party of China," *Peking Review*, 1962, No. 39, pp. 5–8.

[84] "Premier Chou En-lai Reports on the Work of the Government," *Peking Review*, 1965, No. 1, pp. 12–13.

[85] See "Cheng-chih Kung-tso Shih I-ch'ieh Kung-tso ti Sheng-ming-hsien" (Political Work Is the Lifeline of All Work), *Hung Ch'i*, 1964, No. 6, pp. 40–45.

regime's political base for future struggles. With the Third Five-Year Plan beginning in 1966, and with the Party's obsessive opposition to "capitalist and revisionist" influences at home and abroad, it is very unlikely that the CCP will relax its efforts to build unified and disciplined mass support for its objectives.

What distinguishes this period of consolidation from the Great Leap Forward is not any fundamental change in theory but an atmosphere of caution and realism. The mass line and the primacy of politics remain, but so does the restraining influence of the lesson of 1961–1962. Technicians ought to be "red" as well as "expert," but their expertise is highly respected anyway; political consciousness is said to be necessary for increased production, but workers must not have so many meetings that they lose sleep or even a reasonable amount of leisure time. A good illustration of the injection of caution into the mass-line style of thought is the following quotation from Chou's December, 1964, report to the NPC. "We must promote both the revolutionary spirit of daring to think, daring to speak and daring to act *and a scientific and realistic approach.* On the one hand, there must be great enthusiasm in work and on the other, *labour must be alternated with rest.* Innovations must be *put on trial* before they are *gradually* introduced." [86] The recent period is, therefore, close to the Great Leap in language but far from it in spirit. There is patience instead of urgency, calculation instead of enthusiasm. The Party is trying to rebuild and consolidate its political base without giving ground to real or imagined opponents and without the excesses of the Great Leap. The CCP still holds to the central ideas that have determined its attitude toward popular political participation ever since the Yenan period, but it continues to shift the application of these ideas as it responds to, and tries to change, its political environment. Whether or not these shifts establish a long-term trend, or point to a significant change in political participation in China, will become clearer from a closer examination of some of the more important areas of mass political activity in China.

[86] *Op. cit.,* p. 11. Emphasis added.

FIVE

Mass Participation
in the State Structure

The Chinese Communists have tried diligently to put their concept of political participation into practice in the CPR. Even though practice has not always conformed to theory, there is no mistaking the Party's persistent and calculated efforts to remold Chinese political life in accordance with its own theories. These efforts, which have been backed by the CCP's power to manipulate political structure and organizations almost at will, have resulted in an enormous amount of mass political activity, all of which bears the imprint of the Party's concept of political participation. The purpose of the next three chapters is to present a selective description of the most important aspects of this activity in order to demonstrate how the CCP has translated its theory into practice. Chapters Five and Six will discuss mass participation in the state structure and nongovernmental organization respectively; chapter Seven will analyze the most characteristic features of political participation in Communist China.

It is not easy to distinguish between "governmental" and "nongovernmental" activity in China. The distinction is made here primarily for analytical purposes and does not suggest that "nongovernmental" activity is in any sense nonpolitical or beyond the control of state and Party organs. Nevertheless, even though the CCP believes that both governmental and nongovernmental activities may be equally political, it does recognize the formal distinctness of the state structure from other forms of organization. Moreover, this distinction, or lack of it, is of value in assessing the trend and character of Chinese politics, a point to which we shall return later. The discussion of mass participation in the state structure will cover basic-level people's congresses, basic-level elections, and popular participation in legal organs.

PEOPLE'S CONGRESSES

The state structure that existed in the CPR from 1949 to 1954 was a temporary one designed to meet the needs of Communist political construction. The system was marked by considerable variety owing to holdovers of pre-Communist units, differing degrees of administrative stability, and structural experimentation on the part of the CCP. As mentioned earlier, representative bodies were gradually introduced at all levels of government in the form of "people's conferences," but there was little consistency in the progress of these bodies toward the exercise of full powers as "people's congresses." Generally speaking, there was little popular control of government, even in form, throughout this period. Most representative organs, from the Chinese People's Political Consultative Conference (CPPCC) at the national level down to the people's conferences at the lowest level, were initially composed of deputies appointed by the Party or higher levels of government and were defined essentially as consultative or advisory bodies. In 1953–1954, however, the CCP conducted elections throughout China and established a uniform system of people's congresses. This system, which was formally adopted at the First Session of the First National People's Congress in September, 1954, laid down the basic legal characteristics of congresses at all levels. These characteristics have technically remained unchanged even though they were substantially modified in practice by the formation of the rural people's communes in 1958.

At the top of the administrative heirarchy is the central government with the National People's Congress (NPC). Under the central government are the provinces and a few "special municipalities" (since 1959, Peking and Shanghai have been the only cities directly under the central government). The provinces are divided into *hsien* (counties) and municipalities; the special municipalities are divided into urban *ch'ü* (districts). *Hsien* are divided into either *hsiang* (townships) or *chen* (rural towns); municipalities may be divided into *ch'ü* or remain undistricted, depending on size. Each of the levels mentioned has a people's congress, designated as the organ of political power for its particular level, and an executive body called the people's council.[1] For purposes of this discussion, the lowest level of the hierarchy will be referred to as basic-level government. Therefore, basic-level congresses include *hsiang* congresses, *chen* congresses, urban *ch'ü* congresses, and municipal congresses in undistricted cities. Local government is defined as including the following levels: provinces, special municipalities, districted municipalities, and *hsien*.

---

[1] "Constitution of the People's Republic of China," *Documents of the First Session of the First National People's Congress of the People's Republic of China,* Arts. 21, 53–55. This list omits the administrative divisions provided for national minority areas (nationality *hsiang,* autonomous counties, autonomous *chou,* and autonomous regions). It also omits other administrative units, such as the special regions (between province and *hsien*) and the rural *ch'ü"* (between *hsien* and *hsiang*), that were simply subdivisions of the next higher level and had no congresses of their own.

The NPC and local people's congresses are not included in the following analysis as they are not organs for mass political participation. Although all congresses in China claim to be organs of popular political power, only the basic-level congresses are elected directly by the people; the NPC and local congresses are elected by the next lower level of congresses.[2] The NPC, for example, is twice or thrice removed from direct popular election. Theoretically, indirectly elected deputies might still have regular contact with the masses, or at least make a genuine effort to represent them in higher levels of government. In China, however, it is all too obvious that this does not happen. Although there are scattered instances of higher-level congresses and deputies serving as media for popular political expression, all significant mass participation in the state structure takes place at the basic level.

Basic-level congresses hold an impressive list of formal powers. In addition to electing the people's councils at their level, they are empowered to hear and examine work reports of the council, revise or annul "inappropriate decisions and orders" of the council, adopt and issue decisions within the limits of their powers, examine financial revenue and expenditure, and make plans or give approval on a variety of more specific subjects. They may recall any officials elected by them, that is, members of their own councils, presidents of the people's courts at their level, and deputies to the next higher congress. All of their decisions are made by a simple majority vote. Material facilities and expenses, including traveling expenses for deputies attending congresses, are provided by the state. Basic-level deputies are required to bring popular opinions and demands to the attention of the congress and council and may be recalled by the voters who elected them. Basic-level congresses and their councils are elected for two-year terms. *Hsiang* and *chen* congresses are to meet four times a year, while urban *ch'ü* congresses are to meet twice a year.[3]

In spite of such provisions, however, the formal statement of basic-level congress functions reveals that these congresses are not genuine centers of political power. Basic-level people's councils, which are defined as the executive organs of the congresses, are also responsible to higher state administrative bodies and are "subordinate to and under the co-ordinating direction of the State Council."[4] People's councils are to carry out the tasks assigned to them by higher councils, and to issue decisions and orders in accordance with those of higher organs of state administration. They are empowered to convene and submit proposals

[2] *The Electoral Law of the People's Republic of China* (Peking, 1953), Art 3.
[3] "*Organic Law of the Local People's Congresses and Local People's Councils of the People's Republic of China,*" *Documents of the First Session of the National People's Congress of the People's Republic of China,* chap. 2.
[4] *Ibid.,* Arts. 23–25.

to their congresses. "Inappropriate decisions" of both basic-level congresses and councils can be revised or annulled by the next higher
councils and congresses.[5] In accordance with the CCP theory of political participation, basic-level congresses are enjoined to "ensure the
observance and execution of laws and decrees." Deputies must publi-
cize laws, decrees, and policies and assist people's councils in their
work. Each deputy is also expected to work among certain groups of
voters and to organize with other deputies to promote the work of the
people's council.[6] Therefore, the most significant aspect of basic-level
government is its subordination to higher administrative levels and its
obligation to assist in the propagation and execution of state policy.

As stated above, the formation of the rural people's communes in
1958 substantially modified the formal position of basic-level congresses. The central point in this change was the statement that the
rural communes were to replace the *hsiang* as the basic unit of administration in the countryside. Before examining the implications of this
substitution, it will be useful to note the general trend in the number of
basic-level units and the size of the basic-level congresses since 1954.
During the first general elections in 1953–1954, the limits on the number of deputies to a *hsiang* or *chen* congress were fixed at a minimum of
7 and a maximum of 50, with 15 to 35 being the normal range; the
number of deputies to an urban *ch'ü* congress was not less than 35 or
more than 200.[7] These limits resulted in the election of a total of
5,699,144 basic-level deputies in China, most being elected from the
220,466 *hsiang* and 821 urban *ch'ü*.[8] The limits were revised in 1956,
raising the maximum number of deputies for *hsiang, chen,* and *ch'ü*
congresses to 70, 90, and 350 respectively.[9] Then, before the 1958
general elections, a decision of the Standing Committee of the NPC
permitted all basic-level congresses to exceed the specified number of
deputies with the approval of the next higher level of government.[10]
The primary reason for this sharp rise in the size of basic-level congresses was the amalgamation of administrative units. By January 1,
1958, the number of *hsiang* had been reduced to 95,843 and that of
urban *ch'ü* to 388.[11] The reduction in number of units was faster than
the rise in congress size, resulting in a lower ratio of representation in

[5] *Ibid.*, Arts. 11, 27–28.
[6] *Ibid.*, Arts. 7, 20.
[7] *Electoral Law*, Arts. 9, 18.
[8] Chou En-lai, "Report on the Work of the Government," *Documents of the
First Session of the First National People's Congress of the People's Republic of
China*, pp. 108–110.
[9] *JMJP*, May 13, 1956.
[10] *Ta Kung Pao* (Impartial News) (Peking), March 20, 1958.
[11] *CB*, No. 529 (October 29, 1958), p. 69.

basic-level congresses. This could be seen in the 1958 elections when about 4,500,000 basic-level deputies were elected, as contrasted to the 5,669,144 elected from a smaller population in 1953–1954.[12]

The amalgamation of *hsiang* was still in progress in the summer of 1958 when the rural communes were formed, but the communes accelerated this trend. By August, 1959, 99 percent of the rural population had been organized into about 24,000 people's communes averaging approximately 5,000 households each.[13] Since the communes replaced the *hsiang* in the administrative structure, the number of basic-level rural units (and congresses) had been reduced from over 200,000 in 1954 to about 24,000 in 1959. The result was to make rural people's congresses much larger and more difficult to convene than they were in their early years. Commune congresses are expected to meet only twice a year, in contrast to the formal requirement of at least four yearly meetings for *hsiang* congresses, and communes are urged not to be "afraid of too many deputies" when calling congresses.[14] Examples of commune congresses with several hundred deputies are common.[15] Although urban *ch'ü* were also reduced substantially in number between 1954 and 1958, they were not replaced by communes as were their rural counterparts. In spite of the experimental organization of many urban communes, some of which exceeded the size of the *ch'ü,* the *ch'ü* remains the basic level of urban administration.

The cumbersome size of many rural communes, coupled with admitted changes in the distribution of management power at lower commune levels in 1959 through 1962, raised doubts about the permanence of the 24,000 communes. In the fall of 1963, Minister of Agriculture Liao Lu-yen confirmed these doubts by stating that there were "over 70,000" communes in China.[16] Subsequent references indicate that there are now about 75,000 communes, thus restoring the number of basic-level rural units to approximately the number of *hsiang* that existed in the summer of 1958. Nevertheless, although the Party has retreated from the drastic changes of the early commune years, basic-level units remain substantially larger and more complex than in the

---

[12] *JMJP,* July 4, 1958.

[13] *JMJP,* August 29, 1959.

[14] Tso Wei, "Jen-min Kung-she ti Tsu-chih Yüan-tse Shih Min-chu Chi-chung Chih" (The Organizational Principle of the People's Commune is Democratic Centralism), *Kung-jen Jih-pao* (Workers' Daily), August 4, 8, 1961.

[15] During the 1963 elections in Kwangtung, ten communes in various *hsien* elected a total of 2,584 deputies, or an average of over 250 per commune. *Nan-fang Jih-pao* (Southern Daily), May 10, 1963, in *SCMP,* No. 3002 (June 19, 1963).

[16] Liao Lu-yen, "Agricultural Collectivization in China," in *Socialist Industrialization and Agricultural Collectivization in China* (Peking, 1964), p. 24. The article appeared originally in *Cuba Socialista* in October, 1963.

early 1950's. In view of the CCP's desire to maintain close political ties with the masses at the lowest possible level, this is a particularly interesting development. In 1951, for example, *hsiang* and rural *ch'ü* were reduced in size precisely to make the connection between government and people more intimate and to facilitate the execution of state policies.[17] Apparently, the CCP reversed this policy and encouraged larger rural units in order to reduce the number of administrative personnel, to maintain governmental direction over the growing agricultural cooperatives, and to make basic-level political units correspond to natural marketing areas.[18] Administrative and economic considerations were important in themselves, but the declining political usefulness of basic-level government made them decisive. With the growth of rural cooperatives and urban residents' organizations, basic-level government came to have less and less impact on the lives of the people. Since the Party maintained close contact with the people through these organizations, the growing sterility of basic-level congresses did not limit the CCP's ability to mobilize the masses for political action. The operation of basic-level congresses is still important, however, for what it reveals about problems of political participation in China.

When people's congresses were first universally established in 1954, there was some evidence, admittedly drawn mainly from the best examples, of significant activity and discussion at the basic level. In Shihchingshan *Ch'ü,* an industrial district on the outskirts of Peking, the June, 1954, congress meeting made several recommendations on educational and sanitation problems of workers' dependents, demanded a reduction in rents for worker housing, decided to repair a main road leading from the housing area to the factories, voted to intensify punishments for criminal activities and vagrancy in the district, and resolved that all factories should carry out an educational campaign on safety regulations.[19] Another report on two *hsiang* congresses in Szechwan cited a case of a deputy who was recalled by the voters for "negative work" and "catering to landlords." In one of these *hsiang* (Sup'o *Hsiang,* Wenchiang *Hsien*), the congress was praised for discussing and clarifying the "alleged grain deficiency problem" and for "exposing the harmful activities of landlords"; the congress was criticized, however, for

[17] See the directives in *CB,* No. 131 (October 25, 1951).

[18] See Roy Hofheinz, "Rural Administration in Communist China," *China Quarterly,* No. 11 (July–September, 1962), and G. William Skinner, "Marketing and Social Structure in Rural China," Part III, *Journal of Asian Studies,* 24:3 (May, 1965). Skinner argues that the coincidence of basic-level governmental units and natural marketing areas was roughly attained in 1958 and then grossly overstepped in 1958–1959; realization of the communes' disruptive effect on marketing was a prime reason for their later subdivision into units approximating the *hsiang* (and natural marketing areas) that existed in 1958.

[19] *KMJP,* December 10, 1954.

not showing even more initiative in the exercise of its powers by passing a resolution and forcing the council to act on these matters.[20] These examples do reveal some congressional initiative, but it is significant that the "initiative" in each case helped to implement current Party policies. The actions of the Shihchingshan *Ch'ü* congress were praised because they would raise worker efficiency and morale and increase industrial production. The Sup'o *Hsiang* congress was obviously supporting the Party line on the baselessness and reactionary origins of talk about a "grain deficiency."

Other examples give even more specific evidence of the channeling of congressional energies into support for state plans and CCP objectives. When the various urban *ch'ü* congresses in Tientsin convened for their first meetings from June 28 to July 1, 1954 (the length of the session is itself revealing), virtually all of their time was occupied with discussion of the draft constitution and passage of resolutions in its support; every congress resolved unanimously to support the draft and work for its realization by educating the voters.[21] Some light is shed on the apparently fantastic number of proposals submitted by deputies in a story about a *hsiang* deputy in Shansi who had presented thirty-two proposals to his congress. Two-thirds of his proposals were on the subjects of "developing a mutual aid and cooperative movement" and practicing "emulation in production"—scarcely original demands on his part.[22] Finally, a *hsiang* chief's personal account of how he directed a campaign to improve agricultural production illustrated the Party's view of the primary function of basic-level congresses. This chief stated that the fundamental obligation of his office could be met only by "leading the masses to produce better, harvest more grain and support industrial production." Accordingly, he secured a resolution to this effect from his congress and began to mobilize the masses to fulfill it. Resistance was encountered, however, so he called on the deputies and other personnel to educate and propagandize the masses. Whenever certain measures were met with suspicion, he would set up experimental plots or teams, call in the deputies to observe the results and then have them spread the word among the peasants. In all of this, of course, he "relied on the leadership of the local Party branch." [23]

Since it was apparent from the first that basic-level congresses had

---

[20] Wang Ch'ing, "Chung-fen Fa-hui Chi-ts'eng Jen-min Tai-piao Ta-hui ti Tso-yung" (Fully Develop the Functions of Basic Level People's Congresses), *JMJP*, December 2, 1954.

[21] *Ibid.*, July 8, 1954.

[22] *KMJP*, March 29, 1954.

[23] Liu Hsien-yung, "Wo Tang-hsüan Hsiang-chang Hou Shih Tsen-yang Ling-tao Ch'ün-chung Sheng-ch'an ti" (How I Led the Masses in Production After I Was Elected *Hsiang* Chief), *JMJP*, April 13, 1954.

little freedom to act except when they were ratifying or amplifying a policy adopted at higher levels, the congress system was never genuinely healthy. By 1956, there was a surprising amount of criticism of the system in the Chinese press. The writer of a letter to *Kuang-ming Jih-pao* observed that the people's congresses have a "prominent function in educating the people and in mobilizing the people to participate in the state's cause of socialist construction and reform," but that there are still "serious weaknesses" and even direct violations of the Organic Regulations for people's congresses.[24] He cited four suburban *ch'ü* in Anshan where not a single congress had been called since September, 1954, and complained that even when congresses were convened they were of short duration and filled with routine speeches and resolutions rather than genuine discussion. Finally, he charged that many basic-level deputies did nothing between congresses, neither meeting with their constituents before congresses nor reporting to them afterwards. Criticism of this sort was frequent throughout 1956, the main points emphasized always being failure to convene congresses regularly (if at all), absenteeism and apathy on the part of deputies, and "formalism" in the speeches and reports presented to the congresses. At the 1957 session of the National Committee of the CPPCC, Tung Pi-wu made the curiously cautious remark that "as a whole, the convening of local people's congresses has gradually become a regular system."[25] At the same time, Tung tacitly acknowledged the sterility of these congresses by saying that some deputies who "lacked an overall view" sometimes differed with reports presented to congresses, but that "after discussions, all the deputies achieved agreement and gave active support to the correct measures taken by the government."[26]

By 1956–1957, however, "formalism" in representative institutions was clearly a secondary problem, as the CCP was pushing ahead with its plans for cooperativization and the amalgamation of *hsiang*. The pressing nature of organizational work in the countryside and the expansion in the size of rural administrative units created, from the Party's point of view, a need for even tighter control of the basic level by *hsien* government and Party organs.[27] With the formation of the communes, basic-level congresses became even less significant as media for mass participation in the state structure. The formal structure and powers of the

[24] Wang Yung-kuei, "Wo Tui Ti-fang Jen-min Tai-piao Ta-hui Kung-tso ti I-chien" (My Opinions on the Work of Local People's Congresses), *KMJP*, June 7, 1956.

[25] NCNA, Peking, March 12, 1957, in *CB*, No. 444 (April 3, 1957).

[26] *Loc. cit.*

[27] For example, see the *Chi-lin* [Kirin] *Jih-pao* (Kirin Daily) (Changchun) editorial, "Chia-ch'iang Tui Hsiang ti Kung-tso ti Ling-tao" (Strengthen Leadership Over Work in the *Hsiang*), April 15, 1956.

commune members' congresses and management committees were not notably different from those of their predecessors, the *hsiang* congresses and councils; if anything, commune organs were given a wider scope of powers consistent with their wider scope of operations.[28] But in practice the commune congress system was observed with even less regularity than in previous years.

When the CCP faced the problem of establishing the commune management system in place of the existing *hsiang* and cooperative organs in the late summer of 1958, the Central Committee suggested the method of "change above but not below" (*shang tung hsia pu-tung*); that is, unified planning and arrangement of work would be instituted at the top, but the organization of production and the administrative system within the original units would temporarily remain unchanged.[29] Unification of administration was to be carried out by a simple exchange of office: *hsiang* chiefs would become commune directors, *hsiang* congresses would become commune congresses, and *hsiang* councils would become commune management committees.[30] However, while the communes were defined as the administrative equivalents of *hsiang*, they were not necessarily equivalent in size or composition. As the reduction to 24,000 basic-level units shows, some communes were formed by a revision of *hsiang* boundaries or by combining two or more *hsiang;* changes were also being made in lower-level productive units, such as cooperatives and rural factories, that were theoretically to have representatives in the commune congress.

The simplest way to resolve this confusion in accordance with stated principles of basic-level government would have been to hold new elections. The CCP was unwilling to do this since the 1958 elections had just been completed in July and since elections and redistricting would have interfered with the "great leap forward" in agriculture and rural industry. Instead, commune organs were formed by using existing organs where possible and by combining existing organs when the commune encompassed more than one *hsiang*. Where changes in personnel were necessary, the Party itself apparently made the decision. The

[28] Illustrative data on commune management structure can be found in the following sources: Tso Wei, *op. cit.;* "Wei-hsing Jen-min Kung-she Shih-hsing Chien-chang, Ts'ao-an" (Experimental Charter of Weihsing People's Commune, Draft), *JMJP*, September 4, 1958; *Lun Jen-min Kung-she yü Kung-ch'an Chu-i* (The People's Communes and Communism), edited by the Basic Marxism–Leninism Department of the Chinese People's University (Peking, 1958).

[29] "Chung-kung Chung-yang Kuan-yü Tsai Nung-ts'un Chien-li Jen-min Kung-she Wen-t'i ti Chüeh-i" (Resolution of the CCP Central Committee on the Problem of Establishing People's Communes in the Villages), *JMJP*, September 10, 1958.

[30] Wu Jen, "Jen-min Kung-she ho Kuo-chia" (The People's Commune and the State), *Kung-jen Jih-pao*, October 20, 1958.

Hopei Provincial Party Committee directed that "cadres of a people's commune shall be suitably assigned by the next higher level Party committee from among cadres within and outside the Party in the existing *hsiang* and cooperatives." [31] Whatever the particular methods used for establishing commune organs, the confusion of the period and the unwieldy size of many congresses resulted in general neglect of the commune congresses. As late as December, 1958, one writer implied that the system was far from complete by urging that commune congresses and management committees "ought to be established" and that a "guided electoral system should be instituted when the commune, brigade and production team committees are produced." [32]

Judging from newspaper reports, few commune congresses have met regularly or exercised their powers to the full, although some improvements were made after the confusion of the first few months. Regulations specify that commune congresses are to meet at "fixed periods," but the responsibility for calling them rests with the management committees. There is a tendency to convene congresses only when the management committee or Party committee has a particularly urgent problem or decision to be made known to the representatives of commune units.[33] When congresses are convened, leading cadres are urged to discuss matters thoroughly among themselves first so that the congress can concentrate on a small number of vital topics. A few days before the congress meets, these topics and the cadres' proposals on them are given to the deputies for "solicitation of opinion" among commune members.[34] The congress then meets for a day or two, approves the measures presented to it or takes the action requested, and adjourns so that deputies may report to their units on the decision that has been made. Given the fact that commune congresses may number several hundred deputies who have to come from a rather large area (all at commune expense, supposedly) and that so little is accomplished, the cadres' reluctance to convene congresses is understandable.

It might be argued that the decentralization implicit in commune formation gave more autonomy to basic-level government and thereby raised the significance of the commune management system. Initially, at least, the rural communes did increase the self-sufficiency and scope of

[31] "Chung-kung Ho-pei Sheng-wei Kuan-yü Chien-li Jen-min Kung-she ti Chih-shih" (Directive of the CCP Hopei Provincial Committee on the Establishment of People's Communes), *Hung Ch'i* (Red Flag), 1958, No. 8, p. 15.

[32] Chao Han, " 'Ssu-hua' Shih Min-chu Chi-chung Chih ti T'i-hsien" (The "Four Transformations" Are the Embodiment of Democratic Centralism), *JMJP*, December 18, 1958.

[33] See the descriptions of congress meetings in *JMJP*, November 29, 1958, and March 20, 1961.

[34] *Ibid.*, and *JMJP* editorial of January 27, 1961.

operation of basic-level government. This was due to simple expansion in size and also the so-called "integration of government and commune administration" (*cheng-she ho-i*), explained as the "integration, within the commune, of the basic level political structure of our state with the management structure of the people's commune." [35] All agricultural, commercial, and industrial activities within the commune, as well as basic-level political power, were thereafter to be in the hands of the commune government. This situation did not, however, give any more power to popular commune organs. On the contrary, the heavy responsibility vested in the communes was said to make tighter Party leadership necessary.[36] As the following quotation shows, the only organization that could benefit from the increased powers of the commune was the commune Party committee.

The Party organization in the people's communes regularly ought to discuss and examine the work of the congresses, general meetings, management committees and supervisory committees at various commune levels. Important problems of production, mass livelihood, execution of state policies and orders, execution of state plans and other matters, generally should undergo ful fermentation within the Party and be studied with commune members and non-Party cadres. Later, the opinion of the Party organization can be presented to the commune congresses, general meetings, management committees or supervisory committees for discussion; after passage, execution is guaranteed.[37]

There are, then, several reasons for the continued stagnation of basic-level congresses during the commune period. The increase in the size of congresses, the preoccupation of cadres with problems of agricultural production and other commune enterprises, and the Party's insistence on rigid control of all internal commune affairs contributed to this trend. It is also worth noting that the formation of the rural communes raised the question, at least temporarily, of the ultimate disappearance of the state structure. In 1958, the Central Committee defined the commune as a transitional form for the development of a communist society and stated that, as such, the commune was to establish the conditions for the elimination of the internal functions of the state.[38] There is, of course, no evidence whatsoever that the CCP actually contemplated an early

[35] Wang Ch'ung-fa, "T'an-t'an Cheng-she Ho-i" (Discussing the Integration of Government and Commune Administration), *Kung-jen Jih-pao*, November 24, 1961.

[36] Hsü Pang-i, "Keng-hao ti Fa-hui Nung-ts'un Chi-ts'eng Tang Tsu-chih ti Ling-tao Ho-hsin Tso-yung" (Develop Better the Role of Rural Basic Level Party Organizations as Cores of Leadership), *Hung Ch'i*, 1961, No. 21, pp. 21–22.

[37] *Ibid.*, p. 24.

[38] "Resolution on Some Questions Concerning the People's Communes," *Sixth Plenary Session of the Eighth Central Committee of the Communist Party of China* (Peking, 1958), pp. 14, 24–26.

realization of this goal. On the other hand, the Party did try to use the communes to create the desired level of "communist consciousness" for the transition to communism. The commune's role as a schoolhouse for communism was reflected in the statement that "the people's commune is an organization where the masses of people discipline and educate themselves under the leadership of the Party." [39] The result of this conception of the commune was, as pointed out in the previous chapter, a strong emphasis on ideological indoctrination and direct mobilization of the masses. This emphasis reinforced the impression that commune congresses had little to do with the present or future reality of mass political life.

In summary, basic-level congresses are not intended to function as decision-making bodies. They have the right to discuss certain subjects and pass resolutions, but all of their actions are, in effect, subject to review by higher-level authorities. In practice, they are guided and controlled by the basic-level councils and Party committees. Congress sessions are called irregularly and are extremely brief. Topics to be considered are normally determined in advance and meetings are filled with ritualistic speeches and reports. Although deputies may, on rare occasions, raise questions on their own initiative, they cannot offer any comments or proposals that conflict with central policies.

Yet, in spite of all these obstacles to effective action, the CCP insists that the people's congresses are essential parts of the Chinese political system. Whatever their shortcomings, basic-level congresses are tangible signs of popular participation in government. Since elections *do* take place and congresses *do* convene, even though not as frequently as law prescribes, the Party can rightly claim that people who had never taken part in political life before 1949 are now participating in the workings of the state. Because of this "wide mass base," *Jen-min Jih-pao* has editorialized: ". . . our state structure can have the highest prestige and the greatest resources for organization and issuing calls [to the masses]. It can realize popular unity, molding all localities throughout the nation into one unyielding body. It can concentrate the forces of all the people to overcome all difficulties and obstacles in the road ahead, opening a way for the future happiness of our nation." [40]

The primary functions of basic-level congresses, therefore, are to provide a forum for ratification of central policy by each and every local unit, to assist in mobilizing the people behind these policies, and to give

[39] Ouyang T'ao, "A Preliminary Discussion on the Organizational Form of Rural People's Communes," *Cheng-fa Yen-chiu* (Political and Legal Research), 1959, No. 1, in *SMM*, No. 164 (April 13, 1959).

[40] "Wo-men ti Kuo-chia Chih-tu Shih Jen-min Tai-piao Ta-hui Chih" (Our State System Is a System of People's Congresses), *JMJP*, editorial, July 3, 1954.

the people a sense of direct involvement in the state structure. These functions explain why the Party has maintained the congresses in spite of their declining vitality. Basic-level congresses still ratify central policy and still serve as symbols of popular participation; their usefulness in mobilizing the masses has been curtailed but not totally lost. The CCP must know, however, that basic-level congresses cannot retain their value once their claim to represent the masses becomes totally incredible. For this reason, the weaknesses described have detracted from the Party's efforts to realize its concept of political participation.

BASIC-LEVEL ELECTIONS

General conditions By 1966, six general basic-level elections had been held in Communist China. The dates of these elections were roughly as follows: summer, 1953 to spring, 1954; fall, 1956, extending into the early part of 1957; spring, 1958; spring, 1961; spring, 1963; spring, 1966. Except for minor changes, the regulations and patterns established in 1953–1954 have been continued in all subsequent elections. Nevertheless, it is possible to make some broad distinctions concerning the trend of general elections and the specific characteristics of each. The trend has been toward a shortening of the time allowed for each election campaign and a reduction of its national political impact. The emphasis placed on the elections of 1953–1954 has not been repeated in later years, a fact that is readily explained by the circumstances of the various elections.

According to Party propaganda, the 1953–1954 elections had in common with all other basic-level elections the performance of two general functions: first, the education of both masses and cadres in the operation of socialist democracy; second, the creation of higher incentives for fulfilling production goals and carrying out Party policies. The first election also had five specific goals that reflected the circumstances in which it was held: (1) to do a good job of voter registration, so that no one would be wrongfully deprived of his vote or allowed to vote if not entitled to do so; (2) to complete the national census during the registration campaign; (3) to mobilize the masses for conscious and enthusiastic participation so that a very high proportion of the electorate would vote; (4) to combine election work with the then current struggle against bureaucratism, commandism, and instances of illegality and disorder so that all cadres would benefit from the scrutiny of the masses; (5) through the elections, to remove from office those elements found guilty of illegal and disorderly acts or other serious faults and elevate to office those people who had earned the particular respect of the masses.[41] The first, fourth, and fifth of these goals reflected the CCP's desire to use the elections as a vehicle for checking and testing the political and social changes of its first four years in power: decisions were to be made on all people whose political status was in doubt; cadres who had ignored the mass line during the hectic early years were to be chastised; remnants of the old society who had somehow retained positions of authority were to be weeded out; and the new activists who had emerged during land reform and other movements were to be rewarded.

The 1956 basic-level elections were carried out more quickly and reported in much less detail than those of 1953–1954. Two features are evident, however, from the material available. First, the 1956 elections were largely devoted to advancing the movements for cooperativization and increased agricultural production. Second, the elections were poorly handled and probably caused considerable dissatisfaction within the leadership. Part of the difficulty lay with the CCP's inability to complete the elections on schedule, a serious point because of the heavy organizational and production work then going on in the countryside. When the first announcements were made in May, 1956, directives specified that basic-level elections throughout the country should be started in July and completed by November and that, in view of production tasks, election work in each unit should be completed within a twenty-day period.[42] In spite of these injunctions, however, basic-level election work was not completed until the early months of 1957. As late as December 9, 1956, only seven out of 112 *hsien* in Kwangtung had completed the elections; several *hsien* had simply stopped after conducting experimental elections, five *hsien* had not yet started experimental work, and six *hsien* had not even established election committees to administer election work.[43]

The major difficulty, however, was "formalism" rather than delay as such. In a speech to the Shantung Provincial People's Council, the deputy governor of Shantung acknowledged that formalism was "rela-

---

[41] "Chung-yang Hsüan-chü Wei-yüan-hui Kuan-yü Chi-ts'eng Hsüan-chü Kung-tso ti Chih-piao" (Directive of the Central Election Committee on Basic Level Election Work), *Ta Kung Pao* (Tientsin), April 6, 1953.

[42] *JMJP*, May 13, 1956, and "Kuo-wu-yüan Kuan-yü 1956 Nien Hsüan-chü Kung-tso ti Chih-shih" (Directive of the State Council on 1956 Election Work), *JMJP*, May 31, 1956. The 1953–1954 elections had also run well behind schedule, but that result had apparently been accepted as inevitable because of the census and registration problem. The twenty-day limitation was a substantial reduction, as the first elections had required about fifty days per unit; see *Shan-hsi* [Shensi] *Jih-pao* (Sian), August 7, 1956. Since elections since 1956 have been held in the spring, it appears that the fall harvest was regarded as the major cause of delay in 1956.

[43] *Nan-fang Jih-pao*, December 19, 1956.

tively widespread" in his province.[44] He cited three main manifestations of formalism. First, many leading cadres did not understand the significance of elections and entrusted the work to subordinates; the result was "aimless and leaderless" election work in which election committees did little, cadres in election work were transferred to other jobs, plans were never completed, and experimental work was never utilized. Second, some cadres monopolized work without consulting either the masses or other cadres; the result was arbitrary decisions on candidate lists, leading to great mass dissatisfaction and a dampening of political enthusiasm. Finally, some election work was not linked up with production, indicating a failure to understand that "basic level elections are to mobilize mass forces for the completion of various tasks, and foremost is the effort to complete production tasks." A report in *Jen-min Jih-pao* confirmed the fact that formalism had appeared in several areas throughout China. This report linked election problems to the previously noted stagnation of basic-level congresses by pointing out that many people were indifferent to elections because the congresses elected in 1953–1954 had not fulfilled their functions.[45]

Criticism of the 1956 elections may have been partly due to the relatively tolerant attitude toward political discussion in late 1956 and early 1957. Nevertheless, the type of criticism offered suggests that there was a noticeable decline in enthusiasm for the elections on the part of both people and cadres. The Party had apparently hoped that the enormous efforts at education and propaganda in the first election would bear fruit in 1956, permitting equally effective elections with a smaller investment of time and labor.[46] This hope was not realized and the Party has since avoided such disappointments by lowering its expectations. The elections since 1956 have been of relatively minor importance in comparison to the earlier elections or to other movements of the years between 1957 and 1965. In all probability, the problems of 1956 have recurred, but reporting has been so minimal that it is only certain that basic-level elections have fallen, at least temporarily, into secondary significance in the Party's ranking of political activities. The declining importance of basic-level congresses has, of course, contributed to this trend. Judging from scattered reports, the elections of 1958, 1961, and

[44] Yang Hsüan-wu, "K'o-fu Hsing-shih Chu-i P'ien-hsiang, Pao-cheng Tso-hao Chi-ts'eng Hsüan-chü Kung-tso" (Overcome the Tendency of Formalism, Guarantee a Good Job of Basic Level Election Work), *Ta-chung Jih-pao* (Masses Daily) (Tsinan), November 6, 1956.

[45] Ch'üan Chien-ch'in, "Kung-ku Chi-ts'eng Hsüan-chü ti Ch'eng-kuo" (Consolidate the Achievements of Basic Level Elections), *JMJP*, January 5, 1957.

[46] For explicit recognition of this hope, and the dissatisfaction with reduced efforts that resulted from it, see *Ch'ang-ch'un Jih-pao* (Changchun Daily), November 24, 1956, in *Union Research Service*, Vol. 6, No. 15 (February 19, 1957).

1963 have served mainly to reinforce other political movements, such as elimination of rightists in 1958 and extolling the superiority of the socialist "road" over the capitalist "road" in 1961 and 1963. The apparent postponement of the 1965 elections into early 1966 suggests a further decline in the Party's emphasis on this aspect of Chinese political life. It is possible that elections of some commune congresses now occur on a sporadic, unsystematic pattern that discourages national reporting.

Decreasing emphasis on basic-level elections has not involved a departure from the general principles that guide the CCP's management of elections. These principles might be summarized as maximizing the extent of popular participation in the electoral process and minimizing the opportunity for election of candidates unacceptable to the CCP. Both of these principles are obvious derivations from the Party's concept of political participation, but it remains to be seen how systematically they are put into practice.

Maximizing participation   Mass participation in basic-level elections is maximized by placing very few qualifications on the right to vote and by careful propaganda and organization to encourage all eligible voters to take part. Article Four of the Electoral Law states that all citizens who have reached the age of eighteen shall have the right to vote and be elected "irrespective of nationality or race, sex, occupation, social origin, religion, education, property status, or residence." Article Five of the Electoral Law lists the following groups who do not have electoral rights: (1) elements of the landlord class whose status has not yet been changed according to law; (2) counterrevolutionaries who have been deprived of political rights according to law; (3) others who have been deprived of political rights according to law; (4) insane persons. These limitations have great theoretical importance since they allow the government to exclude all political opponents, past or potential, from the electorate. They are, therefore, a concrete expression of the CCP's belief that political participation must be confined to activities that support socialism as defined by the Party. In numerical terms, however, the limitations cited have had little impact on the size of the electorate. In the 1953–1954 elections, only 1.52 percent of the total population was deprived of political rights, and this figure dropped to 0.62 percent in 1956.[47]

[47] Li Yu-i, "On Our Country's Electoral System," *JMJP,* November 29, 1957, in *Union Research Service,* Vol. 9, No. 22 (December 13, 1957). Those deprived of political rights in 1953–1954 totaled less than 3 percent of the potential voters, that is, all men and women who were eighteen or over. Other sources give different percentages on this point, but the difference is not significant. For

The CCP has been moderately successful in its attempt to attain high voting percentages. For example, the percentages of eligible voters who actually cast ballots in the 1953–1954 and 1956 elections were, respectively, 85.88 percent and 86.42.[48] These figures are not as high as those reported from some Communist nations, but they nonetheless represent a substantial organizational achievement in view of traditional political and cultural obstacles to electoral participation in China. The Chinese Communists realize that granting suffrage to virtually the entire adult population is only the first step and that it must be coupled with successful organizational work if a heavy turnout is to be attained. On the one hand, the Party insists that "the number of voters participating in an election completely reflects the democratic nature, or lack of democracy, in a nation's political system," thereby giving itself a favorable basis for comparison with "bourgeois democracies"; on the other hand, the Party acknowledges that the voting turnout "also reflects the degree of organization and consciousness among the masses." [49] Accordingly, the CCP has planned the election campaigns so as to produce a high degree of "organization and consciousness among the masses."

Propaganda and exhortation are the major means for leading eligible voters to cast their votes, but they are supplemented by procedural and organizational techniques that facilitate a high degree of participation. Article Fifty-five of the Electoral Law allows basic-level elections to be conducted either by ballot or by show of hands, thereby eliminating illiteracy as a voting deterrent. In practice, elections in urban areas have generally used the ballot, with literate electors marking the ballot for those unable to read the ballot or record their own vote. Most rural areas, of course, have had to use the hand vote. Party statements have claimed, in each successive election, that more and more votes were being taken by secret ballot, but voting by show of hands remains common in the countryside.

Another technique that has been extremely important in maximizing the vote is the division of *hsiang, chen,* and *ch'ü* into electoral districts, which are laid out by the election committees on the basis of natural living conditions. An undistricted basic-level unit votes as a unit on a day fixed by the higher-level government. Where electoral districts have

---

instructions on how these limitations were to be interpreted in the 1953–1954 elections, see Chung-yang Hsüan-chü Wei-yüan-hui, "Kuan-yü Hsüan-min Tzu-ko Jo-kan Wen-t'i ti Chieh-ta" (Answers to Certain Questions About Voters' Qualifications), *Ta Kung Pao,* April 3, 1953.

[48] Li Yu-i, *op. cit.* The 1956 figure reported here is substantially below reports from early 1957, which were based on partial returns and claimed that the voting percentage had increased to over 90 percent. The 1956 election was presumably a disappointment in this respect as well as in the ways noted above.

[49] *Kung-jen Jih-pao,* August 1, 1953.

been established, however, each district has its own election date and meeting, fixed by the basic-level election committees.[50] Districting is the more common practice for obvious reasons. It permits election dates and meeting places to be adjusted to local schedules and activities and, of course, reduces to manageable proportions the number of people who must be brought together in those localities where voting is by hand. Electoral districts in urban areas are usually based on the area of jurisdiction of the *ch'ü* government's street offices, whereas rural electoral districts were initially based on the natural village and later on the agricultural producers' cooperative; factories, enterprises, state organs, and schools that are large enough to elect one or more deputies may also be designated as electoral districts.[51] Urban electoral districts may still be quite large, but since urban voting is usually by ballot, enough polling booths can be established to meet the demand. It is in rural areas, where elections are normally held at meetings, that districting becomes an essential technique for keeping meetings small and within easy walking distance of the electorate.

Since each deputy is elected from a specific district, districting no doubt promotes popular interest by making candidates better known to the electorate. The small rural districts especially make personal acquaintance with deputies likely, thereby enhancing the public-recognition element in office-holding and encouraging the election of candidates who hold some degree of natural group support. On the other hand, many districts, especially in urban areas, are large enough to elect more than one deputy. Since the Electoral Law does not specify that a deputy must be a resident of his district, there is clearly no guarantee that all deputies will be known to their constituents. In general, popular interest in elections probably depends as much on the concentrated campaign that districts facilitate as on personal acquaintance with representatives. Whatever else might be said about Chinese elections, there is unquestionably a large number of basic-level deputies per unit of population. As mentioned earlier, over five and a half million deputies were elected at the basic level in 1953–1954, or an average of roughly one deputy for each one hundred people. This average was maintained primarily in the rural areas; in contrast, deputies in the urban *ch'ü* were elected on a ratio of one deputy for each 500–2,000 people.[52] In 1956,

[50] See Arts. 39, 52, and 53 of the Electoral Law.

[51] See "Kuo-wu-yüan Kuan-yü 1956 Nien Hsüan-chü Kung-tso ti Chih-shih," *op. cit.* Actually, a street office might be one or more electoral districts, and one or more cooperatives might constitute a rural electoral district.

[52] See Arts. 9 and 18 of the Electoral Law. The fact that rural areas have markedly better representation than urban areas at the basic level is simply a reflection of differing population densities. At the provincial and national levels, where deputies from the two areas meet in the same congresses, the urban areas are over-represented.

a more detailed decision on apportionment retained the one to one hundred ratio only for the smaller *hsiang* and laid down a scale of much poorer representation for *ch'ü, chen,* and the larger *hsiang*. Even so, in 1958, the average number of people per basic-level deputy did not exceed two hundred.[53]

The degree of popular representation in the rural communes has been blurred by the scarcity of information on commune elections. Although it is certain that elections continue and that the production team serves as the primary electoral district within the commune, reliable figures on the number of deputies per unit of population are difficult to obtain. Judging from reports of the 1961 elections, about five to seven deputies were elected in each production team, giving a ratio of somewhere around one deputy for each twenty to thirty people. However, all of these deputies cannot possibly serve in the commune congress as this would result in congresses of astronomical size. In all probability, all the deputies elected in the production team serve in the production brigade congress, but team deputies to the commune congress (the basic level) are limited in some unspecified way. This supposition is supported by a report from the Rural Work Department of the Liaoning Provincial Party Committee, which stated that brigade congresses should be composed of one deputy for each twenty members but that commune congresses should only have about one deputy for each one hundred members.[54] There may be an understanding that the production-team chiefs, and perhaps some assistant chiefs, serve as team deputies to the commune congress, or the brigade congress may simply decide who will attend the commune congress. In any case, the large size of commune congresses indicates that the general ratio of one deputy for each 100–200 people in the countryside is being maintained.

Small districts and large numbers of representatives encourage popular interest in elections, but it is doubtful if they have overcome the "formalistic" aspect of basic-level elections. In the last analysis, electoral participation is maximized more by organizational techniques than by spontaneous mass support for individual representatives. The Party's handling of districts and representation makes a modest contribution to high electoral participation by generating popular interest; it makes a much greater contribution to this goal by keeping the elections simple and accessible to Party leadership.

Minimizing opposition   The second general principle that has characterized all elections in Communist China is the CCP's effort to minimize the opportunity for election of candidates who might oppose Party

[53] See *JMJP,* May 13, 1956, and the comment above (footnote 12).
[54] *Lun Jen-min Kung-she yü Kung-ch'an Chu-i,* pp. 88–89.

policies. This cannot be done by limiting the electorate, except in obvious cases that are not numerically significant, because of the Party's desire to maximize the number of people exposed to the electoral process. Rather, it is done by a variety of formal and informal arrangements in the nomination process that effectively limit nearly all candidates to Party supporters. The most concrete control mechanism is the basic-level election committee, which is appointed by the next higher level of government and is given general authority over the entire election procedure. Specifically, it registers and announces the list of eligible voters, registers and publishes the list of candidates, delineates electoral districts, fixes dates and methods of election, counts the vote, and announces results.[55] This work is carried out under strict supervision from above. Chairmen of basic-level election committees are to be "competent, non-local cadres," and work teams from higher-level election committees are assigned to guide election work at the basic level.[56]

The heart of the election committee's control is its power to produce a formal candidate list. Initially, nominations can be made by the CCP, the "democratic parties," various people's organizations, and individual electors or representatives, all acting jointly or separately; however, joint nomination by the CCP and other parties and organizations is the preferred method of nomination.[57] There is no limit to the number of candidates that may be produced in this way, but ultimately, after thorough discussion of all nominees, the election committee reduces the candidates to the number that are to be elected and issues a formal candidate list that is presented to the voters for approval on election day. Nothing requires the number of candidates on the formal list to be the same as the number of deputies to be elected, but in practice this is a uniform rule. According to Party explanations, the election committee is justified in issuing a list equal to the number to be elected because previous discussions have produced a "majority opinion" as to which candidates ought to be elected. The list is "entirely for convenience" in carrying out the elections since it concentrates the ballots on the favored candidates and ensures that each will receive sufficient votes for election.[58] Article Fifty-one of the Electoral Law provides that an elector may vote for a candidate of his own choice, rather than the official list, but a write-in vote for someone not on the list cannot possibly succeed.

[55] Electoral Law, Arts. 35 and 39.
[56] Teng Hsiao-p'ing, "An Explanation on the Electoral Law," *The Electoral Law of the People's Republic of China*, pp. 44–45.
[57] *Ibid.*, p. 40, and Art. 47 of the Electoral Law.
[58] Ting Chien-sheng, "Wei-shen-ma Tsai Chi-ts'eng Hsüan-chü Chung Tai-piao Hou-hsüan-jen Ming-o I-pan Ying Yü Tang-hsüan Tai-piao Jen-shu Hsiang-teng" (Why Should the Number of Candidates for Deputies in Basic Level Elections Generally Be Equal to the Number To Be Elected?), *KMJP*, August 30, 1953.

In practice, it is not always necessary for the election committee itself to make the final decision on the candidate list because the process of nomination and discussion encourages prevote unanimity on those candidates favored by the CCP. The candidate list proposed by the CCP and other parties and organizations (the "joint list") is, by definition, a "fully representative" list from the start. Although the joint list is open to mass discussion and criticism and to comparison with individually proposed candidates, no major changes can be expected in a list that is already approved by the leaders of all important local organizations, including the Party itself. At best, a few names that arouse particular hostility may be stricken from the joint list. In most cases, however, even mass criticism will not remove a candidate from this list if he "accepts" the criticism and promises to correct his mistakes in the future. This is not to say that the process of nomination and discussion of candidates is unimportant from the Party's point of view. By dividing electors into small groups for this process, basic-level cadres are able to solicit acceptable nominations, explain the "representativeness" of the joint list, and persuade electors to withdraw nominations (after discussion) that conflict with the joint list. In this way, "prevote unanimity" on a candidate list equal to the number of positions to be filled may be reached even before the election committee announces the formal list.

Underlying the CCP's effort to secure professed unanimity before the election takes place is the assertion that there are certain criteria for office-holding which, if understood and observed, will eliminate all disputes over whether a candidate should or should not be elected. On the basis of this assertion, the Party urges voters to "elect those candidates who ought to be elected" and focuses preelection debate on general qualifications for office rather than on competition between candidates. These qualifications are informal standards set by the CCP, rather than expressly stated legal requirements, but they have a controlling effect on the final determination of candidate lists.

Specifically, two types of criteria are imposed: first, criteria on the personal qualities and views ideal candidates should possess; second, criteria on the overall representativeness of the candidate list. The first type is illustrated by the following statement, which acknowledges that all citizens over eighteen are eligible for election but then adds:

But when we nominate our candidates, we must pay attention to choosing those persons who have a clean personal history, who are enthusiastic in serving the people, positively responding to the call of the Communist Party and the People's Government, and who are positive in their work. We should choose those persons who show their love for the masses, who concern themselves with the sufferings of the masses, who do not resort to commandism, and who consult the masses in all matters. And we should choose those persons who are impartial, who think always in terms of the interests of the masses, and who do not show favoritism to their relatives or friends.[59]

The second type is demonstrated by the admonition that the elected deputies should include advanced producers and workers who have emerged during the course of socialist construction (i.e., model workers); a number of worker representatives consonant with the "leading position" of that class; representatives from all walks of life, including private personnel in joint enterprises; female representatives; representatives of national minorities; and a "definite number" of cadres in office.[60] These statements refer to the 1956 election but have been matched by similar themes in all mainland elections.[61]

The criteria for personal qualifications clearly limit candidates to those "activists" who support the Party line, especially the mass line, and who have no questionable class ties or activities in their backgrounds. The demand for "representativeness" also follows the CCP's concept of political participation which regards basic-level congresses primarily as organs for ritualistic ratification of Party decisions and transmission of these decisions to all elements of the population. Strictly speaking, the Party wants neither proportional representation nor absolute majority control. It does not want proportional representation because there are always certain groups that it wishes to overrepresent (workers, poor peasants, etc.). It does not want majority control, in any real sense, as this might deprive certain minority groups (national minorities, business and professional elements, etc.) of any representation at all. What it does want is *some* representation from all significant social and economic groupings, coupled with numerical dominance by those groups that *ought* to dominate from an ideological point of view. The nominating process is designed to ensure this mixture, a mixture which might be lacking if electoral choice were unrestrained.

These informal criteria, backed by the Party's ultimate control, certainly restrict an open choice of representatives by the electorate. One must interpret this fact with caution, however, for the electorate's and the Party's choice may at times coincide. The CCP tries to exclude opponents or potential opponents from office but it also hopes, as the above criteria indicate, that deputies will be "close to the masses." A

[59] *Tsing* [Ch'ing]-*tao Jih-pao* (Tsingtao), September 12, 1956, in *Union Research Service,* Vol. 6, No. 15 (February 19, 1957).

[60] *Ibid.*

[61] In the 1961 elections, the slogan on qualifications was that every candidate should meet the "five conditions": good class origins; a clear history; active in labor; public-spirited in management of affairs; supported by the masses. See *JMJP,* March 29, 1961.

deputy's ability to command popular support is sufficiently important that the Party may make some compromises to have such people in office; it must make an effort to ascertain popular feelings in order to know if this is in fact the case. Nevertheless, it is the Party that makes the decision, bearing in mind the theory that popular interests are ultimately made known and guaranteed through the leadership of the Communist Party. So far as their selective (as distinct from educational) aspects are concerned, elections are designed to produce deputies who will best carry out the function of ratification and implementation of Party policy. The masses are encouraged to assist in determining whether or not the candidates are "qualified" to do this, but they are not free to select whomever they choose.

One important result of the Party's restraints on the electoral process is the tendency to elect, and retain in office, those people who already bear the Party's stamp of approval. In some cases, there are explicit requirements that certain officeholders be deputies. For example, the draft charter of Ch'iliying Commune in Hsinhsiang *Hsien,* Hopei, stipulated that commune congress deputies should include all members of the commune management committee, the heads of commune departments, the members of the Commune Party Committee, the chiefs and vice-chiefs of all the production brigades, the members of the brigade management committees, and the chiefs of all the production teams.[62] However, even in the absence of such regulations, the high percentage of cadres elected as deputies and the relatively low turnover from election to election are striking. Partial statistics for the 1953–1954 elections indicated that over 70 percent of the deputies elected were already basic-level cadres.[63] Sample figures from subsequent elections suggest that 70–80 percent of basic-level deputies are usually reelected. The only apparent exception to this pattern was 1958 when an estimated 43 percent of the deputies were newly elected.[64] The abnormally high turnover in 1958 was probably a result of the lengthy rectification campaign of 1957–1958, coupled with far-reaching changes in the cooperatives and *hsiang* after 1956. Even so, those deputies who were newly elected in 1958 fit the general pattern noted, as they were mainly cooperative directors, labor models, and activists who had distinguished themselves in the 1957–1958 rectification campaign.[65]

The foregoing discussion of the general characteristics of elections in Communist China has emphasized the imposition of formal and infor-

[62] *Lun Jen-min Kung-she yü Kung-ch'an Chu-i,* pp. 82–83.

[63] "Ch'ing-chu Ch'üan-kuo Chi-ts'eng Hsüan-chü ti Wan-ch'eng" (Celebrate the Completion of Nation-wide Basic Level Elections), *JMJP,* editorial, June 20, 1954.

[64] *JMJP,* July 4, 1958.

[65] *Ibid.*

mal Party controls, but has given little concrete description of the electoral process itself. Since the CCP regards this process as a means of political education and mobilization, the presence of restrictions and controls is not a sufficient answer to the significance of mainland elections. Nor is it sufficient to say that elections are meaningless because they have declined steadily in vitality since 1953–1954, for even one such experience is important in the context of modern Chinese politics. We turn to a closer look at the first general elections, therefore, to demonstrate the impact of the most successful election and, concurrently, to illustrate the thoroughness with which the CCP conducts its mass movements.

The 1953–1954 elections The Central Election Committee's Directive on Basic Level Election Work, issued on April 3, 1953, specified the process to be followed throughout the country.[66] It announced that basic-level election work would start immediately and should be completed in all areas by October, 1953. After noting the broad objectives of the campaign, the Directive emphasized the importance of higher-level leadership by outlining the responsibilities of *hsien* and municipal election committees in preparing the way for elections at the basic level. These responsibilities involved three major steps.

1. Initiation of propaganda. *Hsien* and municipal election committees were to carry out propaganda and explanation of the Election Law among the people, concentrating on the following points: (a) make the masses see the significance of the election and their relation to it, the seriousness of electoral rights, and the importance of active participation; (b) make the masses understand who should have electoral rights and who should not, and encourage them to present their views and accusations on this point during voter registration; (c) make the masses understand which people ought to be elected, and elicit universal discussion and examination of candidates to elect or remove cadres according to this standard.

2. Selection and training of cadres. *Hsien* and municipal election committees were to select cadres to serve as chairmen of basic-level election committees and lead basic-level election work. The Directive specified that each 2,000 people would require one election cadre for three-months work, and that each 500 people would require one election worker for one month of work. The Directive stated that cadres needed about seven days of training and workers about three days before being sent down to the basic level; it also listed the major study items in this

---

[66] "Chung-yang Hsüan-chü Wei-yüan-hui Kuan-yü Chi-ts'eng Hsüan-chü Kung-tso ti Chih-piao," *op. cit.* The following summary is based entirely on this Directive.

short training course. Each election cadre was to select three to five workers to form a basic-level work team. In rural areas, a work team might actually handle one to three *hsiang,* but in such cases work would be divided within the team so that each *hsiang* had a trained election worker responsible for it.

3. Final preparations. Before ordering the work teams to commence work, *hsien* and municipal election committees were to complete the following tasks: establish plans, agenda, and policies for all elections under their jurisdiction; confirm the appointment of the basic-level election committees; set the size of basic-level congresses in their area so that the proper number of deputies could be apportioned to the electoral districts; announce the election committees' seals and issue the appropriate documents under these seals; disburse funds for election expenses.

The Directive was equally specific in outlining the procedures to be followed by the basic-level election committees. Here six stages might be described.

1. Establishment of basic-level election committees. The first task of the work teams and election committee chairmen on arrival in their basic-level units was to set up election committees of four to eight members in rural areas and six to twelve members in urban areas. Election cadres were to choose as committee members "capable and representative" people whose appointment was then confirmed at higher levels.

2. Establishment of electoral districts. The basic-level election committees were to establish electoral districts in accordance with natural living conditions. Generally, electoral districts would produce two or more deputies, but single-member districts (or even one deputy for two districts) were permitted in areas of scattered population. As a general rule, electoral districts were not to exceed twenty *li* (a *li* is approximately one-third of a mile) in diameter.

3. Management of census and voter registration. After demarcation of electoral districts, election committees were to set up census and registration stations in each district. These stations would collect information for the district by consulting one representative (the household head or an adult familiar with household data) from each household. For each station, the election committee appointed an "election qualifications examination team" to determine, through consultation with local residents, which persons were eligible to vote. Whoever was "commonly believed or through local deliberation decided" to have the qualification was to be registered accordingly. Disputed and undecided cases could be appealed to the election committee or, ultimately, the people's courts.

4. Proclamation of voter lists and election day. After the conclusion

of census-taking and voter registration, the election committee was to set a time and place for the election and publicly post this information with the list of approved voters. At the same time, all voters in each electoral district were to be divided into "voters' small groups," with one person in each group designated as leader. Voters' small groups were based on place of residence and were under the general leadership of the election committee. Their first task was to scrutinize the published voter list and uncover any remaining objections to the names on the list.

5. Nomination of candidates. The Directive noted that nominations could be made by either groups or individuals, but suggested that the best method was for the election committee to call a meeting of representatives of the CCP and other parties and groups to produce a joint candidate list. This list was to be forwarded to the voters' small groups for discussion at least twenty days before election day. On the basis of these discussions and "in accordance with majority opinion," the election committee would then draw up a formal candidate list and announce it to the voters at least five days before the election. This list would normally be equal to the number of deputies to be elected.

6. Election and completion of work. The Directive specified in detail the election-day procedure, with most of the detail pertaining to rural election meetings rather than to voting at polling booths. After the votes were counted, the basic-level election committee was to issue credentials to those elected as deputies and make an immediate report on the results and voting percentage to higher levels. Finally, the election committee was to dispose of all documents, settle accounts, make a financial report to the people and to higher levels of government, and make a summary report to the higher-level election committee; when this was done, the basic-level election committee was dissolved.

The 1953–1954 basic-level elections followed very closely the rules that have just been described. The overall timing was faulty, as elections were not completed until May, 1954, but this delay had little effect on the general character of the elections. There were also individual cases of violation or disregard of the rules, but the Directive still presents an accurate picture of the procedure that was followed. With this procedure in mind, we can look more closely at certain points that are particularly relevant for mass political participation.

One striking point is the scope and thoroughness of the propaganda effort that accompanied the elections. Although closely integrated with registration, nomination, and election work, propaganda work was separately organized and was itself a mass campaign of impressive dimensions. Localities throughout China followed the same general practices and gave out the same general line, all designed to inform the electorate of the procedure and significance of the elections. Almost every conceivable technique and medium was used—general meetings and lectures, small-group discussions, home visits, private conversation, newspapers, radio broadcasts, movies, posters, songs and plays, and so forth. Wherever possible, existing talents and resources contributed to the propaganda campaign. Movie houses were required to show propaganda films, libraries were transformed into election propaganda stations, and artists and writers were called in to produce the necessary "cultural" propaganda.[67]

The organizational and personnel requirements of this effort were severe. In the Canton area, plans called for about thirty propaganda workers in every street and ten to fifteen in every *hsiang* or *chen*. To ensure proper direction, over 3,000 Canton cadres were transferred into election propaganda work. The key organizational and supervisory agencies were the basic-level governments and Party committees.[68] In addition to all those who were officially designated as "propaganda workers" or "reporters," large numbers of unofficial workers were mobilized through place of employment and the mass organization. The Tientsin Election Committee's plan for election propaganda stated: "Every member of the people's organizations or democratic parties, workers in state organs, factory workers, students and faculty and staff in the schools, etc., in addition to their own active participation in study related to the general elections, must also assume responsibility for carrying on propaganda and explanation about the election movement within the scope of their activities and especially toward their own families, relatives and friends." [69]

The impact of election propaganda did not rest on its volume alone, great as that volume was, but rather on the *style* in which it was carried out. Ideally, this was a mass-line style of propaganda that sought and gained active response from the recipients. Where successful, the propaganda campaign went beyond passive mass reception to active mass participation. Two examples will illustrate this point. In the first example, drawn from a village in Kirin, the propaganda campaign failed because the cadres were irresponsible and superficial in their attempts to communicate with the masses. Meetings were unsuccessful because the cadres came late and kept the people waiting; the "blackboard newspaper" was unintelligible to some peasants because sentences were long and characters were written in artistic style; information was not thor-

---

[67] See the Plan for General Election Propaganda Work in Canton, *Kuang-chou Jih-pao* (Canton Daily), January 16, 1954.
[68] *Ibid.*
[69] *T'ien-chin Jih-pao,* June 5, 1953.

oughly disseminated because notices were changed frequently before everyone had seen them. In short, the cadres presented their propaganda ritualistically without testing mass response.[70]

A report on election propaganda in a Kwangtung *hsiang* provides the contrast.[71] Here the campaign was well organized from the first. A *hsiang* propaganda conference, which was based on Party and Youth League members but also included village activists and primary-school teachers, selected a *hsiang* propaganda team of twenty-seven people and divided it into four groups, one for each electoral district in the *hsiang*. Within each district team, responsibility for certain jobs (management of blackboards, radio broadcasts, newspaper reading, etc.) was assigned to specific individuals; those team members whose "cultural level" was low were assigned to direct, oral propaganda. In spite of these measures, however, a first meeting in one village failed to draw more than 30–40 of the 180 village residents. Thereafter, the propaganda teams concentrated on small-group discussion, home visits, and other informal contracts. With this approach, propaganda could be varied from group to group, related to personal experiences of the listeners, and combined with other types of discussion or recreational activities. Ultimately, these techniques not only aroused mass interest in the elections but provided the basis for a revival of attendance and participation in village meetings. The key to success was presenting propaganda in such a way that the peasants could respond with questions and comments as well as listen. Where this was done, the propaganda campaign combined mass participation with political education.

A second point that deserves further attention is the nomination and discussion process leading up to the election. The Party handled this stage in the 1953–1954 elections with great care, including an enormous amount of experimental work in every province and major city before moving on to general elections in each area. According to a NCNA release, experimental elections were not completed until about the end of September, 1953; over 3,500 electoral districts, of all possible varieties, served as testing and training grounds for the wider application of national and local election regulations.[72] The extent of experimental work was undoubtedly a major factor in the Party's generally successful implementation of the nomination procedure outlined in the national Directive.

There were, of course, some practices that had not been fully anticipated in the Directive. One of these was the solicitation of nominations

[70] *JMJP*, August 4, 1953.

[71] *Nan-fang Jih-pao*, April 9, 1954. The unit is T'angko *Hsiang* in Mouming *Hsien*.

[72] *KMJP*, September 27, 1953.

from the voters' small groups before the first joint nomination meeting of
the Party and other organizations. This practice had mixed results. On
the one hand, it encouraged nomination and discussion of candidates as
well as frequent small-group meetings, thereby giving the process an
aura of permissiveness that would have been lacking if the favored joint
list had been fixed from the start. On the other hand, it complicated the
Party's effort to produce agreement on a number of candidates equal to
that to be elected and it revealed unmistakably the Party's willingness to
replace popular nominations with its own favored list. Thus, in one
electoral district in Peking that was to elect five deputies, the initial
nominations from all the voters' small groups produced over a hundred
and thirty names. Four rounds of small-group meetings still left twenty-
nine names on the nomination list. The official list of five candidates
was chosen from these names by the election committee, but it was
actually the same as the list drawn up at an earlier date by the joint
conference of the Party and other groups.[73]

Another problem not anticipated in the Directive was the parochial-
ism of voters and the difficulty of finding candidates who were both
acceptable to the Party and known to the masses. This problem was
particularly acute in the cities, where electoral districts were relatively
populous and each deputy was to represent, on the average, about a
thousand people. Judging from many reports, there was a pronounced
tendency for small groups to nominate only people from their own
groups and for individuals to restrict their nominations to personal
friends of their own class or status. In one sense, of course, this was
precisely the purpose of small-group discussions—to encourage individual nominations by reducing the unit of discussion to such a small size.
Nevertheless, once it had broken mass political inertia by soliciting such
nominations, the Party had no wish to nourish any expression of frac-
tionalized "interest." The problem was how to secure small-group
approval of a single list which the Party said was "representative" in
terms of the entire district and yet which included many names unknown
to most of the small groups. The Party-controlled list could, of course,
be imposed arbitrarily, but so far as possible, election cadres tried to
solicit at least a formal expression of approval of the joint list before the
election committee made its final pronouncement on the official list.
This could be done partly by explanation and guided discussion within
the small group, but other techniques were also used to break down the
voters' ignorance and suspicion of unknown candidates. One very
common practice was to organize exchange visits among the joint-list
candidates and the voters' small groups; another was to combine two or

[73] KMJP, December 5, 1953.

more groups for discussion of candidates so that a group's support for its own members would be placed in better perspective and, presumably, withdrawn.[74]

The Party was certainly only partially successful in replacing support for natural favorites with genuine approval of the joint list. Given the highly limited and particular character of political attachments for most Chinese, strong resistance to unfamiliar candidates was to be expected even when their technical qualifications were self-evident. What is more significant is that the CCP so explicitly recognized and combatted the persistence of particularistic loyalties in these first general elections. Even though the results were not entirely satisfactory, the Party at least exposed most voters to a wider range of candidates and political considerations than they had ever experienced previously. The voters had no choice but to accept the Party candidates, but in registering their formal acceptance of the candidate lists for the electoral district or basic-level unit they were taking the first step toward active membership in a political unit that transcended particular groupings and linked up with all higher levels of the state.

A third important aspect of the 1953–1954 elections was the scale of popular participation. Two obvious qualifications should be kept in mind in considering this subject. The first is that all electoral activities were led by the Party and that the act of participation itself did not represent an exercise of significant political choice. Nevertheless, electoral participation was voluntary in the sense that coercive measures were not used to secure it. Moreover, the impact of participation for most Chinese was certainly measured more against the apolitical standards of the past than against the principles of free electoral choice that were known to only a minority of the population. A second qualification is that there is no precise method of stating the actual extent of electoral participation. Some of the most precise statistics, as on the voting percentage, may be least meaningful as measures of significant participation. Other figures that are more meaningful must be deduced from fragmentary materials that are not easily verifiable. Given these qualifications, there is little point in trying to go beyond a few general statements that have substantial evidence.

The primary distinction to make in analyzing popular electoral participation, or mass participation in any political movement in Communist China, is that between activists and ordinary citizens. The activists are those who fill official or unofficial positions of more or less regularized responsibility during the course of the movement. Together with the permanent cadres of the Party, state and mass organizations who are the basic-level leadership in its usual sense, they constitute a segment of the

[74] For illustration of these points, see *Ta Kung Pao,* August 29–30, 1953.

population that invests a disproportionately high degree of time, energy, and commitment in political activity. In the 1953–1954 elections, this group included small-group leaders and volunteer propagandists in addition to all the election cadres who served on the previously mentioned committees and teams. For these people, electoral participation meant almost daily meetings, lectures, and contacts with voters over a period extending from one to several months, depending on the official or unofficial position held. The election movement in Tientsin required 1,963 basic-level election cadres, 3,416 technical cadres, over 600 reporting officials (those who delivered reports or lectures), and over 46,000 propagandists and street activists.[75] Approximately 52,000 cadres and activists were thus needed to organize and lead basic-level elections in a city with a population of roughly 2.7 million. It is doubtful if these figures actually include all the activists who emerged in the campaign, but even so the ratio is about one cadre or activist for every fifty people. In Hopei, with a population of 36 million, 1.3 million cadres and activists were used in election propaganda alone.[76] The ratios suggested by these examples are borne out in detailed reports on individual electoral districts. It is safe to conclude that one out of every thirty to fifty people (or one out of every twenty to thirty voters) participated extensively in the elections as an activist.

Estimates of the scale of participation among ordinary citizens are even more difficult. For purposes of generalization, we may start with the assumption (not literally true, of course) that participation in various election activities was universal in terms of its intended participants. In any given locality, election activities lasted for a period of about two months, starting with the local propaganda campaign and ending with the election itself. For the ordinary citizen, there were four types of election activity. The first might be called diffuse propaganda, consisting of basic information on the elections and their significance as transmitted through the press, radio, loudspeaker diffusion, posters, films, and dramatic performances. Popular exposure to these forms of propaganda was universal and frequent, but it did not necessarily involve any response on the part of the recipient. The second type was propaganda meetings, of which there were a great variety. All such meetings theoretically provided the opportunity for questions and response, but in fact the extent of response varied greatly. General meetings, such as public lectures or meetings of local mass organizations, probably involved little popular participation outside of attendance itself; it is likely that attendance was erratic in any case. On the other hand, meetings of smaller groups and individuals were apparently

[75] *JMJP*, March 15, 1954.
[76] *JMJP*, April 27, 1954.

quite effective in transmitting the propaganda message and soliciting a response from the citizens involved. Performance was erratic here, too, as success depended on the ability and diligence of the cadres, but everyone must have been exposed to this form of personal discussion of the electoral process on several occasions.

The third and most important type of popular participation in the election campaign was the voters' small group. Here the citizen was encouraged to make nominations and could hardly avoid at least minimal participation in the discussion of candidates. Attendance was undoubtedly high owing to the smallness and fixed membership of the group. On the average, small groups probably met at least three or four times during the nomination and discussion process. The fourth type of participation was voting itself, which may have been anticlimactic but which nonetheless fulfilled an important symbolic function. In rural areas, election day meant a final public meeting complete with parades, songs, and other festivities. Voting participation was measured at 86 percent of the electorate.

In sum, the assumption that popular participation in the election campaign was universal and frequent is generally justified even though there were exceptions in some localities and in some forms of election activity. For those who served as cadres and activists, the elections were a truly significant form of political activity. For ordinary citizens, they represented a concentrated exposure to the basic-level operation of the political system and a memorable experience in political education.

The fourth and final aspect of the 1953–1954 elections that demands discussion is the way in which the elective function of the campaign was submerged in a flood of competing functions. As the preceding analysis demonstrates, the supposedly primary task of electing basic-level deputies was in no sense ignored. Some incumbent cadres were removed, new names were proposed, popular opinions on candidates were recorded, and decisions were ultimately made on the composition of the new congresses. Nevertheless, Party propaganda about mass control of the state machinery notwithstanding, the fact remains that the election campaign was not a vehicle for popular selection of deputies. The key decision-making point in selecting deputies was the joint conference of Party members and representatives of other organizations, supplemented in some cases by a final decision on difficult choices in the basic-level election committee. Lack of concern with popular control was graphically demonstrated by election reports that persistently glossed over the critical decision-making process. Again and again, joint conferences reduced dozens of popularly nominated names to a list equal to the number to be elected with no explanation other than that the new list met with the "unanimous approval" of the voters. Popular choice among candidates was solicited only at earlier stages to assist the Party in distinguishing "progressive" and "backward" cadres. In these cases, the masses could influence a candidate's future, but their decisions were based on criteria supplied by the Party rather than on personal choice. The masses could help decide whether a cadre "ought to be elected" or not (that is, whether he actively supported socialism and the Party or not), but they could not make a final decision on which cadres would ultimately serve as deputies.

In contrast, several other functions emerged as major aspects of the election campaign. According to the Party press, the accomplishments of the basic-level elections can be summarized as follows: [77]

1. Raising of mass political consciousness. This point refers to the transmission, through propaganda and political action, of the election campaign's ideological message: a greater understanding of the necessity of proletarian (Party) leadership; a greater awareness of class distinctions and, therefore, a greater ability to distinguish between the "people" and "enemies of the people"; a growth of activism, measured in willingness to work, to struggle, to display "revolutionary alertness" against the enemy, and so forth; a greater understanding of the evils of the old society and the promise of the new.

2. Increasing production. No discussion of the elections omitted the assertion that the campaign would improve productive organization and increase production itself, and election propaganda dwelt heavily on this point. In the cities, election activities were used to encourage emulation and competition among workers. In the countryside, they were to advance and improve the organization of mutual-aid teams and cooperatives. In all areas, higher political consciousness was to be directed into greater productive efforts.[78]

3. Strengthening unity. This goal includes not only the ritualistic demonstration of unanimous approval of Party favorites and identification with the new state system, but also consolidation of permanent organizational gains that can be used to "create" unity in the future—for example, the establishment of propaganda networks, the recruitment of new activists, and so forth.

4. Democratic education for masses and cadres. The masses were to gain from the elections a greater knowledge of the state structure and

[77] This discussion is based on a final report on the Tientsin elections in *JMJP*, March 15, 1954, and "Ch'ing-chu Ch'üan-kuo Chi-ts'eng Hsüan-chü ti Wan-ch'eng," *op. cit.*

[78] The notion that higher political consciousness raises production is one of the most characteristic ideas of Chinese communism. It was carried to its extreme in the Great Leap Forward, but with the difficulties that followed, it was temporarily replaced by the statement that higher production raises political consciousness. See the comments in chap. Four.

their rights and obligations within it. Cadres were to learn to avoid bureaucratism, to remain "close to the masses," and to listen to mass opinions and demands.

5. Securing demographic and political information. Through the census and organized mass discussion of voters' qualifications, a great deal of information that would be "useful for economic, cultural and defense construction" was accumulated and verified.

The Party press regarded these five points as "accomplishments" and all were probably achieved to some extent. Whether fully achieved or not, however, they reveal the multifunctional role of elections in Communist China. In the eyes of the CCP, the elective function is a relatively minor aspect of popular participation in an election campaign, a fact which emerges from the following illustrative report on the election campaign in a rural *hsiang* in Shansi.[79] Before the elections, this was a "backward" *hsiang* in which Party leadership was loose and the mutual-aid teams and cooperatives were poorly developed. According to local leaders, it was always a case of "organized in the spring, fragmented in the summer and collapsed in the fall." Election cadres started their campaign, therefore, with a drive to rectify agricultural organization. This succeeded, producing sixty-three new mutual-aid teams and one new cooperative in the process. The cadres then turned the drive toward the elections by posing the questions, How can mutual-aid teams and cooperatives be well managed and plans for increased production realized? The answer, of course, was proper leadership, and thus election work and increased production were tied together.

Preliminary election agitation concentrated on the differences between the old and new societies, with particular attention to the crimes of the old landlord and his cohorts who had controlled the village before liberation. Once the advantages of the new economic and political structure were made clear, census and registration work began. The masses were encouraged to correct any false information given, and ultimately 320 cases of false information on such matters as age and marital status were corrected. Mass discussion of voter lists was initially unenthusiastic as many said it was too much trouble and that old matters should be forgotten. The election team quickly attacked this attitude, pointing out why bad elements had to be excluded from positions of power; as a result, the lists were examined and several "bad elements" were uncovered. The campaign then moved on to nominations and discussions. At this point another difficulty arose in that the masses tended to avoid criticizing candidates and to cite only their good points; moreover, they compared candidates on such grounds as cultural level,

[79] *JMJP*, March 11, 1954. The unit is Chaoyang *Hsiang* in T'aiku *Hsien*.

literacy, and number of children rather than on their ideology and political consciousness. The cadres quickly corrected this tendency, too. After the elections, which were held during the Chinese New Year festival, the new deputies reaffirmed the results of the campaign by criticizing the local people's government for its failure to support mutual-aid teams and cooperatives and for the inaccessibility of many cadres. Reports of this sort are not necessarily accurate in every detail, but they reveal how popular participation in the 1953–1954 elections contributed to the CCP's efforts to bring about fundamental changes in production, organization, political leadership, and political attitudes. In this way, they underscore the fact that the political significance of elections in Communist China lies mainly in functions other than the selection of representatives.

LEGAL ORGANS

In comparison with the system of congresses and elections, the CPR's legal organs provide relatively little opportunity for popular participation in the state structure. This is not to say that the popular role in law enforcement is insignificant or that the masses are excluded from informal settlement of disputes. Quite the contrary is true, as later discussion will show. At this point, however, we are concerned only with popular participation in the more formal aspects of the legal system.

The legal system of the CPR is not, and does not pretend to be, a politically neutral force. As Tung Pi-wu said in his speech to the Eighth Party Congress, the legal system is "an important instrument for the exercise of the people's democratic dictatorship in our country." [80] For this reason, in addition to their judicial functions, the people's courts are enjoined to "ensure the successful carrying out of socialist construction and socialist transformation" and to "educate citizens in loyalty to their country and voluntary obedience of law." [81] For this reason also, the courts are no exception to the general rule of ultimate Party supervision and absence of popular control. However, in keeping with the mass line and the educative function of all political institutions in China, the CCP has attempted to draw the masses into the operation of basic-level legal organs. The two most prominent illustrations of this attempt are the people's tribunals (*jen-min fa-t'ing*) and the people's assessors (*jen-min p'ei-shen-yüan*).

[80] "Speech by Comrade Tung Pi-wu," *op. cit.,* p. 79.
[81] "Organic Law of the People's Courts of the People's Republic of China, Art. 3, in *Documents of the First Session of the First National People's Congress of the People's Republic of China.*

People's tribunals People's tribunals were special legal organs set up to deal with the enormous number of cases, involving settlement of disputes as well as trial and punishment of "criminals," that emerged during the great mass movements of 1950–1955. "Regulations Governing the Organization of People's Tribunals" were promulgated in July, 1950, in accordance with a provision of the Agrarian Reform Law which stated that tribunals would be established in every *hsien* to ensure the completion of land reform.[82] Even from the first, the jurisdiction of the tribunals extended far beyond the specifics of land reform alone. In addition to disposing of cases concerning demarcation of land lots and other land reform matters, the tribunals were empowered to penalize "despots, native bandits, special agents, counterrevolutionaries, and criminals who violate the laws and orders pertaining to agrarian reform, who endanger the interests of the people and the state, plot sabotage activities, and undermine social security. . . ."[83] Subsequently, the tribunals received formal powers to handle cases in connection with the suppression of counterrevolutionaries campaigns, the Three-Anti and Five-Anti movements, and disputes arising in the 1953–1954 elections. After 1955, however, they dropped from public notice.

Throughout their existence, the people's tribunals held an ambiguous position between formal state organs and instruments of direct popular action. On the one hand, they did have regular legal status as component parts of the local people's courts, and, in this sense, were supposedly designed to lighten the case load of a court system that was not yet fully established.[84] Moreover, there were frequent assertions that they would lend a "judicial" air to the mass movements by curbing tendencies toward illegality and spontaneous mass justice.[85] On the other hand, the performance of the tribunals suggested that their role in mass education and mobilization was far more important than their contribution toward the judicial settlement of cases emerging from the mass movements. Although *Jen-min Jih-pao* insisted that the tribunals should never let the peasants take justice into their own hands, it could also argue that the tribunals were "powerful instruments in the promotion of mass movements" that would mobilize the masses behind the peasants, encourage them in their antifeudal struggles, and educate the peasants to

[82] See *The Agrarian Reform Law of the People's Republic of China* (Peking, 1950), Art. 32. The "Regulations" for people's tribunals are found in *CB*, No. 151, (January 10, 1952).

[83] "Regulations Governing the Organization of People's Tribunals," *op. cit.*, Art. 1.

[84] *Ibid.*, Art. 3, and "Organic Law of the People's Courts of the People's Republic of China," *op. cit.*, Art. 17.

[85] See the *JMJP* editorial of July 21, 1950, in *CB*, No. 151, and Liu Shao-ch'i's comments in "On the Agrarian Reform Law," *The Agrarian Reform Law of the People's Republic of China*, pp. 83–84.

understand and participate in the people's democratic dictatorship.[86]

The mobilization function of the people's tribunals demanded mass participation, which took two main forms. First, there were a number of popular representatives who served as "judges." According to the regulations on tribunal organization, the tribunals were composed of a presiding judge, a deputy presiding judge, and a number of ordinary judges. The head judges and half of the ordinary judges were to be appointed by the *hsien* people's government, while the remaining half of the judges would be elected indirectly through local people's conferences and mass organizations.[87] Although this system retained majority control for the appointees of higher government levels, it also opened up a large number of official positions to be filled by popular organizations. Second, the people in general were allowed and encouraged to attend meetings of the tribunals and speak out if they wished, so long as they did not "disturb the order" of the tribunals.

These points support the observation that the tribunals were primarily instruments for political agitation of the masses. It is true, of course, that there was a genuine shortage of judicial personnel in terms of the case load created by the mass movements and that the tribunals did help dispose of these cases. However, there was little in the quality of the "judges" or the procedure of the tribunals to suggest that cases were settled by consistent legal standards or that this was their intended purpose. Mass participation was undoubtedly extensive, at least during those periods when the mass movements were at their peak in a given locality, but there is no reason to believe that participation was perceived as taking part in the judicial administration of the state. On the contrary, exposure to the people's tribunals must have been quite similar to exposure to many other types of political meetings and rallies that were held during the mass movements.

People's assessors With the development of the people's courts, opportunities emerged for popular participation in more regular legal processes. As early as September, 1951, provisional regulations for the organization of people's courts had stipulated that popular representatives should take part in trials in some cases.[88] For the next two years, there was little systematic observance of the provision. "People's assessors," as these nonprofessional participants in trials were called, were chosen by people's conferences or mass organizations to attend trials when these organizations were particularly interested in the case in question. Assessors did not have the same powers as judges and had no

[86] *JMJP* editorial of November 13, 1951, in *CB*, No. 151.
[87] *Op. cit.,* Art. 4.
[88] Text in *CB*, No. 183 (May 26, 1952).

regular terms of office or method of selection. In some cases, the elected "judges" who served on people's tribunals doubled as assessors when there was a demand for popular representation in a people's court. In 1953, after a national conference on legal work, it was decided to give the assessors more permanent office and more specific functions within the legal system. In the 1953–1954 elections, many localities made a point of electing assessors, although not necessarily directly by the people, to get away from the previous practice of *ad hoc* appointments for certain cases.

People's assessors became an integral part of court operations after the adoption of the "Organic Law of the People's Courts" in September, 1954. This law stated that any citizen who was twenty-three or over, who had the right to vote, and who had never been deprived of political rights was eligible to serve as an assessor. Assessors were to be members of the divisions of the courts in which they served, were to have equal rights with judges, and were required to attend court at times appointed by the people's courts. The Organic Law also stipulated that courts would use assessors in all cases of the first instance, "with the exception of simple civil cases, minor criminal cases and cases otherwise provided for by law." [89] Some of the remaining questions about assessors were answered by a Ministry of Justice directive in July, 1956. This directive left the number of assessors to the determination of each local court, but it stated that the ratio of two assessors for each judge in a trial should be generally followed; it also set assessors' terms at two years and stated that each assessor should serve an average of ten days a year in court. [90] As a result of these measures, the assessor system began to operate with a reasonable degree of consistency throughout the country after the 1956 elections.

The number of people's assessors increased steadily throughout the early years of the CPR and exceeded 200,000 after the 1956 elections. [91] The practice of *ad hoc* appointment was apparently replaced by the election of all assessors by about 1954. Direct popular election has also slowly been replacing election by people's congresses or other meetings of representatives, but it is unlikely even now that all are chosen by direct election. Obviously, the people's assessors system, which includes some 200,000-plus assessors who may or may not be directly elected and who serve in court only ten days a year, does not compare with either basic-level congresses or elections as a vehicle for mass political participation. Nevertheless, it does add to the total volume of such participation and deserves at least brief analysis.

[89] *Op. cit.*, Arts. 8, 35–37.
[90] *KMJP*, August 11, 1956.
[91] *JMJP*, March 14, 1957.

Party literature claims that this system, like people's congresses and elections, makes a variety of healthy contributions to the political life of the masses. One typical article cites four such contributions: (1) participation in the courts makes the people feel that they are "masters of their country," and thereby stimulates their enthusiasm for production and [socialist] construction; (2) the system enables the assessors, who are mass representatives, to supervise the work of the people's courts and make suggestions and criticisms to the judges; (3) the assessors are close to the masses and local conditions, which the judges are not, and are better suited to investigating and resolving local problems; for example, they would be more capable at fixing just compensation for draft animals than the judges; (4) through their participation in court activities, the assessors gain knowledge of law and policies which they can pass on to the masses, thereby strengthening law-abiding spirit among the masses, preventing crimes, and reducing the number of disputes.[92] Judging from scattered reports and the nature of the system, there is little foundation for the first two assertions. The act of participation undoubtedly has considerable political significance for the individual assessor, but the system is in no sense a means of exerting popular control over the courts. The latter two assertions, however, must be accepted as partially valid. Even though the assessors do not fulfill these functions to the extent implied, the system does provide for a modest exchange of ideas between the people and professional legal personnel and for a general broadening of popular knowledge about the legal system.

Under ideal conditions, service as a people's assessor can be one of the fullest political experiences open to a Chinese citizen. After the initial selection, which is something of an honor in view of the relatively few people chosen, the assessor may be led through a series of orientation lectures and discussions, be briefed by the judges on more specific legal matters, serve his days in court as an equal voting partner of the judges, engage in investigations of his own (usually personal interviews), perhaps "solve" a case by personal mediation, and make a variety of lectures and reports to members of his own organization or production unit. Unfortunately, these ideal conditions are seldom realized, mainly because of two problems that have plagued the assessor system.

The first problem is the unwillingness of some judges to accept the assessors as equal partners, compounded by the legal ignorance and natural reticence (under these circumstances) of the assessors themselves. Whether because of the judges' attitude of superiority or the

[92] "What Is the People's Assessors System?" *Shih-shih Shou-ts'e*, 1956, No. 16, in *Union Research Service*, Vol. 5, No. 13 (November 13, 1956).

assessors' reticence, the assessors have frequently not fulfilled their assigned role in the courts. Along this same line, there have been complaints about judges who used assessors as personal clerks or who assigned unreasonably heavy work loads to assessors to overcome their deficiencies in legal knowledge. The second problem has been difficulty in arranging the court schedules of assessors and in getting them to put in their time. One logical explanation of this would be insufficient interest, but that is too simple an answer even though it is probably appropriate in some cases. The main reason for poor attendance is simply that the assessors are too busy with their regular jobs, that either they or their superiors are unwilling to donate the time required. Behind this reluctance to excuse assessors for court work lie two factors: first, the enormous emphasis on meeting production goals; second, the fact that most people chosen as assessors are cadres or activists who are genuinely unexpendable at work or whose time is already fully consumed by other meetings and responsibilities. This problem reflects the fact that assessors are very carefully chosen (even more so than basic-level deputies) for their demonstrated activism and conformity to Party standards. At the same time, it reflects the perpetual shortage of cadres who are genuinely qualified from the Party's point of view.[93] Although neither of these two problems is insoluble, they have detracted greatly from the CCP's attempt to inject the mass-line style of participation into the legal system.

CONCLUSION

In concluding this discussion, there are three points that deserve emphasis. First, the institutions designed to encourage mass participation in the state structure have been declining in effectiveness since about 1956. The reasons for this decline are complex but certainly include the following: an increase in the size and complexity of basic-level administrative units that reduced the element of spontaneity and popular interest in these units and invited tighter Party leadership; the emergence of the Great Leap philosophy that tended to replace institutionalized political activities with constant and direct mobilization of the masses; persistent "commandism" and "formalism" in the Party's efforts to maintain popular participation in state organs without allowing popular control, resulting in reduced enthusiasm for the process among both masses and cadres.

Second, institutional sterility has adversely affected the functions that

[93] For illustrations of these problems, see the articles in *Union Research Service*, Vol. 5, No. 13, and Tso P'ing, "Tsen-yang Chieh-chüeh Yao-ch'ing Jen-min P'ei-shen-yüan ti K'un-nan" (How To Solve the Difficulties in Inviting People's Assessors), *KMJP*, August 11, 1956.

mass participation in the state structure is expected to perform. The popular-control function, by which the Party has actually meant an opportunity for the people to express their views on cadres and policies rather than popular decision-making power, has become weaker; the state system does provide some criticism of cadres and some expression of popular "opinions and demands," but close examination shows that these expressions are generally neither spontaneous nor effective. The implementation-of-policy function was reasonably effective in the early years of the regime but has since declined. The 1953–1954 elections, the early people's conferences and congresses, and the people's tribunals helped secure direct popular execution of Party policies and objectives. In later years, however, the major responsibility for implementing Party policies has moved outside the state structure, even though congresses and elections continue to ratify Party policies and call for their execution. The most important aspect of mass participation in basic-level government now appears to be the educative function, broadly defined to include the encouragement of attachments to, and understanding of, new levels of political community as well as transmission of information on laws and policies. The effectiveness of this function has also been limited by the trends noted above, but it is still the major justification for continued mass participation in government under the present system.

Finally, reference should be made to the influence of the past on the manner in which the CCP has handled popular participation in government. In the first place, it is evident that the Party's experience in the Kiangsi Soviet and the Yenan period provided the foundation for nearly all of the popular political institutions adopted after 1949. Broadly speaking, the governmental forms and practices of the Yenan period have served as the model for basic-level government in the CPR. And, although the Party did not continue the three-thirds system and the direct election of higher-level congresses that existed in the wartime period, it had a precedent for indirect elections and more open Party control in the Kiangsi Soviet. More generally, the CCP's experience with mass political participation after 1949 reflects the absence of a democratic tradition in China. To a considerable extent, this absence explains the CCP's desire to claim modernity by being the first to initiate "democratic" institutions and also its difficulties in securing popular participation in such institutions. Like so many other Chinese leaders of the twentieth century, the Chinese Communists have seen "democratic" institutions as instruments of political tutelage and mass mobilization for national purposes. Even in its most democratic phase during the Sino–Japanese War, the Party's real successes lay in the realm of mass movements and national struggles rather than in the practice of democracy.

These influences from China's past and the Party's own experience help explain a curious ambivalence in the Chinese Communists' attitude toward state institutions in general and democratic institutions in particular. On the one hand, the Party exhibits a compulsive desire to have these institutions and to believe that they are even more democratic than those of the West; partly for this reason, the Communists will go to great lengths to maintain the institutional façade of their Party-controlled state. On the other hand, the CCP also seems to have an intuitive suspicion of the formal and legalistic aspects of the state. The best expression of this is the idea that "nature" rather than "form" determines the character of a political system. In some cases this may be a defensive posture, as when a Communist leader argues that Chinese elections are more democratic in nature than those of the West even though they are less democratic in form because of the absence of the secret ballot and direct election of higher-level congresses.[94] Still, the argument is cast in more general terms, as the constant concern with "formalism" and the contempt for bourgeois legalism show. The materials discussed in this chapter have demonstrated the Party's conviction that it is the quality and behavior of men in office, and not the institutional structure, that determines the character of government.[95] Behind this conviction lies not only the "guerrilla mentality" of a revolutionary movement but also the influence of Confucian principles of government.

[94] Teng Hsiao-p'ing, "An Explanation of the Electoral Law," *op. cit.,* pp. 27–28.
[95] See also *ibid.,* p. 45.

SIX

Nongovernmental Organization

Nongovernmental organization includes a wide variety of organizations that have in common only their formal separateness from the state structure. The distinction between state organs and nongovernmental organization in China is not the same as that between "public" and "private" government in the West. There is no "private" government in China, in any real sense, as all nongovernmental organizations perform some "public" functions and are controlled, in varying degrees, by the state and Party hierarchy. However, the distinction is useful for analytical purposes even though it is somewhat artificial.

There are two general types of nongovernmental organization in Communist China. The first is the secondary association which is organized, at least theoretically, on the basis of the common interests, occupations, or class viewpoints of its members. With no significant exceptions, these organizations are national associations with branches at various local levels and operate, again theoretically, on the principle of voluntary membership. The main secondary associations are the "democratic parties" and the mass organizations. The second type is the production or residential unit, of which the urban residents' committee and the production team in the rural communes are the primary examples. These units differ from the secondary associations in two respects. First, they have no higher-level organization of their own, although they are connected in some ways to basic-level state organs and may cooperate informally with their neighboring units. Second, membership is involuntary and automatic for all those living or working in a given unit; there are qualifications on this point but they will be discussed later. Production and residential units may serve as electoral districts for basic-level congresses and as administrative units for basic-level government. They also serve, in fact if not in name, as governing agencies for their members. Nevertheless, they have no legal status as part of the state structure and their organization is too varied and incomplete to constitute a single *de facto* level of government beneath the basic-level state organs.

Nongovernmental organization is supremely important in the Chinese Communist political system. It is the primary mechanism for transmitting Party policies to the people and mobilizing them for the execution of these policies. It also gives the masses their best opportunity for participation in the management of their own immediate affairs. Nongovernmental organization is too vast and varied a subject to describe fully in this study, but a general discussion of its major forms will indicate its role in mass political participation. This discussion will cover the democratic parties, mass organizations, urban residential organization, and rural production units.

DEMOCRATIC PARTIES

According to the annual listings in *Jen-min Shou-ts'e* (the *People's Handbook* of mainland China), there are eight "democratic parties" in China. They are the Revolutionary Committee of the Kuomintang, the China Democratic League, the China Democratic National Construction Association, the Chinese Association for Promoting Democracy, the Chinese Peasants' and Workers' Democratic Party, The China Chih Kung Tang, the Chiu San Society, and the Taiwan Democratic Self-Government Society. The oldest is the Chih Kung Tang, which traces its origins back to the Taiping Rebellion although it was organized in its present form by a group of overseas Chinese in San Francisco in 1925. With the exception of the China Peasants' and Workers' Democratic Party, which claims 1927 as the year of its origin, all the other parties date from the 1940's. The youngest is the Revolutionary Committee of the KMT, which was organized in Hong Kong in January, 1948. Each party claims to speak for, and organize specific segments of, Chinese society, but there is much overlapping. It suffices to say that the parties as a whole represent the nonlaboring elements within the United Front —intellectuals, bureaucrats, professional and technical workers, merchants and industrialists, and overseas Chinese.[1]

The democratic parties are not associations for mass political representation or mobilization. Their membership is small and limited mainly to the relatively well-educated social strata mentioned above. Although they play a prominent role in discussion and endorsement of Party policy at the national level through their representation in the NPC and the CPPCC, their activities and organization are isolated from popular political life at lower levels of government. In 1957, the democratic parties held over 22 percent of the seats in the NPC, but less than 9 percent in provincial congresses.[2] At the basic level, they are

[1] See the brief descriptions of these parties in *1957 Jen-min Shou-ts'e* (Peking, 1957), pp. 249–257.

[2] Ch'ang Shu, "Kuan-yü Wo-kuo Hsüan-chü ti I-hsieh Ts'ai-liao" (Some Data on Our Election System), *Kung-jen Jih-pao* (Workers' Daily), October 19, 1957.

mentioned scarcely at all in connection with mass political activities. The parties do have local organizations at the provincial level and in the major cities, but their local work concentrates on political study and ideological education among their own members. In the context of this study, therefore, the role of the democratic parties illustrates the CCP's general attitude toward other political organizations rather than mass political participation itself.

United Front theory determines the political role of the democratic parties. As noted in chapter Four, the CCP accepted support from other parties as a tactical move in the Yenan period and then permitted them to continue after 1949 on the grounds that all classes counted among the "people" needed their own organizations for political representation. However, the CCP fundamentally limits the United Front by insisting that the Chinese revolution is following the socialist road and that CCP leadership is necessary at all stages of the revolution. Li Wei-han, director of the United Front Work Department of the CCP Central Committee, has explained the significance of United Front theory for the democratic parties by elaborating on these basic points.[3] According to Li, the CCP recognized early in the Sino–Japanese War that class distinctions remained within the United Front. After 1949, when the "new democratic" revolution transformed itself into a socialist revolution, the critical distinction within the United Front became that between the "basic" worker-peasant alliance and the "subsidiary" worker-bourgeoisie alliance. The worker-peasant alliance includes the Party's "reliable allies"—the peasants, revolutionary intellectuals, and some of the urban petty bourgeoisie. The worker-bourgeoisie alliance includes the nonlaboring "wavering allies"—the middle bourgeoisie and the upper section of the urban petty bourgeoisie (that is, the national bourgeoisie), the enlightened gentry, and all other social forces willing to cooperate in the socialist revolution. Toward the "wavering allies," whom the democratic parties represent, the Party adopts a "two-faced policy" of "uniting with and struggling against"; that is, it unites with them to further the revolution, but, at the same time, struggles to transform their bourgeois character and bring about their elimination as a class.

In more concrete terms, United Front theory has made subtle yet significant distinctions in the democratic parties' role at different stages of the revolution. During the new democratic revolution and at the beginning of socialist construction, the democratic parties were to

[3] The following discussion is based on Li Wei-han, "The United Front—A Magic Weapon of the Chinese People for Winning Victory," *Peking Review*, 1961, Nos. 23–24, and "The Chinese People's Democratic United Front: Its Special Features," *ibid.*, 1961, Nos. 33–35. The two articles appeared originally in *Hung Ch'i* (Red Flag), 1961, Nos. 11 and 12 respectively.

broaden the basis of national unity under CCP leadership. But after socialist construction was "basically completed on the economic front" in 1956, the democratic parties were to assist in their own extinction by the ideological transformation of their members. Of course, the democratic parties still contribute to the façade of multiclass support for CCP leadership and, as the slogan "long-term coexistence and mutual supervision" indicates, this function will continue for some time to come. Nevertheless, the Party no longer relies as heavily as it once did on the support and prestige of non-Party figures and it now uses the democratic parties as a weapon against their own class base.

The organization and activities of the democratic parties have conformed closely to the implications of United Front theory. As early as 1950, the democratic parties held a series of meetings under CCP guidance to focus their work on the organization and "education" of Party supporters among limited segments of the population. For example, the Democratic League's decision on this point, adopted in December, 1950, defined the league's organizational tasks as unifying the progressive intellectuals by bringing them into the league, carrying out education and study to achieve common and uniform progress, and struggling for the realization of the Common Program and the completion of the new democratic revolution.[4] Although the league was to concentrate on organizing intellectuals in various cultural, professional, and governmental pursuits, the decision prohibited the recruitment of members from the army, public security organs, intelligence agencies, revolutionary universities, foreign-office organs, and minority nationalities. It also excluded from league membership all past or present secret agents; those who spoke or acted against the Soviet Union, the CCP, or land reform; members of former "reactionary organizations"; and those who were particularly "evil and criminal" or "corrupt and degenerate." Moreover, the league was to require evidence of political activism before accepting a member and was to propagandize all prospective members on the Common Program and the league's constitution.

An article by Ch'en Ming-shu, a member of the Standing Committee of the Revolutionary Committee of the KMT, spelled out the full extent of CCP control over the organizational activities of the democratic parties in the early years of the CPR.[5] Ch'en emphasized the inseparability of the United Front from Party leadership by use of an organic metaphor. The connection, he said, was like flesh and blood or a man's

---

[4] "Chung-kuo Min-chu T'ung-meng 'Kuan-yü Fa-chan Tsu-chih ti Chüeh-ting'" (The China Democratic League's "Decision on Developing Organization"), *Hsin-hua Yüeh-pao* (New China Monthly), 1951, No. 16.

[5] Ch'en Ming-shu, "Wei Kung-ku Fa-chan Min-chu Tang-p'ai Tsu-chih erh Nu-li" (Strive for the Consolidation and Development of the Organization of the Democratic Parties), *Ch'ang-chiang Jih-pao* (Yangtze Daily) (Hankow), June 30, 1951.

nervous system; the Party is the brain or nerve center while the democratic parties are the nerve endings in the limbs and trunk. The relationship imposes mutual rights and obligations. The CCP has the right to lead and the obligation to assist the democratic parties; the democratic parties have the obligation to follow CCP leadership and the right to "overtake" its example. Concretely, the Central-South Bureau of the CCP had accepted its "rights and obligations" with a decision to send some CCP members to join the democratic parties and assist them from within, to aid the parties in persuading progressives to join, and to help the parties in cadre training classes. Throughout the early 1950's, therefore, the democratic parties measured the success of their political activities in terms of the "progressive" example that their members set for the Chinese bourgeoisie in study, increased production, bond subscriptions, participation in mass movements, cooperation with state regulations, and general support for the CCP program.[6]

Li Wei-han signaled the shift to dominant emphasis on ideological education in a 1956 report to the NPC in which he called for a program of political and ideological study among members of the democratic parties.[7] Thereafter, all meetings of the democratic parties and the CPPCC echoed the refrain of laying the ideological foundations for the transformation of the bourgeoisie into "socialist workers."[8] The most prominent agencies for this ideological transformation were the "Institutes of Socialism" and other political education courses that were set up after 1956 in various cities under the auspices of national and provincial levels of the CPPCC. These schools, which were attended by non-Party intellectuals and businessmen as well as members of the democratic parties, offered courses in communist theory, revolutionary history, and current policies, with intensive readings, lectures, discussions, and debates; "students" also engaged in labor (so far as possible, since most were middle-aged or elderly) as part of their "orientation" to socialist ideology.[9] The objective was not simply to educate the students in Party

[6] For example, see Chang Nai-ch'i, "Report on the Work of the China Democratic National Construction Association," NCNA, April 14, 1955, in *CB,* No. 327 (May 16, 1955).

[7] Li Wei-han, "The Democratic United Front in China," NCNA, June 25, 1956, in *CB,* No. 402 (July 24, 1956).

[8] In 1960 the Chairman of the Democratic League called on his party, which supposedly represents the bourgeoisie, to "promote the cause of the proletariat and destroy the bourgeoisie." See Shen Chün-ju's speech to the Central Committee of the Democratic League, *KMJP,* July 29, 1960, in *CB,* No. 639 (November 12, 1960).

[9] See Chang Chih-yi, "Political Study Is an Important Means of Helping Bourgeois Elements, Bourgeois Intellectuals, and Democratic Groups Remold Themselves," *KMJP,* January 1, 1959, in *CB,* No. 547 (January 27, 1959); Nieh Chen, "Problems Concerning Studies and Reform of the Students of the Institute of Socialism," *JMJP,* April 8, 1960, in *CB,* No. 628 (July 22, 1960); and the articles in *Union Research Service,* Vol. 21, No. 2 (October 7, 1960).

policies but to implant an anti-individualist and antibourgeois outlook that would erode the ideological foundations of the democratic parties.

The CCP's insistence that the democratic parties devote their main energies to ideological self-reform is intensified by the warning that there is no alternative to acceptance of socialist transformation. Although no one in China can escape this situation, it applies most directly to the democratic parties. The reasons for this particular concern lie generally in the fact that these parties are the only organizations whose members have any significant exposure to Western political theory and specifically in the fact that some of their members attacked the emptiness of the "mutual supervision" slogan in the "hundred flowers" campaign of 1957. Although the CCP was committed to ideological remolding of the democratic parties before 1957, the events of that year strengthened their determination to carry out the transformation without the slightest concessions to bourgeois democratic principles. For the Chinese bourgeoisie and democratic parties, Li Wei-han has said, the antirightist struggle of 1957–1958 was a "historical turning point" on the road to acceptance of socialist transformation; the rightists' belief that they could resist transformation was proven to be a mistake.[10]

The "rightist" attack of 1957 failed to lessen the totality of Party domination, but it was nonetheless a significant attempt. For a few weeks, some of the political tensions that lie beneath the surface in Communist China were brought into the open. Not the least of these tensions was the democratic parties' desire to establish their position as political parties by gaining a greater voice in political decisions and greater freedom in recruiting their members.[11] The CCP's response was that the democratic parties themselves would have to take the lead in eradicating such bourgeois democratic notions, but the experiment forced the Party to admit that its concept of political participation prohibited any significant debate over political decisions even within the United Front.

MASS ORGANIZATIONS

The term "mass organizations" sometimes refers to all forms of organization in China that give political direction to large numbers of people at the basic level. In this sense it includes cooperatives, communes, residents' committees, and basic-level congresses. For purposes of this discussion, however, the term is used in a more limited sense to

[10] Li Wei-han, "Study Chairman Mao's Writings and Gradually Change the World Outlook," *JMJP*, September 25, 1960, in *CB*, No. 639 (November 2, 1960).

[11] See the "hundred flowers" criticism by democratic party members translated in MacFarquhar, *The Hundred Flowers Campaign and the Chinese Intellectuals*, pp. 40–58, 226–230, and especially Lo Lung-chi's comment on pp. 42–43.

refer to those secondary associations that recruit their members on the basis of common interests, characteristics, or occupations and have national as well as local organization. This definition excludes many local groups (mainly recreational or cultural in nature) that have no national organization and little political significance, but it still takes in an enormous range of organizational activity. The *1957 Jen-min Shou-tse'e* lists forty-three national *jen-min t'uan-t'i* (that is, mass organizations in our sense), and this figure does not include the twenty-three national industrial unions that belong to the All-China Federation of Trade Unions, the forty national societies that make up the All-China Federation of Natural Science Societies, or the eight national associations in the All-China Federation of Literary and Art Circles.

In terms of mass participation, there are three general types of mass organizations. The first type includes those organizations that have relatively large memberships and that are primarily devoted to the political mobilization of their members and the population at large. By any standards, these are the most important mass organizations in China as they assume the greatest responsibility for transmitting official policies to the lowest level and organizing the masses for political activity. The Communist Youth League (the Party youth auxiliary), the Trade Unions Federation, the Women's Federation, and the Students' Federation are the major organizations of this type.[12] The second type includes those organizations that are frankly political and propagandistic but which have relatively little contact with the Chinese people. Most of these are designed to advance the Party line in international relations; examples are the various "friendship" associations with foreign countries, the Chinese People's Association for Cultural Relations with Foreign Countries, the Chinese People's Institute of Foreign Affairs, the China Afro–Asian Solidarity Committee, and the China Peace Committee. In some cases, these organizations may claim mass membership (the Sino–Soviet Friendship Association once had about seventy million members) but they offer few genuine opportunities for mass participation. Their work consists mainly of high-level exchange visits and propaganda releases.

The third type of mass organization is the professional or technical association that has a relatively small and exclusive membership and that engages in some "private" activities of a professional or scholarly nature. These associations may put out scholarly publications, engage in national and international exchange of information, and so forth. They are not as constantly involved in political mobilization and propa-

[12] The membership of these organizations is roughly as follows: Youth League, 25 million (1964); Federation of Trade Unions, 20.8 million (1965); Women's Federation, 76 million (1953); Students' Federation, 4 million (1955).

ganda as the other types and they do not have a significant range of contact with the masses. Nevertheless, they are in no sense isolated from politics. All recognize the political leadership of the CCP and all exhort their members to implement the Party line in areas pertaining to their special interests. Although some of their activities may be nonpolitical, they must participate in national political movements and subordinate their professional activities and opinions to political considerations whenever the Party so demands.

The remainder of this discussion will concentrate on the first type of mass organization which plays such an important role in mass political participation in China. Broadly speaking, mass organizations of this type have four common characteristics.[13] First, they are firmly controlled and supervised by the CCP through the placement of Party members in leading positions. In practice, the combination of Party members and non-Party activists within the organization, coupled with the obvious futility of resisting Party wishes and policies, is sufficient to ensure that the organization will follow the Party's lead. However, as a result of central government regulations adopted in late 1950 and early 1951, the state has ample power to control all forms of secondary associations by legal means.[14] According to these regulations, all "social organizations," including both local organizations and mass organizations as defined here, were to register with the people's government at the level at which they were organized; branches of national organizations were also to register at their local level. Organizations were required to submit, at the time of registration, full information on their name, location, objectives, constitution, leading personnel, size of membership, organizational structure, and economic condition (including sources of revenue). They were also enjoined to accept the "guidance" of the government with which they registered; to cooperate with it in carrying out various tasks of economic, cultural, and national construction; and to submit to it regular reports on their conferences, general meetings, work plans, and financial status. Any "reactionary" organization harming the "interests of the state or people" or any organization violating the regulations could be disbanded.

[13] Although now rather dated, Chao Kuo-chün's *The Mass Organizations in Communist China* (Cambridge, Mass., 1953) remains an extremely useful study of the general organization and activities of the major mass organizations.

[14] "She-hui T'uan-t'i Teng-chi Chan-hsing Pan-fa" (Provisional Methods for the Registration of Social Organizations), and "She-hui T'uan-t'i Teng-chi Chan-hsing Pan-fa Shih-hsing Hsi-tse" (Detailed Regulations on the Operation of the Provisional Methods for the Registration of Social Organizations), *Chieh-fang Jih-pao* (Liberation Daily), November 17, 1951. These regulations exempted most of the major organizations already established from petitioning for registration but did not exempt them from compliance with the operating restrictions.

Second, the constitutions of all these mass organizations proclaim "democratic centralism" as their guiding principle. As is the case in state and Party structure, "centralism" (minority submission to majority, and lower levels obeying higher levels) is much more conspicuous than "democracy" (regular convening of congresses at all levels and free discussion before decisions are reached). All major decisions are made at the top, and higher levels can review and revoke the decisions of lower levels. In effect, the centralized structures of the mass organizations supplement and reinforce the state structure as channels for transmitting central policy down to the basic level.

Third, the major mass organizations have in common a well-developed basic-level organization to encourage maximum participation and obedience to higher directives by individual members, to develop as many activists as possible, and to expand the amount of contact between members and nonmembers. There are, of course, variations in the basic-level organization of different mass organizations and in the effectiveness with which they are run, but there is no doubt about the general desire to maintain vital branches at this level. In the case of the trade unions, a primary organization may be established in any enterprise or establishment with ten or more trade union members.[15] In larger enterprises, the primary committee may set up subordinate committees at the workshop level and trade union groups on the basis of production or office units. Trade union groups elect their own leaders, while the primary committees are elected by general meetings of members or by congresses of members' representatives.[16] The creation of such small branches facilitates frequent meetings, direct personal contact between leaders and ordinary members, and the existence of a trade union organization in even the smallest production unit. It also requires the services of large numbers of activists who are regular workers, rather than full-time trade union cadres, but who engage in official union work in their off-duty hours. In 1957, there were almost four million such activists, about 30 percent of the national trade union membership.[17]

Finally, all the major mass organizations perform the same general function in the Chinese political system. They are the Party's "transmission belts," as the Soviet writers say, or the "essential ties with which

[15] See Art. 28 of the revised "Constitution of the Trade Unions of China," adopted at the Eighth All-China Federation of Trade Unions Congress in December, 1957, in *CB*, No. 484 (December 19, 1957). In the previous constitution, 25 members were needed to set up a primary committee. Where there are fewer than the minimum, the union members may join the nearest primary trade union organization.

[16] *Ibid.*

[17] Hsu Chih-chen, "Report on the Revision of the Constitution of the Trade Unions of China," in *CB*, No. 484.

the Party links itself to the masses." Through its control over the mass organizations, the Party produces the popular support of policies that the mass line demands. "Outside the state structure, the Party also organizes the strength of the masses in support of the work of the state structure in order to guarantee the realization of state tasks. Through the trade unions, the Youth League, the Women's Federation, the cooperatives and other mass organizations, the Party produces intimate ties with the working class and broad masses, organizing and mobilizing them to respond to the call of the state structure." [18] While Party statements on the mobilization function of mass organizations are usually quite vague, the constitutions and major statements by leading figures of these organizations leave no doubt about the specific actions and attitudes that they are expected to produce. Thus, Article II of the Constitution of the Students' Federation defines the tasks of the Federation as follows:

Under the leadership of the Chinese Communist Party, to unite the students throughout the country, in enthusiastic response to Chairman Mao's call "to have good health, to study well, and to work properly"; to thoroughly implement the party's policy of "letting education serve the political interests of the proletariat, and combining education with productive labor"; to make efforts to cultivate ourselves to be both red and expert intellectuals of the working class, so as to struggle to build China into a great and strong Socialist country with highly developed modern industry, modern agriculture, and modern science and culture; to strengthen the unity with the students of Socialist countries; to develop friendship and cooperation with the students of various countries; to support the struggle against imperialism and colonialism, so as to exert efforts for the cause of bringing about a lasting peace and the progress of mankind.[19]

The specific tasks of different mass organizations vary with the policies that apply to the particular segment of the population for which they are responsible, but the general function is always the same. They are to serve, as one writer has said of the trade unions, as "the honest executors of the lines, guiding principles, and policies of the Party."[20]

Since the primary function of the mass organizations is clearly similar to that of basic-level government, one might ask whether or not these organizations duplicate or even replace the lower levels of the state structure. The answer is that the combination of mass organizations, urban street organization, and rural production units has largely re-

[18] Chou Fang, ed., *Wo-kuo Kuo-chia Chi-kou* (Our State Structure) (rev., Peking, 1957), p. 58.

[19] NCNA, February 10, 1960, in Leo A. Orleans, *Professional Manpower and Education in Communist China* (Washington, 1961), Appendix H.

[20] Ku Ta-ch'un, "A Trade Union Must Take the Initiative and Active Step to Play the Part of a Good Lieutenant to the Party," *Chung-kuo Kung-jen* (China Worker), 1959, No. 19, in *SMM*, No. 198 (February 1, 1960).

placed basic-level government as the effective location for mass political mobilization and participation, but that significant differences between the mass organizations and the governmental structure remain. The essential difference is that the mass organizations are continually engaged in educating and mobilizing their members so that every individual will take part in the execution of Party policies, whereas basic-level government must devote most of its energies to handling the administrative tasks imposed by higher-level ministries and governments. The state structure encourages mass participation and mobilization through congresses and elections, but the earlier analysis of these activities indicates that they are more effective as symbolic political participation than as constant and thorough means of mass mobilization.

At the same time, mass organizations do assume some administrative responsibilities. The peasants' associations, which will be discussed briefly in a later section, were the "legal executive organizations" for carrying out land reform.[21] The Women's Federation, through its participation in legal proceedings and its own investigations and mediation, has assumed a major share of responsibility for administering the Marriage Law. The trade unions also carry out certain administrative functions, notably as the basic units for the administration of the Chinese labor insurance program.[22] The "employees' and workers' congresses" (chih-kung tai-piao ta-hui) might be mentioned in this context since they are referred to as a form of popular participation in administration even though they have little genuine authority. These congresses are representative bodies set up in state enterprises after 1956 to discuss and make proposals on the management of production and workers' welfare in their respective enterprises. Although not technically trade union organs, they operate under trade union sponsorship and leadership. According to one account, they can hear and discuss work reports of the factory director; examine and discuss enterprise plans for production, finances, technology, and wages; and examine and discuss expenses for bonuses, welfare, labor insurance, and trade union operating expenses.[23] The employees' and workers' congresses are clearly consultative bodies rather than administrative agencies, but they do reflect trade union attempts to encourage mass participation in enterprise management.

---

[21] The Agrarian Reform Law of the People's Republic of China, Art. 29.

[22] See Arts. 25–29 of the "Labour Insurance Regulations of the People's Republic of China," in Labour Laws and Regulations of the People's Republic of China (Peking, 1956).

[23] Li Jun-chih, "Kuan-yü Kuo-ying Ch'i-yeh Chung ti Chih-kung Tai-piao Ta-hui Chih-tu" (The Employees' and Workers' Congress System in State Enterprises), Hung Ch'i, 1962, No. 2, pp. 33–37.

The discussion thus far has omitted any reference to the representative function of the mass organizations. On paper, these organizations are responsible for defending the interests of their members and making their wishes known to higher authorities. For example, Article VII of the Trade Union Law states: "It is the duty of trade unions to protect the interests of workers and staff members, to ensure that the managements, or the owners of private enterprises, effectively carry out labour protection, labour insurance, wage standards, factory sanitation and safety measures as stipulated in the laws and decrees of the government and other relevant regulations and directives, and to take measures for improving the material and cultural life of the workers and staff members."[24] Among the revisions in the new trade union constitution adopted in 1957 was the stipulation that trade union members had the legal right to "demand protection and support from trade unions when the material interests and democratic rights of trade union members are being infringed upon as a result of violation of the state policy and law by enterprises, government organs and schools."[25] There is no question that the mass organizations are technically responsible for representing their members' interests and that, from time to time, efforts are made to tighten this responsibility. However, because of the supremacy of the collective interest in China, the mass organizations devote more attention in both theory and practice to organizational support of Party policies than to members' interests.

Defense of members' interests has been a prominent issue only in women's and trade union organization. The Women's Federation has been the most consistently outspoken of all mass organizations in asserting the rights and aspirations of its membership. However, this assertiveness is not due to greater independence or concern with the masses but rather to the fact that women are perhaps the only "underprivileged" group in China in the eyes of the CCP. As one women's leader has pointed out, ideas held over from the "old society" still cause disdain and discrimination against women in schools, employment, government, and various aspects of marriage and family life; therefore, women need an organization that will ". . . unite their forces, give expression to their aspirations, protect their rights and interests and those of their children, and supervise the implementation of the policy and decrees regarding the equality of men and women."[26] Since Party leaders agree with these opinions, the Women's Federation has been able to push the interests of its members in a way that other organizations have not. For

[24] *Labour Laws and Regulations of the People's Republic of China.*

[25] Hsu Chih-chen, *op. cit.*

[26] "Speech by Comrade Teng Ying-chao," *Eighth National Congress of the Communist Party of China,* II (Speeches), pp. 227–229, 234.

example, in the 1953–1954 elections a leading cadre of the federation openly urged all women to nominate and elect female candidates in order to demonstrate female equality and better protect women's interests.[27]

The trade union debate over workers' interests has been much more complex. On the one hand, there have been consistent complaints from the workers and even from high-ranking union officials that the trade unions have sacrificed workers' interests in their efforts to maintain industrial harmony and increase production. These complaints have undoubtedly been encouraged by high expectations about labor's position in a socialist society and by the Party's reluctance to stifle mass initiative in the proletarian ranks. On the other hand, the Party has insisted that workers' interests cannot take precedence over national interests. It has acknowledged that some trade union cadres and organizations have failed to represent the workers and that the unions must improve in this respect, but it has also branded as "economism" or "trade unionism" all attempts to use the unions as political weapons in the defense of workers' interests. Without going into detail, we can say that the trade unions have shown tendencies toward greater representation of their members' interests but that all of these tendencies have been checked and heavily criticized.[28]

In summary, the mass organizations are the CCP's primary assistants in transmitting Party policies to the mass level. In the process of mobilizing their members for political action, they provide much greater opportunities for popular political participation than does the state structure. Although they have suffered from their general inability to advance the interests of their members and from the effects of excessive centralization and Party control, they have nonetheless been relatively successful in making the mass line a reality. The mass organizations have been particularly useful in organizing the urban population through the trade unions, the Students' Federation, and the various intellectual, professional, and technical associations. Moreover, through the Youth League and the Women's Federation, they bring large numbers of youth and women, in both urban and rural areas, into organized political life. Nevertheless, the majority of peasants and urban housewives do not belong to any of the major mass organizations. These critical gaps in the Party's organizational network are filled by "residents' committees"

[27] Li Ch'i-yang, "Tung-yüan Fu-nü Ch'ün-chung Chi-chi Ts'an-chia P'u-hsüan Yün-tung" (Mobilize the Masses of Women for Active Participation in the General Election Movement), *JMJP*, June 9, 1953.

[28] Cf. Lai Jo-yu's speeches at the Eighth Party Congress and the Eighth Trade Union Congress, cited in chap. Four. See *Union Research Service*, Vol. 8, No. 12 (August 9, 1957) for a collection of documents criticizing trade union neglect of workers' interests; the criticism is taken from basic-level cadre conferences held throughout China during the "hundred flowers" period.

(*chü-min wei-yüan-hui*) in the cities and basic production units in the countryside. The last two sections of this chapter will consider the role these units play in mass political participation.

RESIDENTS' COMMITTEES

The CCP's policy on urban administration changed several times in the first few years of the regime. Immediately after "liberation," there was a proliferation of urban administrative units with many cities establishing governments at street, *ch'ü,* and municipal levels. The Party soon decided that this "fragmentation of power" was harmful and ordered the abolition of street government and the reduction of *ch'ü* government structure and powers. By the middle of 1950, however, the desire to maintain closer contacts with the urban population resulted in the establishment of *ch'ü* people's representative conferences and a new expansion of *ch'ü* government, but with the warning that *ch'ü* government should not become "independent" and that street government should not be reestablished.[29] During the next few years, *ch'ü* government became the basic level of state power in the cities. At the same time, a great variety of organizations and committees sprang up at the street level to cope with problems of urban security and welfare and with demands for mass mobilization imposed by the great political campaigns of the early 1950's. The CCP never retracted its prohibition against street government as such, but it recognized that the existing structure of government and mass organizations could not reach the housewives, children, street merchants (hawkers), and unemployed who did not belong to any of the major urban organizations. After a substantial amount of experimentation, the Party ultimately proposed regulations for residents' committees and street offices in 1954.[30] We should remember that these units have always aimed primarily at the organization and mobilization of urban housewives and other politically isolated groups.

From 1950 on, there were scattered reports of the emergence of "residents' small groups" and residents' committees in various Chinese cities, but the main experiments took place in Shanghai and Tientsin. In Shanghai, the residents' committees grew out of street associations for security, welfare, and mutual aid, some organized by basic-level government and some by the residents themselves. By the latter part of 1951, over 80 percent of Shanghai residents were involved in these associa-

[29] "Ta Ch'eng-shih Min-chu Cheng-ch'üan ti Hsin Chien-she" (New Construction of Democratic Political Power in the Large Cities), *JMJP,* editorial, May 16, 1950.

[30] Street offices (*chieh-tao pan-shih-ch'u*) are administrative branch offices of basic-level urban government.

tions, which were renamed residents' committees and used to carry out the Resist America–Aid Korea and Suppression of Counterrevolutionaries campaigns as well as to handle welfare problems at the street level.[31] Work in Tientsin proceeded more slowly but more systematically. In November, 1952, Tientsin announced its "provisional methods" for establishing residents' committees.[32] According to these regulations, residents' committees would be based on "natural residential conditions and social relations" and would range from a hundred and fifty to five hundred families in size. Residents' small groups of ten to thirty households would be formed within each committee area; each small group would select a representative and these representatives in turn would elect the residents' committee. Committees were under the leadership and supervision of the *ch'ü* government, and were responsible for propagandizing government policies and orders among the people, reflecting residents' views to higher levels, and carrying out a variety of security, welfare, and mediation functions. These regulations formed the model for the national regulations later adopted.

By December, 1954, according to a report from the Ministry of Internal Affairs, experimentation with street organization in over eighty cities had demonstrated the value of residents' committees and street offices.[33] The report stated that the major value of such organization was that it reduced excessive confusion and duplication in work at the street level. It cited cases in which the establishment of residents' committees had reduced the number of street organizations from twenty to three and the number of activists' meetings per month from twenty to four. There is no reason to doubt this argument as duplication of organization and overworking of activists was, and has remained, a serious problem for the CCP. Where street organization had already sprung up in response to Party and popular needs, residents' committees and street offices merely simplified existing organization and provided a more systematic way of recruiting additional activists. However, there were also areas in which organizational efforts lagged behind, and in these areas the establishment of residents' committees was a fresh Party effort to extend its control and contact among the masses.

The Standing Committee of the NPC passed regulations governing the organization of urban residents' committees and street offices on December 31, 1954.[34] Residents' committees, defined as "organizations of a mass self-governing character," could be established under the leader-

[31] See *Chieh-fang Jih-pao* (Shanghai), May 28, 1951, and *Ta Kung Pao* (Impartial News) (Hong Kong), November 5, 1951.

[32] *Chin-pu Jih-pao* (Progressive Daily) (Tientsin), November 28, 1952.

[33] *JMJP*, December 6, 1954.

[34] Text of these regulations is in *JMJP*, January 1, 1955.

ship of a basic-level urban government or its authorized organizations (i.e., street offices) to "strengthen organizational work among urban street residents and to advance residents' public welfare." Their specific tasks were as follows: "(1) to manage items concerned with the public welfare of residents; (2) to reflect the opinions and demands of residents to the local people's council or its subordinate organization; (3) to mobilize the residents to respond to government appeals and to respect the law; (4) to lead public security and protection work of a mass character; (5) to reconcile disputes among the residents." A committee area would include one hundred to six hundred households, which could be divided into residents' small groups of fifteen to forty households each, but no committee was to establish more than seventeen small groups. The residents' committee itself would consist of seven to seventeen members, with one member elected from each small group; each small group would also elect a group leader who would normally serve as the group's representative on the residents' committee. Members of the committee would divide responsibility among themselves for the committee's work, but additional activists could be recruited to serve on work committees if the work load was heavy. So far as possible, no one would have more than one job.

According to the regulations, units such as state organs, schools, and large enterprises would not participate in the residents' committees but were to send delegates to meetings that concerned them and respect the committees' decisions on residents' welfare. Miscellaneous expenses of the committees and supplementary living allowances for their members would be provided by local government, but public welfare funds were to be raised by "voluntary collections and contributions" from the residents. In all of their activities, committees were to develop "democracy and mass voluntarism" through democratic centralism and to avoid compulsion or commandism. In most cases, urban street offices provided immediate leadership for the committees. Street offices could be established by basic-level people's councils specifically to direct residents' committee work in accordance with council directives and to keep the councils informed of residents' opinions and demands. They were to have a chairman, several secretaries, and three to seven cadres for specialized work, all appointed by the basic-level people's council.

The establishment or reorganization of residents' committees moved ahead rapidly after the issuance of these regulations. By August, 1955, 129 cities, or 80 percent of those expected to set up the new street organizations, had established residents' committees.[35] As might be expected, residents' committees and small groups received greatest pub-

[35] *KMJP,* August 9, 1955.

licity in 1954–1955 but they also played a major role in the rectification campaign of 1957–1958 and in organizing urban residents for productive activities in the early stages of the Great Leap Forward. However, Party experimentation with urban communes after 1958 greatly confused the general picture of urban street organization. Up until the latter part of 1960, it appeared that urban communes would drastically alter the existing structure of urban government by merging political and economic organization, much as rural communes had done in the countryside. For example, one writer stated:

> The street office is no longer simply an organ for the management of administrative affairs. . . . [It] has become an organ for the organization, leadership and management of street production; it has become the unifier and organizer for production, exchange, distribution and welfare among street residents; it is in the process of gradually becoming a basic level organization for the unification of political and economic affairs and is gradually taking shape as a unit which combines urban basic level political power with mass organization of the street residents.[36]

Nevertheless, the old governmental structure remained in spite of many such statements implying that new politico-economic units would emerge at the basic level of urban government. By 1961, it was evident that the urban commune movement was coming to a standstill and that most communes had existed only on paper.[37]

The residents' committees themselves never actually disappeared, even at the height of the urban commune movement in 1960. They remained intact in those areas where communes were not established, and some of them apparently became subordinate units (perhaps under different names, such as urban production "teams" or "brigades") in those urban communes that were established. The committees certainly changed in character in 1958–1961 when they devoted nearly all their energies to small-scale production and the management of public mess-halls. However, scattered reports since 1961 indicate that they are continuing their welfare activities and that the attempt to transform them into "street enterprises" or branches of larger economic units has been dropped.

The regulations on residents' committees suggest that these committees have two main functions: (1) to provide greater direction and organization of urban residents in order to secure their active support of Party policies and state directives; (2) to resolve as many community problems as possible at the street level, thereby reducing demands on the energies and financial resources of formal government. To carry out

[36] Kuan Ta-t'ung, "Ch'eng-shih Chieh-tao Chü-min Kung-tso ti Yüeh-chin" (Leap Forward in Urban Street Residents Work), *Hung Ch'i*, 1960, No. 1, p. 31.
[37] See Henry J. Lethbridge, *China's Urban Communes* (Hong Kong, 1961).

these primary functions, the committees aim at a high degree of internal
"democracy" and participation. A brief discussion of each of these
points will illustrate the role of the committees in popular political
activities.

The most important of these functions is to organize mass support for
Party policies. In general terms, the committees have carried it out by
transmitting directives downward to every household and by organizing
the masses for political study. Almost every committee has its newspaper reading groups, street bulletin-boards, and general meetings to keep
the residents informed on current policies and tasks. Mass movements,
such as the rectification campaign of 1957–1958, increase the intensity
of political education by transforming the residents' small groups into
forums for ideological discussion and indoctrination. Constant exposure
to political education and propaganda provides the foundation for the
execution of Party policies at the street level.

More concretely, the residents' committees have devoted particular
efforts to securing mass participation in two major programs. The first
of these was strengthening public-security work in the cities. As noted
earlier, the Suppression of Counterrevolutionaries movement was an
important factor in the Party's desire for tighter street organization
before the adoption of the 1954 regulations. In an editorial discussing
these regulations, Jen-min Jih-pao placed great emphasis on the fact that
urban growth had greatly complicated problems of control in the cities
and that the residents' committees could aid in ferreting out counterrevolutionaries and controlling illegal behavior; is also suggested that the
committee's assumption of welfare functions, many of which public-
security organs had been handling, would leave these organs free for
more effective security work.[38] This concern faded after 1955, although
it never disappeared, and was replaced by the demand to mobilize
surplus urban manpower for productive purposes. Pressure to organize
residents for production had been evident from the first, but it became
the major task of the residents' committees in 1957–1958. In 1957,
committees began recruiting urban residents for work in the countryside,
and this was followed in 1958 by the organization of housewives into the
street production and service groups that led directly to the urban
commune movement. Under such slogans as "change consumers to
producers" and "change individual household duties to collective labor,"
the residents' committees took the lead in mobilizing housewives for the
Great Leap Forward. Street offices and Party members within the
committee area provided the leadership for mobilizing residents on

[38] "Kai-chin Ch'eng-shih Chi-ts'eng Cheng-ch'üan Kung-tso ti Chung-yao Ts'o-
shih" (Important Measures for Advancing Basic Level Political Power in the
Cities), JMJP, editorial, January 2, 1955.

specified projects. The Party general branch at the street level provides overall leadership on current work projects, deciding which programs will be emphasized, when and how political study will be organized, and so forth. Individual Party members are responsible for maintaining contact with activists within the residents' committees, thereby ensuring committee action on Party goals, and for testing and raising mass political consciousness. The street offices handle more specific tasks by calling regular meetings of committee chairmen, passing on assignments for day-to-day work, and disposing of problems that the committees are unable to solve by themselves.[39]

The governmental function of the residents' committee (i.e., attending to various minor problems of its people) is definitely subordinate to the more general goal of political education and mobilization. *Jen-min Jih-pao* has made it quite clear that the committees' governmental activities are expected to benefit socialist and economic construction.[40] Nevertheless, the committees' ability to solve some of the daily problems of urban residents, even when the solutions are linked up with broader Party goals, adds to its significance as a unit for mass political participation. Specifically, residents' committees manage some or all of the following tasks in their areas of jurisdiction: welfare—preferably finding or creating minor employment for the unemployed and needy rather than dispensing funds; health and sanitation—organizing "antipest" campaigns, inspecting and installing toilet facilities, disposing of manure, and organizing neighborhood sweeping and cleaning details on a rotation basis; mediation—resolving disputes among neighbors and married couples; cooperative services—organizing nurseries, kindergartens, playgrounds, clothing repair teams, and mess halls; minor administrative tasks —assisting in rationing administration and the collection of rents and utilities payments.[41] Of course, basic-level Party and state organs guide and encourage the committees in these tasks on the grounds that healthy, harmonious neighborhood life reduces labor absenteeism and raises popular morale, that service activities free more hands for "productive labor," and even that nurseries, playgrounds, and other group activities provide education in the "superiority of collective life." Whatever the Party attitude might be, however, the residents and their repre-

---

[39] See the report on daily street office work in Canton in *Kuang-chou Jih-pao* (Canton Daily), March 2, 1957, and a report on Wuhan street organization by Chang Wei, "Min-tsu-chieh Ju-ho Fa-hui Tang ti Ling-tao Tso-yung" (How Mintsu Street Brought Out the Party's Leading Role), *JMJP*, August 8, 1958.

[40] "Kai-chin Ch'eng-shih Chi-ts'eng Cheng-ch'üan Kung-tso ti Chung-yao Ts'o-shih," *op. cit.*

[41] For illustrations of these activities, see *T'ien-chin Jih-pao* (Tientsin Daily), November 19, 1952; *KMJP*, March 6, 1955; *Ch'ang-chiang Jih-pao*, May 6, 1955; and *South China Morning Post* (Hong Kong), November 13, 1961.

sentatives do participate in some of the decisions and nearly all of the management on such neighborhood projects.

The preceding point raises the question of "democracy" in residents' committee work. There is no doubt that the numerous responsibilities and small size of the committees encourage extensive mass participation. To cite just one example, a street area in Tientsin embracing 2,957 households (divided into seven residents' committees) had a total of 1,072 committee members, committee workers, and other activists, or more than one activist from every three households.[42] The recruitment of such large numbers of residents to take part in managing neighborhood affairs guarantees a certain amount of public discussion and debate on those matters that are left to neighborhood decision. However, the election of residents' committee members does not mean that the committees are democratic, self-governing units in a fuller sense. Elections are held without any sign of the Party-determined lists that prevail in basic-level congressional elections, but their importance is minimal. Regulations demanding yearly re-election are sometimes disregarded and there is little meaningful debate over who will serve on the committees; as in basic-level elections, reelection of incumbents after token criticism is the general rule. In all probability, the major problem is simply finding enough people who are willing to serve. Given the relatively low level of political consciousness among urban housewives, willingness to serve is in itself sufficient "activism" to secure Party acceptance. In any case, close supervision by street-office and Party cadres sharply limits the political importance of these positions.[43] "Democracy" in the residents' committee, then, is largely a matter of natural informality and equality in such a small unit and widespread popular participation in managing certain internal affairs. It is not popular control of officials who hold genuine authority and can represent the residents at higher levels.

The greatest weakness of the residents' committees has been precisely this absence of authoritative leadership within the committee itself. In some cases, residents living in a committee area but working outside it have resisted committee proposals on sanitation, fund collections, and attendance at meetings. Moreover, real control over committee affairs has remained in the hands of street-office and Party cadres who are still overworked in spite of all the activists recruited within the committee.[44]

[42] T'ien-chin Jih-pao, May 16, 1953.

[43] Sample reports on such elections can be found in Hsin Wan-pao (New Evening News) (Tientsin), June 30, 1956, editorial, and July 4, 1956; (Kuang-chou Jih-pao, December 14, 1956; Chang-chia-k'ou Jih-pao (Kalgan Daily) (Kalgan), May 11, 1957.

[44] See the comments on these problems in Chieh-fang Jih-pao, June 24, 1956, and Kuang-chou Jih-pao, December 12, 1956.

Nevertheless, these problems do not nullify the committees' usefulness. They have served remarkably well as organizations for mobilizing urban housewives in support of Party policies. They have encouraged urban residents to participate actively in neighborhood affairs, but always within the limits of the Party's general policies and without lessening higher-level control over the more important matters. As a result, the committee is always subject to control and interference from above, while the residents' political activities are focused mainly on their own small unit without any significant upward influence or contacts.

RURAL PRODUCTION UNITS

In rural areas as in the cities, the CCP has created small-scale units beneath the basic level of government that have become the focal points for popular political activities. In the cities, such units include the residents' committees based on neighborhood groupings, the enterprise trade union organizations, the students' groups in schools or classes within the schools, and the local branches of various mass organizations that do not have a common place of work, study or residence. The rural counterpart of these units is the basic agricultural production unit, currently the production team within the rural people's commune. Since the production team did not emerge until 1958–1959, at least in name, a brief look at its forerunners is in order.

Basic-level rural government has relied upon other forms of rural organization for assistance in mobilizing the peasants for political action ever since the CCP came to power in 1949. From 1949 until the completion of land reform, the peasants' associations provided this assistance. The peasants' associations were "mass organizations of peasants formed on a voluntary basis," drawing their membership from all "antifeudal" rural strata except the rich peasants.[45] Although regulations called for ascending levels of organization up to the provincial level, the *hsiang* peasant association was in fact the most important unit. Coordination of peasant association policy came through basic-level government and Party organs rather than the higher levels of peasant organization. The primary purpose of the peasants' associations was to organize and educate the peasants in preparation for land reform and to serve as the "legal organs" for this reform. However, in keeping with Party theory, they were also to defend the peasants' interests, unite the peasants for various antifeudal social reforms, organize the peasants for production, and raise the peasants' political and cultural level.[46]

[45] See "General Regulations Governing the Organization of Peasants' Associations," Arts. 1, 4, in *The Agrarian Reform Law of the People's Republic of China.* Rich peasants could apply for membership after the completion of land reform.

[46] *Ibid.,* Arts. 3–4.

Party members and peasant activists led in organizing the peasants' associations and guiding them through the land reform program, but the associations' influence on peasant political life was still profound. Although the CCP opposed "spontaneous" peasant action, there were simply not enough rural Party cadres in the early years to supervise adequately the staffing and operation of the associations. As a result, the peasants sometimes had a significant control over the election and removal of peasant leaders, and peasant meetings were generally quite open to expression of popular opinions. This is not to say that peasants' associations were totally independent, except in isolated cases, or that the peasants as a whole took full advantage of their new political opportunities. Nevertheless, the fact that the associations did provide new opportunities for peasant political action was, and is, of great importance. A large proportion of rural cadres in China today emerged as activists or cadres during land reform. For the most part, these new rural elites are poor or lower middle peasants who may now be Party members but who nonetheless gained their credentials in the course of a populist upheaval that was deeply intertwined with long-standing peasant aspirations. It may be that much of the CCP's difficulty in leading the peasants into cooperatives and communes stems from the fact that many of its trusted rural cadres are products of the land reform period. In any case, the activities of the peasants' associations symbolized, perhaps better than any other events or actions, the fundamental change that the CCP was trying to make in the political life of the Chinese people.

The peasants' associations disintegrated after the completion of land reform and the consolidation of the new political structure. For a few years, roughly 1953–1955, *hsiang* people's congresses and councils were the centers of rural political participation, although they still relied on elected leaders in the villages for grass-roots contacts. The vitality of *hsiang* government at this time was due to its relative smallness and simplicity. With a rural population of approximately 110 million households and a total of 220,000 *hsiang,* each *hsiang* averaged only 500 households. Moreover, the early forms of agricultural production units were not sufficiently complex to demand governments of their own. Mutual-aid teams and the early agricultural producers' cooperatives (APC's) organized regular political education and frequent meetings of members to discuss organizational affairs, but did not need any particular management structure.[47] In any case, neither the mutual-aid teams nor the early APC's ever approached total membership among the

---

[47] See the CCP Central Committee's "Decisions on Mutual Aid and Cooperation in Agricultural Production" in *People's China,* July 1, 1953 (Supplement), and "Decisions on the Development of Agricultural Producers' Cooperatives" in *People's China,* April 1, 1954 (Supplement).

peasant population; even in 1955, only about 15 percent of peasant households belonged to APC's.[48]

The "high tide" of cooperativization in the latter half of 1955 and throughout 1956, in which virtually all peasants joined the new "higher" APC's by the end of 1956, radically changed this picture. The higher APC was a self-governing economic unit organized under the "leadership and assistance of the CCP and the People's Government" and guided by the state economic plan. In addition to organizing collective agricultural production, it exercised a wide range of political, cultural, welfare, and recreational functions that made it, in effect, a governmental unit.[49] The extent of the higher APC's controls over and services to its members demanded a relatively complex management structure. According to regulations, this structure was democratic and totally independent of basic-level government. In fact, Party influence within the APC prohibited real democracy or independence, but the provisions for mass participation in the management structure are of interest in this discussion. The general meeting of members (or members' representative congress in large cooperatives) was to meet at least twice a year to carry out an impressive list of powers, including the following: adoption and amendment of the APC charter; election and removal of the APC director, vice directors, management committee, and supervisory committee; examination and approval of the production plans, budgets, income distribution plans, and reports presented by the management committee; decisions on new members and on awards and penalties to members.[50] There is no evidence that cooperative members or representatives exercised these powers in a real sense any more than basic-level congresses have exercised theirs. The point, however, is that APC regulations provided for total membership participation in these ritualistic meetings or delegate participation at the ratio of one representative for every ten members in all but the largest APC's. Thus, the member's contact with APC management was much closer than his contact with basic-level government.

The organizational aspect of the higher APC had a greater impact on popular political activity than did its management structure. Article XXX of the "Model Regulations" specified that the APC's should be divided into production brigades (*sheng-ch'an tui*), of fixed membership and work area, that would serve as the basic units of labor organization within the cooperatives. Since the brigades were natural residential and

[48] See Chao Kuo-chün, *Agrarian Policy of the Chinese Communist Party,* Table 1, p. 293.

[49] "Kao-chi Nung-yeh Sheng-ch'an Ho-tso-she Shih-fan Chang-ch'eng" (Model Regulations for the Higher Agricultural Producers' Cooperatives) in *1957 Jen-min Shou-ts'e,* pp. 173–179.

[50] *Ibid.,* Arts. 56–57.

work units based on clusters of houses or small villages (although the regulations did not so state), they gave the APC's a solid organizational base in the village that greatly facilitated both economic and political mobilization. The economic aspects of collectivization were probably uppermost in the minds of the Chinese Communist leaders in 1955–1956, but they took full advantage of the new and more thorough rural organization to mobilize the peasants in the CCP style of political participation. The "Model Regulations" specified, in Articles XLV–L, that the Party, the government, the Youth League, and the Women's Federation should guide political work in the APC's; that the objective of political work was to guarantee the completion of production plans, the diligent and thrifty management of the cooperative, the "correct integration of collective and state interests with the individual interests of members," and the ideological and organizational consolidation of the cooperative; that the APC's should use spare time to educate members in current affairs, Party and state policies and laws, and the spirit of patriotism and collectivism; that the APC's should constantly raise the socialist consciousness of their members and overcome the ideological remnants of capitalism; that the APC's should promote democracy, oppose commandism and bureaucratism, encourage criticism and self-criticism, and strengthen unity among members and between leaders and members; that the APC's should raise the "revolutionary vigilance" of members and strengthen internal security work. It is difficult to find a clearer statement of the scope and objectives of political participation in China.

The CCP was apparently reluctant to see the higher APC's displace *hsiang* political structure and was genuinely concerned about the possible development of APC autonomy. In the summer of 1956, one writer stressed that *hsiang* government must continue as the basic political and administrative unit; he argued that even though the cooperatives "seem to be the political, economic and cultural center of their members' lives," they were "only collective economic organizations for the laboring peasants" that could not replace basic-level government.[51] A few months later, a joint directive of the State Council and the CCP Central Committee expressed more specific concern about APC autonomy by insisting that basic-level state and Party organs vigorously assert their leadership over the villages.[52] However, after some efforts to limit the

[51] Hsieh Ch'iu-lun, "I-ching Ho-tso-hua ti Hsiang, Shih-fou Hai Hsü-yao Hsiang I-chi Cheng-ch'üan Tsu-chih?" (Is Hsiang Level Political Organization Still Necessary When Cooperativization Is Completed?) *Hsüeh-hsi* (Study), August 2, 1956.

[52] "Kuan-yü Chia-ch'iang Nung-yeh Sheng-ch'an Ho-tso-she ti Sheng-ch'an Ling-tao ho Tsu-chih Chien-she ti Chih-shih" (Directive on Strengthening Production Leadership and Organizational Construction in the Agricultural Producers' Cooperatives), *Chieh-fang Jih-pao,* September 13, 1956.

further expansion of rural economic organization,[53] the Party pushed on to the formation of the rural communes in the summer of 1958. With the emergence of the communes, as the discussion in chapter V has indicated, the Party formally accepted the principle of the integration of basic-level government and rural economic organization. From the peasants' point of view, however, this was simply acknowledgement of an accomplished fact. Party protestations about the continuing functions of basic-level government notwithstanding, village political life had become increasingly isolated from *hsiang* government ever since about 1954. Once the principle of *cheng-she ho-i* was accepted, a group of Peking University scholars admitted that the early cooperatives had taken over some village political functions as early as 1953 and that the advent of the higher APC's in 1955 had reduced *hsiang* functions to general coordination of the cooperatives while the cooperatives themselves assumed all responsibility for village administration.[54]

After about a year of experimentation, the rural communes settled into the three-level management system that has continued up to the present. The three levels are the commune (*jen-min kung-she*), the production brigade (*sheng-ch'an ta-tui*) and the production team (*sheng-ch'an tui*). In 1959, the then 24,000 communes were divided into some 500,000 production brigades of 200 to 300 households each, which were in turn divided into roughly three million production teams averaging 40 households each.[55] Since chapter Five has discussed the sterility of popular participation in the upper levels of commune management, our attention here will focus on the production team.

In most cases, the production team is simply a continuation of the APC production brigade within a larger economic organization. Although its average size was initially somewhat larger than the suggested twenty households for APC brigades, reductions in team size in 1961–1962 brought many down to twenty or thirty households each. Whatever the exact size, the production team is clearly based on the rural village or on natural residential groupings within the village. From the

[53] A Central Committee directive on APC rectification in September, 1957 stated that one cooperative per village with production brigades of about twenty households was a suitable norm; text in *JMJP*, September 16, 1957.

[54] "Ts'ung Huang-ts'un Jen-min Kung-she ti Chien-li K'an Cheng-she Ho-i ti Li-shih Pi-jan-hsiang" (The Historical Necessity of the Integration of Government and Commune Administration as Seen in the Establishment of Huangts'un Commune), *Hsin Chien-she* (New Construction), August 7, 1959.

[55] *JMJP*, August 29, 1959. None of these figures hold true today. Following the subdivision of rural communes into 75,000 units, some production brigades were also subdivided to give a total of over 700,000 brigades; see G. William Skinner, "Marketing and Social Structure in Rural China," Part III, *Journal of Asian Studies*, 24:3 (May, 1965), p. 399. Changes in the number of production teams are noted below.

first, the team served as the basic unit of labor organization within the communes. During the retrenchment of 1961–1962, it also became the commune's "basic accounting unit" in matters of production and distribution, with considerable freedom from higher commune levels in management of its own affairs.

Production team affairs are administered by an elected team management committee of about five to seven members, some or all of whom may also serve as team representatives to the brigade congress. A team will also have a few "work groups" of fixed or fluctuating membership, each with its own group leader, for major labor assignments within the team. Team "autonomy" does not mean independence from Party leadership. Most teams will have at least a few Party members who occupy the key positions. But whether team leaders are Party members or not, they will be in close touch with Party organs which will make sure that team management is conforming to Party policies and directives. Party influence also extends directly into the team and down to every member through the operation of "leadership cores." A leadership core consists of one or more Party members and activists who recruit additional activists to form a network of direct contacts with everyone in the unit in question. The Party establishes leadership cores in the team itself, in all work groups, and among the various age, sex, and occupational groupings within the team. Through these core leaders, who are guided in their work and political "study" by the Party, the CCP supplements supervision over the management committee with direct access to every individual in the team.[56]

Political participation within the production team is roughly comparable to that within the residents' committee. Team members do have some formal political powers, such as election of the management committee and discussion of major team affairs in general members' meetings, but these activities are not significant mechanisms of popular influence as the issues have normally been settled in advance. Nevertheless, members do influence team decisions to some extent through a variety of informal contacts with their leaders. The leaders arrange some of these contacts by regular consultation with old peasants, periodic visits to members' homes, or special hours when they are available for discussion with members. Prearranged discussion is not necessary, however, in a unit of only one hundred to two hundred people who work and live together and have done so, in most cases, for all their lives. The production team can never embark on a plan of action that violates

---

[56] See Lewis, *Leadership in Communist China*, pp. 232–243, and the materials cited therein, for more detail and analysis on Party leadership within the production team. For reports on "leadership cores," see *JMJP*, August 27, 1960, and November 13, 1960.

Party wishes, but in carrying out its responsibilities for production and the livelihood of its members it tends to make its decisions by collective discussion and debate. For example, popular discussion is common on such matters as assignment of labor quotas within the team; how to make the best use of the team's land; when crops should be planted and harvested and how growing or stored crops should be protected; how the team's manure supply should be collected and distributed; and how team funds should be spent in the repair of roads, buildings, ditches, fields, and bridges within the team's area.[57] In the intimate atmosphere of the village, team leaders cannot avoid a sense of responsibility to popular wishes on these matters.

Like all forms of organization in China, the production team also devotes great efforts to mobilizing its members behind Party policies. The responsibility for this task falls mainly on the "leadership cores"—the members of Party, youth, and women's organizations, as well as other activists, who work with specific segments of the team's population. Through field meetings, informal conversations during rest periods and after work hours, evening lectures, newspaper reading groups, and so forth, they pass on the Party line, try to translate it into meaningful terms for the vlilagers, and exhort all members to put it into practice. Much of this political education obviously involves little action or response by the members. Mobilization occurs only when the peasants are roused to attack a particular object (which might be a person, a work project, or "erroneous" ideology) or when the ordinary conduct of team affairs is invested with political significance. In the latter case, the Party's insistence that the team's management of a particular matter is part of a national struggle for socialist construction transforms the most ordinary human behavior into political action.

Membership in production teams is, in effect, compulsory for all peasants, or roughly 80 percent of the Chinese population. Moreover, unlike the residents' committees, production teams do not face the problem of members whose work or study draws their interests and activities away from the residential unit. The fact is that the rural village is the only level at which the overwhelming majority of Chinese have any significant voice in community affairs, that external politics are interpreted to them in terms of village experience, and that they can respond to external political influences, in most cases, only within the confines of village life. The focusing of popular political participation on the rural village, which is the stronghold of traditional political

---

[57] For a formal statement of matters to be decided at the team level, see Hsü Ti-hsin, "Lun Hsien Chieh-tuan Nung-ts'un Jen-min Kung-she ti Ken-pen Chih-tu" (The Basic System of the Rural People's Commune at the Present Stage), *Hung Ch'i,* 1961, Nos. 15–16, p. 34.

patterns and beliefs, must impede the CCP's proclaimed desire to destroy the particularistic loyalties of the Chinese peasant and change him into a participating member of a national political community. It is impossible to say how strong particularism remains in the Chinese countryside. John Lewis has suggested that village kinship and friendship ties are still prerequisites of successful leadership in the production team.[58] The collapse of commune authority during the rural economic crisis of 1959–1961 also indicates the survival of village tendencies to fall back on their own resources for self-preservation in times of stress. The CCP has, of course, fought against rural particularism in its propaganda and in many of its mass movements against the old social order. These efforts have certainly had some effect. Still, in allowing the production team to emerge as the primary unit for popular political participation, the Party has encouraged the preservation of some of the traditional political attitudes that it has so explicitly attacked in its theory and in its past revolutionary action.

CONCLUSION

Three conclusions emerge from this discussion of what has so inacurately been termed "nongovernmental organizations." First, these organizations are far more effective than the state structure in providing the conditions for fulfillment of the mass line. They have not always done so because of their failure to defend their members' interests consistently and because of the stifling effects of centralization (in the democratic parties and mass organizations) and Party control (in all cases). Nevertheless, they have certainly mobilized the masses behind Party policies and they have given the masses limited opportunities for participation in the management of minor affairs.

Second, nongovernmental organizations, and especially the mass organizations and democratic parties, demonstrate the practical application of the ideological principle that non-Communist thinking is potentially bourgeois thinking. The organizational statement of this principle is that any organization that does not accept Party leadership is potentially opposed to Party leadership. As a result, spontaneous organization is impossible without the risk of charges of counter-revolutionary activity. Theoretically, spontaneity is encouraged, but only in the realm of individual action. All organized group action must have prior Party approval and constant Party guidance.

Third, with the exception of the democratic parties and perhaps some

[58] Lewis, op. cit., pp. 237–238, and "The Leadership Doctrine of the Chinese Communist Party: The Lesson of the People's Commune," Asian Survey, 3:10 (October, 1963), pp. 457–459.

of the minor mass organizations, nongovernmental organizations concentrate the political activities of their members in residential, occupational, and educational units that lie somewhere beneath the basic level of government. These units are always open to controls from above, from state and Party organs or from higher levels of the mass organizations, and they are constantly exposed to propaganda and directives that deal with nonlocal political affairs. Nevertheless, although the Chinese citizen's political education may cover almost any aspect of national and international politics and he may participate in state activities through ritualistic elections, congresses, and rallies, most of his political actions relate to the affairs of small economic and social units that are not part of the formal governmental structure.

SEVEN

Political Life in Communist China

One of the striking features of the Chinese political system is the degree to which a uniform style of participation pervades all popular political activities. To a great extent, this uniformity is a result of the CCP's conscious and persistent efforts to structure Chinese political life in accordance with its doctrine. Nevertheless, the Chinese political landscape has not been totally malleable to Party manipulation, and the Chinese style of participation reveals certain disadvantages and failures, as well as advantages and successes, from the Party's point of view. A description of political life in Communist China must include, therefore, analysis of the main characteristics of the Chinese style of participation and an attempt to evaluate their consequences.

CHARACTERISTICS OF PARTICIPATION

Political participation assumes many forms in China but certain characteristics are common to all of them. The common qualities emerge more clearly from analysis of the organizational setting in which participation occurs, the nature of political relationships among those who participate, the way in which political issues are defined, the primary objective of political action, and the manner in which popular action on major issues is coordinated. Analytical distinctions such as these are not so sharp in practice but they serve to illustrate the main characteristics of mass political life.

The organizational setting—small-group activities The most characteristic organizational setting for political participation in China is the small group. There are, of course, many types of political activity in which people participate in large numbers. Parades, rallies, the mass "trials" of counterrevolutionaries and landlords during the early years of the regime, general meetings of members in production teams and residents' committees, basic-level congresses—all of these are more or less regular gatherings of large numbers of citizens which certainly have some political significance for the participants. For the most part, however, these gatherings involve little discussion or response among those present. They have symbolic and ritualistic importance and they are useful for the transmission of information, but they are inadequate organizational devices for the type of popular participation that the CCP wishes to produce. It is the small group, which can elicit response from every member and check this response against daily behavior, that plays the critical role in the Chinese style of participation.

In the most precise sense, the small group is a unit with a fixed membership of not more than fifteen people who meet regularly (daily or weekly) for well-organized purposes and activities.[1] Its most common form is the political study group in which members engage in lengthy discussion of study materials under the guidance of a group leader. The key aspect of the study group is the "criticism and self-criticism" that requires every member to express his views, criticize himself, and submit to the criticism of others in the group. The small study group is a regular feature in Party life, in "thought reform," in most schools (including colleges and universities, cadre training schools, and the "institutes of socialism" for bourgeois and intellectual elements), and in certain occupational situations, such as government offices and enterprise management, where there is a relatively high educational level among small working groups. It is also an irregular feature of political life for the entire population, appearing during the mass movements or in units not mentioned above where there is a high degree of "activism."

Small-group activity in a more general sense is a universal form of political organization even where the conditions of fifteen-member limits and tightly organized study and criticism are not met. At all times and in all places, the Party follows the general principle of dividing members of social units into groups small enough to permit some discussion and personal contact between leaders and members. Thus, there are small groups in the factories, residents' small groups in the cities, work groups within the production teams, voters' small groups during elections, and temporary small groups among those in attendance at all major meetings and congresses. In addition, there are countless meetings of very small numbers of people which, though informal in composition and manner of convening, are still important and deliberate parts of the Party's organizational arrangement of political participation. In all of these groups, whether they conform closely to the ideal study group or not, that all letters should be carefully handled by referring them to the

[1] For general discussions of the small group, see John Wilson Lewis, *Leadership in Communist China* (Ithaca, 1963), pp. 157–160, and H. F. Schurmann, "Organization and Response in Communist China," *Annals,* Vol. 321 (January, 1959).

there is personal response to guided political discussion and a testing of every individual's political standpoint.

The use of the small group as the typical setting for popular political activity has many advantages. First, by assigning to cadres and activists responsibility for the guidance of small units of specified membership, it enables group leaders to verify by personal observation the transmission of Party policy to the citizenry. The Party's historical experience in mobilizing an illiterate and politically apathetic population has taught it the importance of such verification. Second, the small group makes politics more vivid and memorable by placing it in a setting where face-to-face discussion is possible. The CCP constantly reminds cadres that personal participation makes politics meaningful and that "what is learned in debate is unforgettable"; the small group facilitates the realization of these principles. Finally, since the small group normally consists of people who live or work together, it brings formidable social pressure to bear on its members. The Chinese Communists capitalize on pressures for associational conformity, which are particularly strong in the Chinese tradition, to enhance the persuasiveness of their doctrine and reinforce their demands for political unanimity.

Political relationships—direct contact and moral leadership   The doctrinal assertion that leaders are legally responsible to the masses and that people's congresses are "supreme organs of power" is an inaccurate definition of political relationships in Communist China. In fact, the Party seriously emphasized the legal aspects of the state structure only during 1954–1956. A much more consistent theme than observance of "socialist legality" has been a deep suspicion of the development of "bureaucratism" and "formalism" as a consequence of the necessary institutionalization of Communist political power. As we have seen, the long-term trend of Chinese Communist politics has been toward an emasculation of the state structure in general and representative bodies in particular, even though this trend has not been entirely due to the desires of Party leaders. The ineffectiveness of the state structure in obvious contradiction of Party theory is not due simply to CCP cynicism. It reflects an even stronger theoretical conviction that the mass line and "socialist democracy" depend on an organic, intuitive relationship between cadres and masses rather than on institutional and legal controls. Two important aspects of this relationship are an emphasis on direct contacts between cadres and masses and an insistence on the moral quality of CCP leadership.

The importance of direct contacts has been noted many times in this study, particularly in references to small-group activities, but the best example is the operation of "democratic management" in basic-level political units. "Democratic management" (*min-chu kuan-li*) was one of the fundamental principles of the "Model Regulations" for higher APC's and became the object of a Party enforcement campaign in 1957. A Central Committee statement of March 15, 1957, listed three items as the critical elements of democratic management: (1) APC cadres must make periodic financial statements directly to the members; (2) cadres must discuss all cooperative affairs with the members, and especially with experienced peasants; (3) cadres must participate in production to gain experience and set a good example for the masses.[2] Democratic management in the APC's did not wholly ignore the functions of members' congresses, but a "democratization of management" movement that followed the formation of rural communes in the latter part of 1958 demonstrated that representative bodies played only a minor role in commune "democracy." The literature of this movement focused on two matters: first, the direct solicitation of mass discussion and opinion, and second, the "democratization" of cadre work style.[3]

Solicitation of mass opinion depended mainly on an immense variety of meetings between cadres and masses and on the use of *tatzupao* (large hand-written posters posted publicly for all to read). *Tatzupao* were said to be "powerful means of mass participation in management" because they enabled the masses to express their opinions at any time. Democratization of cadre work style was the "central key to carrying out democratic management." Once a cadre achieved a democratic work style, he would be "one with the masses" and would automatically govern in accordance with their needs. Cadres were to achieve this style by direct association with the masses and by personally experiencing their living and working conditions. The "four-togethers"—eating, living, working, and consulting with the masses—and the "six to's"—making regular visits to the fields, nurseries, "happiness homes" (for the aged), hospital, mess halls, and members' homes—were typical slogans for encouraging cadres to "democratize" management by democratizing themselves.

The systematic way in which the CCP solicits and publicizes letters and visits to officials is further evidence of the directness of political relationships in China. In June, 1951, the central government adopted regulations calling on all local and higher-level governments to establish departments for handling letters from the people and information bureaus or reception rooms for receiving visitors.[4] The regulations stated

[2] "Min-chu Pan-she San-hsiang Ts'o-shih" (Three Measures for Democratic Management of Cooperatives), *JMJP*, March 19, 1957.

[3] This discussion draws on many reports of the movement; in particular, see *JMJP*, November 19, 1958; November 29, 1958; and December 4, 1958.

[4] "Kuan-yü Ch'u-li Jen-min Lai-hsin ho Chieh-chien Jen-min Kung-tso ti Chüeh-ting" (Decision on the Work of Handling People's Letters and Receiving People's Calls), *Chieh-fang Jih-pao* (Liberation Daily), June 9, 1951.

proper departments or officials for speedy answer or resolution and that "model cases" of special educational value should be publicized after disposition. A conference of the North China Bureau of the CCP Central Committee in November, 1952, followed with more detailed regulations. The North China directives specified the bureaucratic procedure for dealing with letters, reemphasized the importance of prompt and careful handling of people's letters and calls, called for closer Party supervision of the process, and noted that basic-level work would have to be strengthened to avoid a growing tendency for people to run to higher levels for resolution of their questions and problems.[5]

The focus of handling letters and calls has shifted over the years. Initially, it was the solicitation of accusations from the people against possible counterrevolutionaries or "bad elements" who had slipped into the Party and government. After 1955, emphasis shifted to rationalization proposals and to complaints about public facilities, marketing, food distribution, and so forth. Whatever their content, however, letters and calls transmit popular views and problems directly to responsible units, where their handling and publicizing builds the image of a Party and government that are intimately connected with the masses. Of course, the system gives the letter-writer or visitor no control over the person whom he petitions. The 1951 "Decision" even stated that "questions of a fault-finding or probing nature that are presented to the government by counterrevolutionaries assuming the name of the people should not be answered." The significant point is that so much of local government's information about popular conditions and so many solutions of the public's minor problems are due to direct letters or visits from the masses rather than to the representative structure.[6]

In the Chinese political system, then, the citizen characteristically enters into direct contact with cadres who, theoretically, have an intuitive understanding of popular problems as a result of personally experiencing the living conditions of the masses. What is missing from this idealistic conception of political relationships is the element of popular control over leaders, since formal institutions do not fulfill this function. The CCP answers by claiming that it is the *quality* of Communist

[5] "Chung-kung Chung-yang Hua-pei-chü Kuan-yü Ch'u-li Jen-min Lai-hsin Chieh-chien Jen-min Ch'ün-chung Kung-tso ti Chih-shih" (Directive of the North China Bureau of the CCP Central Committee on the Work of Handling People's Letters and Receiving the Masses' Calls), *T'ien-chin Jih-pao* (Tientsin Daily), December 9, 1952. A separate directive on procedure accompanied this document.

[6] In 1962, about 500,000 people in Kiangsu alone wrote letters and paid visits to government officials, and 80 percent of their problems had been resolved by February, 1963; NCNA, Nanking, February 20, 1963, in *SCMP*, No. 2937 (March 13, 1963). After the 1953–1954 elections in one *ch'ü* in Port Arthur–Dairen, 3,068 proposals had been forwarded to cadres by the people themselves as compared to only 486 from people's deputies; *Lü-ta Jen-min Jih-pao* (Port Arthur–Dairen People's Daily), April 1, 1954.

leadership, rather than institutional controls, that ensures "democracy" and observance of mass demands. Cadres are "naturally" responsible to the people because of their adherence to a doctrine which demands that they be responsible. The doctrine itself is the real source of authority, basing its claims to legitimacy on its superior morality; those who follow this doctrine have a moral claim to political leadership on the grounds that they alone can lead society along the right path.[7] There is, then, a natural political elite in China composed of those people who accept and follow the superior morality of Communist doctrine. They are the people who "ought to be elected" and who will always deserve their positions if they follow the doctrine correctly. As "good Communists," they will naturally govern in the interests of the people. Obviously, however, they are also obedient to Party orders and, in case of conflict, Party orders take precedence over mass demands. It is equally obvious that an "immoral" cadre may lose his understanding of the masses by failure to maintain his direct contacts with them and yet remain safe from popular (though not necessarily Party) retaliation.

Definition of issues—political education The only political issues in China that can become the rallying point for mass participation are those that the Party introduces and defines. The classic proof of this statement was the "hundred flowers" episode in which some individuals tried to initiate debate on unauthorized issues. The result, after brief success, was either absolute rejection of the issues or continued debate only on grounds defined by the Party. Of course, the Party can neither predict nor totally control the issues and opinions that may arise at any given time. What it can do, however, is prohibit widespread discussion of an issue until it has defined its position and then insist that discussion resolve itself in support of this position. As one writer has said: "In fact, we can have incorrect opinions that differ from Party policy, but only if the masses can say what they wish and support Party policy and if opinions that oppose incorrect opinions can also emerge. This is a very natural thing since opinions that are incorrect and differ from [Party] policy cannot represent mass interests and will receive the opposition of correct opinions that do represent mass interests."[8] The Party, then, assumes responsibility not only for defining all political issues but

[7] See Lewis, *Leadership in Communist China*, pp. 38–47, for a discussion of the relationship between Communist morality and political leadership. The CCP's claim to moral, as well as historical, justification for its rule is prominent in Liu Shao-ch'i's essay, "How To Be a Good Communist." See Howard L. Boorman, *"How To Be a Good Communist:* The Political Ethics of Liu Shao-ch'i," *Asian Survey*, Vol. 3, No. 8 (August, 1963); a Chinese text of the new edition of this essay is in *Hung Ch'i* (Red Flag), 1962, Nos. 15–16.

[8] Wang Han-chih, "I-k'ao Ch'ün-chung, Cheng-ch'üeh Kuan-ch'ieh Cheng-ts'e" (Rely on the Masses, Correctly Carry Out Policy), *Shih-shih Shou-ts'e* (Current Events), 1961, No. 17, p. 9.

also for overcoming spontaneous differences from its position on these issues. The technique by which the Party informs the masses of political issues and the "correct" positions on them is political education.

Political education in Communist China covers an enormous range of topics, but, so far as possible, there is one common theme in the treatment of all of them. This theme is the attempt to present political education in such a way that it relates to the personal experience of the citizen and thereby gives him some grounds for identifying with the Party position. Even more basically, political education must be simple enough at the start to convince the citizen that it is within his rights and abilities to debate political issues at all. The organization of a "political theory study group" in a Shanghai residents' small group illustrates this problem. The women involved in the group were all about forty years old and most were "semiliterate." Understandably, the first attempts at "theoretical study" produced great frustration and disillusionment. Recognizing the problem, the group leaders switched to study materials that were much closer to the "daily lives and tastes of the housewives." Interest grew rapidly thereafter and the "superstitious viewpoint about studying theory was smashed." [9] Even when "superstitions" about political participation have been overcome, however, the Party continues to translate political issues into terms of personal experience.

Two common pedagogical devices demonstrate this process. One is the use of contrasting "models" to highlight the differences in "correct" and "incorrect" policies and behavior and to provide, in the correct "model," an example for imitation. The models employed may be two workers or peasants, two cadres, two labor units, or even two sets of ideas or work styles. In all cases, however, the models clarify Party-approved issues and policies by offering concrete examples of the "good" and "bad" that the people may imitate and reject respectively. A second device is to explain political issues by reference to incidents and personalities that already have personal significance for some or all of the audience. For example, the CCP defends its general program by contrasting living conditions in the "new" and "old" societies and by urging people to talk about the injustice and oppression they suffered before 1949; whenever possible, cadres will identify the old order with specific landlords and local officials who have now been overthrown. Old soldiers will extol the CCP and its leaders with reminiscences about their experiences in the anti-Japanese and civil wars. When the Party attacks American imperialism, cadres urge the people to recall unpleasant incidents with Americans during the years before 1949, while PLA

[9] *Wen-hui Pao* (Literary News) (Shanghai), August 26, 1958.

veterans recite the American "atrocities" they witnessed in Korea. China's "semicolonial" history will be raised to identify with political struggles throughout the Afro–Asian world. By such references, the Party solicits personal involvement and identification with distant political issues and programs. The good cadre, of course, will not limit himself to explaining policies in terms of local experiences, but will reverse the process as well by generalizing on the "political significance" of every local incident or dispute.

Political education takes many different forms that vary greatly in their intensity and scope of application. The most intense and the most limited in scope is "thought reform." [10] Thought reform relies on a tightly controlled environment and the threat or use of force to challenge the subject's entire past life and political beliefs, convince him of his "guilt" and the necessity for reform, and then rebuild a new ideological character by intensive study under constant criticism and supervision. It is unquestionably the most thorough and effective form of political education that the CCP employs and it suggests the Party's general ideological aims for the entire population. Nevertheless, the Party does not, and cannot, subject all Chinese to an "educational" process of such intensity. Those who have undergone thought reform, or a reasonably close approximation of it, include some Party members, most intellectuals and political prisoners, and those who have attended the "revolutionary universities" and other training schools specifically designed to remold the thought of the students.

A second form of political education is political study, which is one of the primary techniques of thought reform but is a far less intensive experience. It demands individual participation in a discussion process that exposes the individual to group criticism, compels him to examine his most basic beliefs, and leads him to at least a surface statement of his acceptance of the Communist viewpoint. Unlike thought reform, however, it does not involve total isolation from outside contacts or the threat of physical punishment, and it does not necessarily lead to a written confession or even a conclusive decision on whether or not the individual has "reformed." Every Chinese has probably participated in political study at some time, but only a minority of the population experiences it as a regular form of political education. The technique is, however, sufficiently familiar to both cadres and masses that the Party can organize political study at the mass level whenever it wishes.[11]

[10] See Robert J. Lifton, *Thought Reform and the Psychology of Totalism* (New York, 1961), especially the analytical definitions of thought reform and "totalism" in chaps. 5 and 22.

[11] For examples of how mass study is organized, see Liu Wan-pang, "Lai-an Hsien Shih Tsen-yang Tsu-chih ho Chien-ch'ih Kung-nung Ch'ün-chung Hsüeh Li-

Probably the major limitation on the overall effectiveness of political study is the great variation in the quality of study. Political study among peasants is not what it is among intellectuals, even though the format may be the same, and the performance of two study groups of similar composition may be quite different, owing to the different abilities of their group leaders. Political study is a powerful technique for political education and participation, but it is extremely vulnerable to variations in the ability and enthusiasm of its participants.

Political propaganda is the least intensive and most universal form of political education in China. It is total in its coverage and virtually continuous, although the intensity will always vary with the political demands of the moment. Many meetings among the masses that are identified as "study" are actually in this category since they involve no outside preparation and very little response by the participants. Political meetings in rural areas, for example, frequently consist of little more than a lecture by a cadre or a current events session (based on a radio broadcast or a newspaper reading to the group). Such meetings are informative and may stimulate some interchange of opinion, but they are not political study in the sense that we have defined it.

Political education in Communist China defines political issues and educates the people in the policies of the ruling party and the nature of the state system, but it also tries to raise their political consciousness and convince them of the necessity for political action. This aspect of political education explains its intensity and pervasiveness. If only understanding and passive obedience were the goal, a lesser effort would suffice. But political education has the task of making the masses see political issues and feel the need for action in the same way that the Party does. The "Socialist and Communist Education Movement" carried out in the rural communes from September, 1958, to the spring of 1959 is a perfect example of this process. Since the communes were already formed when the movement got under way, its purpose was not simply to explain the commune system and ensure mass obedience in joining. The movement's goal was to guarantee the future of the communes by persuading the peasants that the communes were necessary and by destroying the "individualism and particularism" that inhibited voluntary peasant acceptance of the communes. One discussion of the movement pointed out:

Individualism and particularism are like a stubborn skin disease: today you drive it out, tomorrow it rushes back; you drive it out here, it rushes back

lun ti" (How Laian Hsien Organized and Maintained the Worker-Peasant Masses' Study of Theory), *Hung Ch'i*, 1960, No. 3, pp. 30–33; and Yü Ch'ing-ho, *et al.*, "I-ko Shou-huo-yüan Li-lun Hsüeh-hsi Hsiao-tsu" (A Salesclerks' Theoretical Study Group), *Hung Ch'i*, 1960, No. 7, pp. 36–40.

there. In saying this are we saying that individualism and particularism can never be driven out? No, we are only saying that we must use the method of long-term, patient persuasion and education with respect to individualism and particularism; we must use the method of communist ideological education. Individualism and particularism will not be truly exterminated until every commune member possesses communist ideology.[12]

The Party knows that the people must obey its orders, but it cannot be sure that they will actively support Party policies until political education has raised their political consciousness and implanted the communist viewpoint in their minds.

The objective of political action—execution of Party policies   The primary objective of all the acts through which the Chinese citizen participates in politics is execution of Party policies. In a limited sense, some forms of political participation do not aim directly at this objective. There is, for example, mass participation in patriotic ceremonies, in the management of strictly local affairs on which the Party has no specific position, and in many educational activities that do not focus on particular policies. However, the Party tries to link all of these activities to realization of the CCP's political program. Patriotic ceremonies may stress loyalty to the nation or state, but national loyalty is inseparable from loyalty to the Party and must be demonstrated by support for Party policies. Cadres constantly tell members of residents' committees and production teams that proper management of their units is a contribution to socialist construction. And political education, as we have just noted, never loses sight of the ultimate objective of action. From the Party's point of view, therefore, the test of mass political participation is whether or not it leads to active support of CCP policies. One who goes through the motions of participation without developing "activism" is guilty of political passivity which, in effect, is opposition. There is no freedom to abstain from political action in China.

By insisting that the people participate "consciously and voluntarily" in the execution of Party policies, the CCP politicizes all areas of life into which its authority penetrates. This is not to say that all areas of life are political. Although there is no theoretical limit to the extension of Party authority, in practice the Party does not attempt to regulate everything. Nevertheless, the range of behavior that the CCP tries to influence or control is extremely great. Consider, for example, the "socialist" or "patriotic" pact. These pacts are agreements among neighbors to observe certain standards of conduct on the grounds that interests of state or socialist construction are involved. In one "socialist neighborhood pact" in Peking, the residents agreed to the following

[12] *JMJP,* October 9, 1958.

obligations: To strengthen unity and mutual assistance, help neighbors who are busy or sick, criticize others for their shortcomings, and accept criticism in return; to prevent fires, restrain "bad people" from inciting incidents, and observe regulations requiring the reporting of the arrival and departure of visitors; to accept responsibility for cleaning streets, ditches, and toilets and for killing all flies and mosquitoes; to maintain personal health and hygiene by bathing, changing clothes, washing hands before eating, washing all food, and dressing children carefully with an eye to the weather; to be "diligent and frugal" in managing the household, thinking up ways to economize on food, clothing, coal, water, and electricity; to participate in study for the elimination of illiteracy and to read the newspaper regularly; to respect all policies and decrees of the government, respond to every call of the government, participate in all activities and pass on information to those who cannot attend meetings.[13] One might well question the Party's ability, or desire, to hold the signers of such an agreement to their promises. The point, however, is precisely the fact that the signers themselves are to enforce the pact because they have accepted the Party's assertion that all these acts have a wider political significance.

The CCP's insistence on popular support for all of its policies makes the range of political action in China extremely wide. Popular political action includes not only such obvious categories as electoral participation, service as a cadre or activist, or participation in the decisions of small units such as production teams and residents' committees, but also involvement in the execution of tasks that the Party has defined as essential for the victory of socialism over its enemies. By far the most important task of this sort is increasing production. From 1949 to the present, the CCP has consistently cited increased production and willingness to work as the primary evidence of popular political activism. Popular assistance in internal security work—the supervision and apprehension of political and social criminals—has been next in importance, although it no longer receives the emphasis that it did up to 1955. Another critical area is mediation of all kinds of disputes. The mediation committees in the communes and urban neighborhoods, usually dominated by women, perform services that are of great assistance to the Party and which, incidentally, tend to reduce the role of the state legal structure at the lowest levels. The Party also stresses mass implementation of various measures in the fields of sanitation, health, pest riddance, and conservation of scarce products and resources. Social reform was a major field for mass action in the early years of the regime, but it has

[13] *JMJP*, August 17, 1958. For other examples of "patriotic pacts" see *Ch'ang-chou Jih-pao* (Changchow Daily), April 19, 1958, and April 29, 1958.

gradually given way to movements for economic and technological progress and for ideological reform.

Coordinating political action—the mass movement On nearly all major national issues, the Chinese political process culminates in a mass movement that coordinates in one general campaign all the organizational and educational efforts that prepare the citizen for political action. Mass movements are the most characteristic expression of the Chinese style of political participation. Like general election campaigns in Western democracies, they are the most significant events in mass political life and the symbol of the basic objectives of political participation. As "the most concentrated and salient form of expression of the mass line" and "the climax of the revolutionary action of the masses," [14] the mass movement relies on direct action by an enthusiastic and totally mobilized population to bring Party policies to fruition. The essence of the movement is its ability to stimulate mass activism, thus avoiding reliance on specialists and state organs, while retaining Party leadership to prevent spontaneous or undisciplined action.[15]

The CCP adopted the mass movement during its formative years as a revolutionary party when direct popular action had to compensate for other political and material weakness. Even after 1949, widespread popular activism was essential for the success of the far-reaching social, economic, and political changes initiated by the Party. It was not until 1956, at the Eighth Party Congress, that Chinese Communist leaders began to express some reservations about the mass movements, hinting that they were necessary during the "revolutionary" period but that they were unsuitable for a state that had settled its internal political struggles and was erecting a stable governmental structure.[16] It is significant that the CCP recognized the fundamental difference between mass movements and institutionalized political action, and even more significant, therefore, that it chose mass movements as the driving force of the Great Leap. In 1959, Chou En-lai spoke approvingly of the "series of mass movements" that had "advanced like waves" on the economic, political, and ideological fronts of the socialist revolution, enabling the masses to retain their revolutionary enthusiasm without "cooling down" and continually raising their political consciousness for the further development

[14] Li Yu-pin, "The Great Victory of the Mass Line in the Institutes of Higher Education," *Chung-kuo Ch'ing-nien* (China Youth), 1959, No. 24, in *SMM,* No. 199 (February 8, 1960).

[15] See "Speech by Comrade Lo Jui-ching," *Eighth National Congress of the Communist Party of China,* II (Speeches), 109–112.

[16] See the speeches by Liu Shao-ch'i and Tung Pi-wu, cited in chap. iv, notes 64 and 65.

of the revolution.[17] Liu Shao-ch'i stated that mass movements under centralized Party guidance "can certainly become the most dynamic and constant factor facilitating the economic leap forward;" he acknowledged that they would "upset some production regimes," but only those that were already "outdated" and a hindrance to production.[18]

The Party's unrestrained enthusiasm for mass movements subsided after the economic setbacks of 1959–1961. By 1961, the mass movement as a technique for raising industrial production had disappeared.[19] At the same time, the CCP relaxed the constant mass mobilization and indoctrination that had been the foundation of the Great Leap. However, there is no indication that the Party has ceased to regard the mass movement as one of its most potent political weapons. It has conceded that the mass movement cannot substitute for technical competence in production, but the revival of national campaigns for ideological indoctrination in 1963–1965 shows that the Party still relies on the assistance of coordinated mass action in executing its policies. The CCP's reluctance to give up the mass movement is understandable. It has great emotional appeal for Party veterans who rose to power on a movement that seemed to demonstrate the superiority of human enthusiasm and effort over material resources; the "guerrilla mentality" and a mystical faith in mass action help to explain the extravagant use of mass movements in the Great Leap. However, the Party's reliance on the mass movement rests not only on faith but also on its proven ability to concentrate popular energies behind the Party's current tasks.

As various references in this study have indicated, mass movements have been in progress among some portion of the population almost every year since 1949. The scope of these movements prohibits detailed analysis, but some general characteristics and trends should be noted. (The 1953–1954 election campaign, described in detail in chapter Five, is an adequate example of their thoroughness and impact on political life). Movements are launched by central directives, either government or Party, that state the basic scope and objectives. Local governments at municipal, provincial, and *hsien* level follow with their own statements that echo the central directives and specify the timing and operation of the movements within their area of jurisdiction. In practice,

[17] Chou En-lai, "A Great Decade," in *Ten Glorious Years* (Peking, 1960), pp. 55–56.

[18] Liu Shao-ch'i, "The Victory of Marxism–Leninism in China," in *ibid.*, pp. 23–24.

[19] Franz Schurmann, "China's 'New Economic Policy'—Transition or Beginning," *China Quarterly*, No. 17 (January–March, 1964), p. 86. In an editorial of October 26, 1959, translated in *CB*, No. 602 (November 5, 1959), *JMJP* had stated that the belief that mass movements could not be used in industrial production was "bourgeois thinking" on the part of "rightists."

local response tends to be quicker in the northern provinces than in the south; in a very rough way, most major movements have spread outward from the capital with the more distant regions being the last to initiate and complete their work. Within localities, too, the movements develop unevenly. "Experimental work" in "key points" always precedes a more general unfolding of a campaign in any given area. Experimental work not only tests popular response and the effectiveness of techniques but also serves as a training ground for a select group of cadres who will provide leadership when the movement is expanded. There is no need to go into the techniques of mobilization as they are identical to those discussed repeatedly in earlier sections. The mass movement simply steps up the pace of ordinary mass political activities and focuses them on a particular policy or objective.

Up to 1957, the movements that involved widespread mass partici-pation (as opposed, for example, to ideological reform of the intellec-tuals) focused on specific programs of exceptional political, economic, and social significance. They produced ideological indoctrination and debate, but their ideological content was secondary to the specific politi-cal action demanded by the program in question. The Party apparently believed that it could secure mass participation in land reform, aid to Korea, suppression of counterrevolutionaries and so forth, by combining political and social pressure with appeals to personal interest, national-ism, and general support for the Party, and that ideological conversion would follow as a consequence of this participation and the substantive changes produced by the movements. By 1956, from the Party's view-point, the early movements had eliminated the regime's major opponents and established a broad political consensus based on support for social-ist construction. The "hundred flowers" episode shattered this convic-tion. Actually, the liberalization of 1956–1957 was not due solely to Party confidence or complacency about the extent of its popular sup-port. The decision to liberalize was based on a combination of internal and external factors that outweighed what must have been substantial reservations within the Party. Still, it was a gamble that the regime expected to win, and failure lost none of its impact because of prior recognition of the dangers involved. The Party's reaction brought about a significant change in the character of mass movements. A few com-ments on the 1957–1958 rectification campaign at the mass level will clarify this point.

The "hundred flowers" outburst was linked to a rectification campaign launched at the end of April, 1957, against bureaucratism, sectarianism, and subjectivism in higher levels of state and Party organs. This rectifi-cation campaign gave way to an "antirightist" movement during the summer of 1957, and then emerged again at the end of the summer after

the most prominent "rightists" had been attacked and refuted. However, the portion of the rectification campaign that lasted from September, 1957, through the spring of 1958 was quite different from its earlier
phase. Although it continued to "rectify" personnel in the upper levels
of Party and state organs, educational institutions, democratic parties,
and various cultural and professional circles, it was also extended for the
first time to the masses of workers, peasants, and urban housewives.
Rectification at the mass level was definitely not an "antirightist" struggle. Instead, it took the form of a nationwide debate, under the slogans
of "great blooming and contending" held over from the "hundred flowers" period, on the following general questions: whether or not the
revolution and the work of construction had been correct; whether or
not the socialist road should be taken; whether or not Party leadership,
proletarian dictatorship, and democratic centralism were necessary;
whether or not foreign policy had been correct.[20] There was, of course,
only one correct answer to these questions, and the objective of the
campaign was to instill a genuine acceptance of the "correct" answers
in the entire population.

The 1957–1958 rectification movement was, therefore, a new type of
mass movement in that it was primarily dedicated to ideological indoctrination rather than the implementation of more specific Party programs. The source of this difference was recognized by one writer who
stated: "Socialist reconstruction has two aspects: one is reconstruction
of the system, the other is reconstruction of man. At present, the
reconstruction of the system is basically completed but the reconstruction of man is not yet concluded. Old thoughts and habits which reflect
the old system have not been basically eliminated; new thoughts and
habits which reflect the new system are still not well established." [21]
The events of the first half of 1957 had shown the Party that mass
assistance in "reconstructing the system" had not brought about a "reconstruction of man." The people had participated in the great mass
movements of 1949–1955, but without accepting communist ideology.
The 1957–1958 rectification campaign and most mass movements since
then have assumed that the "reconstruction of man" through ideological
indoctrination is essential for the further advance of socialist construction.

The shift from "reconstruction of the system" to ideological indoctrination was mainly one of emphasis. Party theory asserts that political

[20] Teng Hsiao-ping, *Report on the Rectification Campaign* (Peking, 1957), pp.
1–2, 26.

[21] Shen Chieh, "Wei-shen-ma Yao Tsai Nung-ts'un Chin-hsing She-hui Chu-i
Chiao-yü" (Why We Must Carry Out Socialist Education in the Villages), *Cheng-
chih Hsüeh-hsi* (Political Study), 1957, No. 9, p. 11.

action and correct ideology should be inseparable. The earlier movements did not ignore ideology and the raising of consciousness, and the later movements have not ignored political action. The difference is that the later movements have stressed the ideological foundations of action in a way that the earlier movements did not. The 1957–1958 rectification campaign, for example, was clearly an ideological movement in terms of its primary content; it was, in fact, more frequently referred to as a "socialist education" movement, although both terms were used interchangeably in many cases. The core of the campaign, whether among workers, peasants, or housewives, was solicitation of opinions in the small group, followed by intensive discussion of these opinions and popular debate on the general questions referred to above. As these questions indicate, the CCP expected debate to produce popular acceptance of the most fundamental aspects of Party doctrine. Nevertheless, in spite of its emphasis on indoctrination, the movement still tried to channel mass participation in the "great debate" into action on current Party policies.

For one thing, the Party used solicitation of mass opinions to rectify basic-level leadership and organization. The workers, especially, were encouraged to recite their grievances about cadres' work style and various defects in trade union, Party, and factory organization. In one factory in Szechwan, over two-thirds of the 9,074 opinions raised during the campaign pertained to "bureaucratism, sectarianism and subjectivism" among the leadership.[22] Rectification of cadre work style, including reelection in some cases, was also an important part of the movement in the cooperatives.[23] Generally speaking, the campaign uncovered many minor grievances, whether due to leadership errors or not, that were discussed and satisfied before the movement ended.

However, the basic connection between ideological indoctrination and execution of CCP policies lay in the Party's ability to direct the debate over socialism toward critical issues among the various segments of the population. Among the workers, these issues were increasing production and the question of welfare and wages. The Party's position, of course, was that workers should strive to increase production without expecting "unjustified" material gains. Cadres and activists attacked the "irrational welfare benefits" of the old society, such as annual bonuses, free clothing and free housing, maintaining that higher wage scales under communism more than made up for the loss of such benefits.[24] A factory in Chungking devoted a major share of debate to the wage

[22] *Ssu-ch'uan Jih-pao* (Szechwan Daily) (Chengtu), December 1, 1957.

[23] See the CCP Central Committee's directive on rectification in the APC's in *JMJP,* September 16, 1957.

[24] *Kung-jen Jih-pao* (Workers' Daily), August 15–16, 1957.

question after a general meeting in which some speakers "won the applause of backward elements" by stating that no one could "blame the workers for thinking about money if their wages were low." The debate allegedly reduced the number of workers "making trouble over wages" from 54 to 4 (out of about 275 in the factory).[25] In rural areas, the debate moved quickly against the "individualism and particularism," among both APC cadres and members, that was said to be subverting individual loyalties to the APC and APC cooperation with the state. Management of grain supply and distribution within the APC and in the APC's arrangements with the state were critical issues on which enforcement of Party policies was sought. As the movement drew to a close, there were reports that the debate had persuaded many families that had withdrawn from the APCs to apply for readmission.[26] In the residents' committees, which were the last organizations to take part in the movement, debate first encouraged housewives to be "nameless heroes" doing a good job of housework and neighborhood service chores and then, as the massive labor mobilization of 1958 progressed, to volunteer for rural labor or initiate small-scale production activities in the streets. In all of these cases, ideological indoctrination also led to execution of specific Party policies.

Although the Party's 1957 decision to apply the force of the mass movement to the "reconstruction of man" did not signify abandonment of the mass movement's proven effectiveness in the "reconstruction of the system," it is nonetheless true that most campaigns since 1957 have had a pronounced ideological focus. Does this signify any change in the vitality or role of the mass movement as such? Most Party statements would indicate not, as the campaigns of 1963–1965 have been full of glowing testimony to the sweep and power of mass action. There is an air of unreality about such statements, however, because the movements in question do not seem to have developed the revolutionary power attributed to them. For example, in 1964–1965 there was talk of the revival of "poor peasants' associations" to take part in rural "class struggle," but this "struggle" consisted mainly of discussions about class and class consciousness and was a far cry indeed from the rural struggles of the 1930's, 1940's, and early 1950's. In fact, the CCP may actually be more concerned with its own doctrinal purity and the strength of its control over present and future cadres than with converting the masses to socialism. The "learn from the People's Liberation Army" and "cultivation of successors" movements, both of which focused on the guidance and training of cadres, suggest that the primary value of mass

[25] *Ch'ung-ch'ing Jih-pao* (Chungking Daily), January 8, 1958.

[26] See the series of articles in *Ta Kung Pao* (Impartial News), August 29–September 8, 1957, and *Kung-jen Jih-pao,* January 5, 1958.

movements is that they provide a simulated revolutionary atmosphere for those who lack revolutionary experience. In an editorial of August 3, 1964, *Jen-min Jih-pao* made this point explicit by stating that a person's revolutionary quality could be judged only in class struggle, and that all cadres and revolutionary youth must therefore "be organized to take part in a planned way in revolutionary mass movements, which at the present time means taking part in the socialist education movement." [27] If this is the case, the mass movement will remain a characteristic feature of Chinese political life. But it is important to note that a political phenomenon that was originally an alternative (and even antithetical) to institutionalized political action may in the future become an institution for the recruitment and training of political elites.

EVALUATION

Evaluation of mass political participation in China is a hazardous project, since the analyst simply cannot judge precisely the critical elements of popular motivation and response. Documentary sources, refugees, and reports by visitors provide important evidence, but conclusions still depend on inference, intuition, and subjective balancing of conflicting reports. Nevertheless, there is no reason to question the value of logical inferences about the Chinese political process. The Chinese people have not become automatons in the service of the CCP, nor can the Party manipulate their ideas and reactions at will. They have been totally organized for service to the state, but organization has not destroyed the powers of individual judgment. The Chinese Communists regard political study and persuasion as rational enterprises, however much one may dispute their reasoning; they have tried to control popular attitudes by limiting and twisting public communications, but they have not eliminated rationality from Chinese politics. Hence, the Chinese political process provides evidence of real political problems that can serve as a basis for logical projections about the popular role in politics.

The theory of Chinese Communism states, and its practice proves, that the primary function of political participation is to organize the masses for conscious and voluntary execution of Party policies. However, the organizational success of the Chinese style of participation has definitely not meant an absence of difficulties. In organizing the masses under Party leadership and guiding them into political action, the CCP

[27] "Cultivating and Training Millions of Successors to the Proletarian Revolution," in *Peking Review*, 1964, No. 32, p. 15. See also Hu Yao-pang's report to the Ninth Congress of the Communist Youth League in June, 1964, *Revolutionize Our Youth!* (Peking, 1964), especially pp. 22–25.

has encountered problems that have been resolved, if at all, only at the cost of serious doctrinal and political strains. "Organizational success" may be a fair generalization, but it requires additional explanation of the regime's accomplishments and problems in the realm of popular participation.

Organizational success   The organizational accomplishments of the CCP need little elaboration here. The Party has constructed an organizational network that brings political education and Party guidance to every citizen. Through this network, and especially the small group, the Party has mobilized the population for action on all of its major programs. Some of this action has no inherent political content, but the CCP has made it political by stressing its relevance to national goals and by using it as evidence of political commitment. Mass assistance in the execution of Party policies has contributed greatly to all of the regime's accomplishments and remains a significant factor in the regime's future capabilities.

The Party's record in organizing active mass support is by no means perfect. On several occasions since 1949, the implementation of specific central policies has lagged behind, owing, at least partially, to the Party's inability to secure popular support. This phenomenon was most dramatically evident in 1961–1962 when the organizational network itself began to disintegrate at the basic level in the countryside. Some of the reasons for these failures will be discussed later. For the moment, we can simply note that organizational successes far outweigh the failures over the period since 1949 and that the CCP's ability to survive the crisis of 1961–1962 indicates that it retains impressive organizational powers.

Assuming that the CCP's ability to produce organized mass action is recognized, the important question is what motivation lies behind this action. Beyond any doubt, the Party uses compulsion to produce mass action in some cases; to the extent that it does, action ceases to be political. Careful distinctions are necessary in considering this point. In the first place, the Party insists that discussion and persuasion are the only appropriate methods for producing support among the "people" (those classes supporting socialist construction). Most cadres follow this rule in the sense that discussion and persuasion are the *primary* methods for soliciting mass cooperation with the Party. The difficulty arises in connection with those people who do not respond actively to persuasion. There are two rough categories of such people: those who oppose the Party "summons" by acting or speaking against it in an unmistakable way, and those who simply fail to respond with sufficient activism. The Party uses force, or the threat of force, against the first category; fear of physical punishment is probably the major deterrent of active opposition. The second category, or "passivists" as we might call them, is theoretically "opposing" the Party since all failure to support socialism is said to aid the opponents of socialism. Nevertheless, the Party does not expel them from the ranks of the "people" for their sin of omission and they need not fear physical punishment. At the same time they cannot escape some compulsion to conform. This compulsion normally takes the form of social pressure—intensified persuasion by cadres and activists, public criticism and condemnation, and perhaps some form of ostracism. It may also take the form of a justifiable fear on the part of the "passivist" that he is jeopardizing his future by acquiring a bad name, although this fear is much stronger among professional and technical strata than among the masses of workers and peasants for whom individual promotion and placement is a less meaningful question.

Compulsion, then, does play some role in mobilizing the masses for action. For all those who oppose the regime and for those "passivists" whose career prospects are heavily dependent on bureaucratic or Party favor, the threat of physical or material reprisals is constant and powerful; they may act on Party orders, but not voluntarily. However, outside of these categories and with the admission that individual cases of coerced action occur, the bulk of mass action on Party policies is voluntary even though it is never spontaneous and seldom free from some form of compulsion. As noted in the Introduction, voluntarism is always a matter of degree; very little social action is *totally* free from compulsion. The action to which we are referring in China is voluntary in the sense that the consequences of nonaction, in most cases, are not so severe as to compel action unless there is also present some degree of willingness to act. There are two reasons why the consequences of nonaction, which are mainly verbal harassment and social pressure, do not assume a strongly coercive flavor. The first is that the number of "passivists" who do not respond with the desired degree of activism is so great that social pressure loses much of its force. Except in extreme cases, the "passivist" can be fairly sure that much of the criticism to which he is subjected is merely for the sake of appearances by people who are not themselves free from the same sin and that the threat of social ostracism is unenforceable against so many people. The second reason is that the rewards of activism are not so great as to compel universal competition for their attainment. By definition, activism demands more work and less leisure, and yet it is absolutely no guarantee against future criticism and pressure of exactly the sort that the "passivist" experiences. Moreover, given the economic and political structure of Communist China, activism at the mass level promises no significant affluence or power.

Compulsion, therefore, even though an ever-present aspect of Chinese political life, does not explain the Party's organizational success. At the same time, as we have already suggested and will discuss more thoroughly later, the element of "voluntarism" in Chinese political participation is frequently not what the Party means by "conscious and voluntary" action. Some of the Chinese masses may participate with genuine ideological commitment and understanding, but the voluntarism of the majority rests on other factors. Broadly speaking, there are four main sources of the voluntary political participation that has made the Chinese style of participation an organizational success.

The first source is habitual obedience to political authority. Whether or not they approved, or even understood, the CCP program in 1949, most Chinese accepted the political legitimacy of the new leaders. Since central political authority had never held much immediacy for the Chinese people, acceptance of this authority was not a matter of great controversy. It was probably sufficient that the new leaders had demonstrated their military superiority. However, the incorruptibility of the Party, the model behavior of the Red Army, and the Party's professed concern for the people—all widely publicized and all strong traditional legitimizers of political authority—certainly helped to confirm the CCP's authority. Popular acceptance of Party rule encouraged voluntary popular obedience to Party demands, especially when these demands were explained by rational persuasion and justified by moralistic goals.

The second source is positive ideological support for some or all of the Party's objectives without ideological commitment to Party doctrine as such. The two primary appeals here are nationalism and a demand for socio-economic progress; in many cases, of course, the two are inseparable. Many Chinese, and virtually all of the intellectuals, have voluntarily supported the Party because of their belief that it would restore China's international prestige and power and build China into a modern state. The CCP has recognized these appeals and traded on them heavily. In fact, political education has undoubtedly been most successful in implanting the themes of nationalism and progress. Since political education always identifies these themes solely with CCP doctrine, they have been the lure that has drawn some Chinese to the full "socialist consciousness" that the Party solicits. Nevertheless, the testimony of refugees and the "hundred flowers" outburst indicate that most intellectuals, at least, do distinguish between their willingness to sacrifice for the Party and their willingness to sacrifice for the nationalistic and modernizing goals that the Party professes.[28] There are times when nationalism or the demand for progress may cause disaffection from Party policies. The Great Leap policy, for example, alienated many technicians and intellectuals who felt (correctly) that it was a false road to economic progress. In the long run, however, these themes will probably continue to attract considerable voluntary participation in "socialist construction."

The third source of voluntary political participation is satisfaction of personal needs, expecially desires for personal advancement and community status and belonging. Although satisfaction of these needs does not depend exclusively on active political participation, and the degree of satisfaction is not so complete as to make participation compulsive, it is nonetheless true that participation does offer significant personal rewards. Cadres and activists at the lowest level may enjoy little of the power or rewards traditionally associated with official position in China, but they are still in a position of leadership over their neighbors and they have taken the first step toward a political career, however distant and unpredictable the path to the higher levels of power may be. The truly enormous number of ordinary citizens recruited to positions of village, neighborhood, or workshop leadership, on the basis of demonstrated political activism, is a major factor in basic-level support for Party objectives. For those who are not recruited to such positions, active participation still serves as a symbol of community membership and as a basis for a great deal of public commendation in the form of awards to individuals or teams and selection as "models." The psychic value of a sense of belonging and status in the village, neighborhood, or workshop must be considerable in China, especially in view of the importance of associational ties in traditional China. A sense of full membership in these units is more important than ever since they now fulfill functions that were formerly scattered among several types of associations.

Finally, some of the appeal of political participation rests on its connection with popular interests. The CCP has never encouraged the expression of individual interests, but it has always insisted that individual interests will be satisfied with the realization of the collective interest. While this claim is invalid as a universal principle, there are times when a genuine coincidence of individual and Party-defined collective interests exists. This was the case with many of the early mass movements and it would seem to be the case with programs for improvements in sanitation, pest riddance, agricultural technology, and so forth. For all of its hostility toward interest politics, the Party has not been averse

[28] See Mu Fu-sheng, *The Wilting of the Hundred Flowers: The Chinese Intelligentsia Under Mao* (New York, 1963), *passim*.

to stressing group interests on some occasions. Most prominently, the CCP line on land reform, mutual aid, and early cooperativization emphasized the material gains of the peasant. For example, in a 1954 speech, Teng Tzu-hui, the director of the Rural Work Department of the CCP Central Committee, said that the movement to form APC's must invoke the principle of mutual benefit because the peasants are "utilitarian and calculating" and will never join if they stand to lose in the process.[29] When the Party has been able to build a convincing case for coincidence of individual and collective interest, it has attracted some active and voluntary mass support on this basis This certainly happened more frequently in the early years of the regime than it has since 1957; the CCP's growing insensitivity to popular interests during the Great Leap Forward was a major factor in its declining popular support during that period. However, popular participation in the management of minor internal affairs in such units as production teams and residents' committees still gives the Chinese citizen a very modest opportunity for political activity that is related to his own interests.

All of these factors, combined with the effectiveness of the CCP's organizational and persuasive techniques, have produced the popular political participation that has been so critical for the CPR's accomplishments. Another question that is related to the CCP's success in organizing mass participation is what secondary functions participation has performed in addition to executing Party policies. The previous discussion has made some suggestions along this line in noting the personal satisfaction derived from participation. The two most important points, however, are the extent to which mass participation has contributed to the emergence of a national political community and whether participation has given the Chinese people any voice in national political affairs.

National political community depends on such conditions as popular loyalty to a central government, consciousness of the individual's political relationship with this government, and some degree of popular understanding and concern about national affairs. These conditions were absent in the traditional political system of China, in spite of the unifying influence of Chinese culture. They began to emerge in the latter part of the nineteenth century, but were not highly developed even at the end of the Second World War. Since the establishment of the CPR in 1949, however, a sense of national political community has been growing with unprecedented rapidity. Among the factors that account for this trend are the establishment of a highly centralized government

[29] *Chung-kuo Ch'ing-nien Pao* (China Youth News), September 1, 1954, in *CB*, No. 306 (November 22, 1954).

that extended its administrative control down to the smallest social units, the growth of a national transportation and communications system, the assertive political role that the new government has played in international affairs, shifts of large numbers of people from one region to another, and the deliberate attempt to use the educational and communication system to foster a sense of national political community. Mass political participation has also contributed to this process in rather incalculable ways. The contribution is twofold. First, the act of participation itself is a symbol of the individual's loyalty to and identification with the central government. Participation in the formal state structure is particularly important in this respect since the connection with the national level is sharpest there. Party propaganda has tried to establish the same connection with all political acts, but the degree of success is questionable. Second, the prominence of political education in the Chinese style of participation ensures that every citizen will receive a vast amount of information about national affairs. The newspapers, radio broadcasts, and lectures to which the citizen is exposed provide an avalanche of data on central policies, national figures, and political and economic conditions all over China. Mass political participation has, therefore, added to the growth of national political community mainly through symbolic political acts and exposure to propagandistic reporting of national affairs.

The Chinese style of participation limits decision-making power at all levels of government except the very lowest to the CCP. Even CCP theory, for all of its pretensions about popular sovereignty, does not disguise the Party's supreme political power. Nevertheless, it is still legitimate to ask whether the mass line permits some popular influence, though not control, on national political decisions. In other words, does the Chinese political system have any place for pressure groups of even the weakest sort? The answer is No. Even if a pressure group can survive with only a suggestion of influence, it must still have some type of organization, a conscious motivation to influence policy, and some legitimacy within the system. There have been groups in Communist China that have fulfilled one or two of these conditions, but none that has fulfilled all. Perhaps the closest thing to pressure-group activity in Communist China was the intellectuals' attack on the Party in the "hundred flowers" period. Their organization was rudimentary to say the least (it was scattered among the democratic parties, certain educational institutions, and perhaps the newspaper *Kuang-ming Jih-pao*) but they did have specific group complaints and they were consciously trying to influence policy and establish the legitimacy of this influence. The Party, of course, ultimately denied the legitimacy of their action, and further attempts were out of the question. It is the Party's refusal to legitimize any organized expression of particular interest that prohibits pressure-group activity.

What is left to the Chinese people, then, is simply the hope that their leaders will be attuned to popular demands and the knowledge that no government can enforce policies that meet with truly massive, though unorganized, opposition. It is popular "influence" of this sort that the mass line acknowledges and encourages. By insisting that the people express their opinions, by tolerating discussion of "incorrect" opinions so long as they are voiced by unorganized individuals, by relying to such a great extent on mass cooperation for the enforcement of policies, and by forcing basic-level leaders into direct contact with the masses, the CCP is, in fact, exposed to some degree of popular influence. By far the best example was the retrenchment in rural commune organization in 1961–1962, but there have been other cases in which popular response has influenced the execution and formation of Party policies. The Marriage Law, the birth control issue, the urban communes, and concessions to the intellectuals in 1956–1957 are all cases in which the Party has deferred to some extent to popular feelings.

In sum, the Chinese style of participation has been a success in terms of its primary organizational function. It has also contributed heavily to the development of national political community in China and very modestly to exposure of political elites to popular opinions and demands; these are functions that the CCP regards as related to, but secondary to, the organization of the masses for political action. The Party's ability to organize popular political activity derives partly from genuine ideological commitment among the people, partly from the organizational and persuasive skills of the Party, partly from compulsion, and partly from such factors as habitual obedience to authority, support for nationalistic and modernistic goals, desires for career advancement and community status, and coincidence of political interest. These multiple functions and motivations help explain the impressive volume of political activity in China, but they also bear testimony to what are, from the CCP's point of view, some very serious problems in the Chinese style of participation. It is not inconsistent to refer to problems in areas that have already been mentioned under the rubric of "success." Party goals in political participation are so high that one can speak of important shortcomings even where a substantial degree of success is attained. For example, popular political action seldom achieves the total ideological commitment and the high level of consciousness and voluntarism that CCP doctrine prescribes. It is not mere quibbling to cite such doctrinal inconsistencies. The Party insists that results will not be permanent if the people act without sufficient consciousness. The Party may be wrong on that point, but lack of political consciousness does cause extreme tension in the Communist political system because it forces cadres and activists to bear the burden of incessant agitation and mobilization among the masses. The longer this process continues, the greater becomes the strain on Party relations with the masses and the possibility for serious deviations from the mass line. All of the problems that are discussed below relate directly or indirectly to the Party's inability to produce the desired level of consciousness among the people.

Strains in the mass line   The mass line evolved in the 1930's and 1940's from a situation in which there was a relatively high correlation between short-run Party objectives and popular interests and in which cadres at all levels were in relatively close contact with the masses. Because of these conditions, the mass-line formula of Party decision and popular execution was usually realized in practice with a minimum of strain. After 1949, the formula remained but the situation changed. The CCP discovered that mass execution of policies designed to produce major changes throughout China was a very complex matter and that higher-level cadres no longer maintained the popular contacts that were to ensure a "democratic" style in the absence of popular controls. The Party's response was to retain the theory of the mass line while trying to recapture its original spirit through indoctrination of the people and rectification of cadres. The mass movements have been the most tangible sign of this effort to force the political situation into conformity with the theory. But the mass movement, for all of its demands on masses and cadres alike, has been only a temporary solution. It creates mass "enthusiasm" and renews direct cadre leadership of the people, but only by an enormous expenditure of time and effort. Moreover, enthusiasm drops rapidly when the movement subsides and the movements seem to lose more of their impact with each campaign. The problem of the mass line is, therefore, a recurring conflict between theory and reality. The Party recognizes the symptoms of the conflict, but refuses to abandon its theory. And, as the divergence between theory and reality becomes greater, it becomes more and more difficult to produce "conscious and voluntary" action by the masses.

Strains in the mass line appear in many ways. One example is Party interference with the state structure in the face of its insistence that this structure is the instrument through which the people themselves, albeit under Party leadership, will manage the state. As early as 1951, the Party admitted that state organs were stagnating, that people's congresses and councils were becoming "cadres' conferences," and that Party organization was assuming all the responsibilities of government. In one *hsien* in Honan the number of proposals presented at meetings of the *hsien* representative conference dropped from 2,600 at the first meeting to 582 at the third and only 24 at the sixth.[30] Periodically, as during the first elections and congresses in 1953–1954, the Party has breathed some life back into the state structure, but the *de facto* location of political power in Party committees at various levels has always resumed the general trend. By 1956–1957 the problem of "Party serving as government" was widespread.[31] The weakening of congresses and elections at the basic level during the Great Leap confirmed this trend. Ironically, *hsia-fang* (the policy of transferring cadres to lower levels), which was conceived partly as a device for renewing cadres' contacts with mass life, has frequently demonstrated the Party's willingness to interfere with normal state processes as many of the downward-transferred cadres have assumed posts that should be elective.[32]

Another sign of mass-line difficulties has been the tendency toward isolation from the people of all cadres who do not actually work at the mass level. Party literature is full of concern over this problem, whether it is genuinely due to "bureaucratic" and "formalistic" errors on the part of cadres (as the Party usually claims) or whether it is simply an inevitable result of the heavy bureaucratic work load imposed on them.[33] The contradiction between cadres' ignorance of, and isolation from, daily life and the theory of the mass line has been attacked by *hisa-fang,* soliciting people's letters and calls, and so forth. While these efforts add to the direct quality of cadre-mass relations, they do not actually resolve the problem. The fact is that Party leadership can be maintained with the thoroughness that the CCP demands only by vesting direct authority in Party committees. As long as this is the case, cadres will be neither temperamentally nor occupationally suited to follow the mass-line style of leadership. In this perspective, the CCP's performance during the Great Leap appears as a hyperbole of the mass line. The fantastic demands on the energies of the people, made in the name of the mass line, could only have resulted from either general ignorance or general disregard of the actual conditions of popular life. Efforts to restore the mass line by *hsia-fang* merely emphasized the conflict be-

[30] *Ho-nan Jih-pao* (Honan Daily), November 20, 1951. See also the documents on the Conference of North China *Hsien* Magistrates, held in Peking in September, 1951, in *CB,* No. 148 (January 4, 1952).

[31] See Hsü Tai-huang, "Chieh-chüeh I-tang Tai-cheng ti Wen-t'i Yao Ts'ung Shao-pien Chao-shou" (Solving the Problem of Party Serving as Government Must Start From Above), *Kuei-chou Jih-pao* (Kweichow Daily) (Kweiyang), February 27, 1957.

[32] See Lewis's discussion of *hsia-fang* in *Leadership in Communist China,* pp. 220–232.

[33] For a typical discussion, see An Tzu-wen's report at a high-level cadre study meeting, *JMJP,* February 12, 1953, in *CB,* No. 231 (March 1, 1953).

tween theory and practice by making demands for physical labor from cadres, intellectuals, and office workers that few could accept voluntarily.

Finally, the conflict between theory and practice that has weakened the mass line is illustrated by the Party's refusal to give theoretical recognition to conflicts of interest among the people. The CCP admits, of course, that "contradictions" can exist among the people. But "contradictions," in the CCP definition, are due to imperfect perceptions and behavior; they will resolve themselves in a higher stage of unity after appropriate discussion and education. This view is essential to the preservation of the mass line which assumes that *all* the people will eventually accept and execute Party policies "consciously and voluntarily." In practice, however, conflicting interests remain.

Consider the following example reported by a Shensi commune inspection team.[34] The commune was formed from eighteen cooperatives in a single *hsiang* located on both sides of a river. The cooperatives on the north side of the river were relatively wealthy; they had good land, plenty of draft animals, and good equipment (they had recently put new rubber tires on eight of their carts). The southern cooperatives, however, were not so wealthy and, in particular, did not have enough draft animals to work their fields. When the discussion on commune formation started, the southern cooperatives and the Party committee favored one commune for the entire *hsiang*. The representatives of the northern cooperatives, however, did not want to share their animals and tools with the rest of the *hsiang;* they "acted like men possessed" and advocated the formation of two communes, one on each side of the river. The Party committee identified the source of the problem as "particularism" and opened up an educational campaign to overcome it. In the end, everyone saw that particularism could only interfere with commune unity and production and with implementation of the state plan. The plan to form one big commune was "unanimously approved."

In more general terms, the Party frequently notes conflicts of interest in the agricultural situation. But it persistently identifies these conflicts as "contradictions" between "particular interests" and "collective interests" or between cadres and masses, thereby implying that unity will be established as soon as the contradictions are recognized and overcome.[35] In this way, the Party anticipates and justifies the one-sided

[34] "Tung-feng Jen-min Kung-she Tiao-ch'a Pao-kao" (Report on the Investigation of Tungfeng People's Commune), *Hsi-pei Ta-hsüeh Hsüeh-pao (Jen-wen K'o-hsüeh)* [Journal of Northwestern University (Humanities)], 1958, No. 3.

[35] See Teng Tzu-hui, "Lun Nung-ts'un Jen-min Nei-pu Mao-tun ho Cheng-ch'üeh Ch'u-li Mao-tun ti Fang-chen ho Pan-fa" (Internal Contradictions Among the People in the Villages and the Policy and Methods for Correct Handling of Contradictions), *Chung-kuo Ch'ing-nien*, 1957, No. 21.

solution and "unanimous approval" that always results. In fact, however, it is simply refusing to admit that a situation can arise in which genuine popular interests can oppose Party policies even after "patient persuasion and education." These verbal gymnastics cannot be very convincing to the people involved. Like Party interference with the state structure and cadre isolation from the masses, the smashing of interests that conflict with those of the Party demonstrates the CCP's frequent inability to maintain both Party leadership and "conscious and voluntary" execution of its policies by the masses.

Low popular consciousness   Low political consciousness among the masses is the most directly visible weakness of political participation in China. To the Chinese Communists, political consciousness implies not only an awareness of the political significance of social action but also an ability and willingness to see political issues as the Communists do. Lack of participation is obviously a sign of low political consciousness, but, as might be expected, it is not a common phenomenon. There will always be a few who simply abstain from participation, and one can find reports on "backward" units where failure to participate in meetings or other political activities is widespread. However, the Party makes special efforts to correct such cases, and it is doubtful if widespread absence of participation can exist anywhere in China for very long. The more common manifestation of low political consciousness is participation that is not motivated by a rational acceptance of Party objectives and a willingness to act on them. Those who engage in political participation but, from the Party's point of view, for the wrong reasons probably constitute the greatest proportion of the Chinese population. The statement that only a minority of the population has high political consciousness in the Party's sense of the term is necessarily an impressionistic conclusion. It is supported, however, by the general tone of mainland literature that deals with mass political participation and, more specifically, by the criticism of the "hundred flowers" period and the decline in public morale during the crisis of the Great Leap. Of course, low political consciousness among the majority of the population does not mean that the regime is ready to collapse. There is a great divergence between the level of consciousness that the Party hopes to attain and the level that still ensures popular tolerance of the regime. The actual level falls somewhere in between.

There are three general sources of low political consciousness in Communist China. The first source, and the only one that indicates a genuine lack of political consciousness in a neutral sense, is the Chinese tradition of popular political apathy and ignorance. For all of the sweeping changes in "transitional" China, traditional political attitudes were still widespread when the Communists came to power in 1949. Time and again, these attitudes have frustrated the Party's efforts to instill a genuine understanding of its programs among the masses, let alone organizing them to carry out these programs on their own initiative. The problem has naturally been greatest in rural areas, although it is by no means limited to the countryside. To give just one sample of the difficulty of inducing political consciousness in rural China, we may refer to a report on a village in Hupei.[36] Land reform in this village was "comparatively thorough" and the peasants had shown a high degree of activism in production. Nevertheless, within a few months after the conclusion of land reform, a "numb and negligent" ideology had settled over many of the cadres and peasants. Only twelve of the twenty-five members of the peasants' association committee were still working actively; the majority of small-group leaders were becoming lax in their work, and some were frankly looking for "substitutes" to take over their jobs. Among the peasants generally, there was "gratitude to the government for distributing the land"—always, to the CCP, the prime evidence that the peasants had failed to grasp the political significance of land reform. They participated in land reform only with hopes of raising their fortunes and with no understanding of the national significance of their actions. Land reform succeeded only because of the cadres who came into the village to organize it; when they left, there was no one to replace them. Reports of this sort were most common in the early years of the CPR, but, as rural political conditions in 1961–1962 have shown, there are still many peasants who have no significant political consciousness.

A second source of low consciousness is actual hostility to Party objectives. This may be due to a feeling that the Party is pursuing policies that are not in the national interests, a feeling that was evidently widely held by intellectuals during the "hundred flowers" period; or it may be due to Party violation of individual interests, which was a major factor in peasant disaffection during the difficult years of 1959–1961. Needless to say, this attitude is not necessarily indicative of an absence of political consciousness in a real sense. Quite the contrary may be true, as the frequency of hostility toward Party policies among the intellectuals shows. There is a possibility that CCP efforts to raise political consciousness among the students by nationalistic and modernizing appeals may be producing some real dissatisfaction among the future Chinese elite over the Party's failure to modernize at a sufficiently rapid pace.

Finally, low political consciousness may result from dissatisfaction

[36] *Ch'ang-chiang Jih-pao* (Yangtze Daily), November 8, 1951.

with the Chinese style of political participation as such. In this case, the problem lies not so much with objections to substantive policies of the regime as with resentment of the manner in which policies are carried out. Disenchantment with participation has many causes. The most important is undoubtedly the obvious discrepancy between Party theory and practice discussed earlier. There can be little incentive to participate when one believes that all the conventional political phrases and practices are simply a disguise for dictatorial rule by a small group of men. Coupled with this is an undercurrent of caution, if not actually fear, in all relationships with the party. Mao Tun, the writer, may have expressed this more vividly than he intended in a reference to the characterization of Party cadres in current Chinese fiction.

We often see that the vocabulary used by one secretary of the Party committee is the same as that used by another secretary of the Party committee—regardless of the occasion. In some works . . . only the language of the secretaries of the Party committee or branches does not have any individuality. One of the reasons for this is that the language of the secretaries of the Party committee is not only formalized but is also bound by certain invisible taboos.[37]

Disenchantment with participation also stems from personal resentment of the intrusion of seemingly unnecessary political activities into one's private life. During the "hundred flowers" campaign, Yeh Tu-i, a member of the Central Committee of the Democratic League, commented with distaste on the necessity of political participation for any sort of status; he said that many specialists found political activities to be ". . . a great burden that hinders their research work. Some people take part in politics when in fact they have no interest. Even when they attend meetings, although they are wearing their earphones they have pulled out the plugs, and they are thinking over their own research problems." [38] Other sources have commented on a decline in student interest in and knowledge about their political studies, the unreasonable and inefficient way in which political tasks are organized, and general reluctance to expose oneself to criticism and self-examination in political study.[39]

[37] Mao Tun, "A General Review of Short Stories Published in 1960," *Wen-yi Pao* (Literary Gazette), 1961, Nos. 4–6, in *CB*, No. 663 (October 18, 1961).

[38] *JMJP*, May 17, 1957, quoted in Ch'en Ch'üan, ed., *"Ming-fang" Hsüan-ts'ui* (Selections from the Blooming and Contending Campaign) (Hong Kong, 1958), Vol. I, pp. 76–77.

[39] See *Chung-kuo Ch'ing-nien Pao* (China Youth News), November 5, 1955; "Relieve the Students of Their Too Heavy Burden of Social Activities," *Chung-kuo Ch'ing-nien*, 1956, No. 9, in *SMM*, No. 43 (July 16, 1956); and Nieh Chen, "Problems Concerning Studies and Reform of the Students of the Institute of Socialism," *JMJP*, April 8, 1960, in *CB*, No. 628 (July 22, 1960).

A final cause of disenchantment with the Chinese style of participation is the frequent deterioration of small-group discussion into petty
matters that have no real political significance. According to one writer,
criticism at meetings is frequently senseless, trivial, lacking in solemnity,
and directed at irrelevant personal matters.[40] This tendency reflects a
serious conflict in political participation in China. On the one hand, the
Party demands political activism of everyone, urging all Chinese to
engage in "struggle" and assert their "initiative and creativity" in the
cause of socialism; on the other hand, it limits opportunities for truly
spontaneous action and reserves for itself the right to pass judgment on
the "correctness" of all political action. As a result, much that passes
for political action is forced or false attacks on the behavior and personality of others, which seems to be a relatively safe form of "activism."
Much of a small group's energies may go into the resolution of personal
rivalries and struggles for power that have little to do with the political
issues that are supposed to be debated. Some of this activity may
actually develop into a surprisingly democratic form of internal group
"politics" but, interesting though that may be, it cannot help but detract
from the value and appeal of the type of political participation that the
Party is trying to produce.[41]

Basic-level cadre problems   Throughout this study, there has been
frequent reference to problems connected with basic-level cadres. The
essence of the difficulty is a shortage of people who are willing and able
to meet the rigorous demands of mass-line leadership. The qualitative
nature of this problem demands emphasis. There is no shortage in the
total number of cadres, and the CCP is constantly trying to reduce their
number in order to avoid excessive bureaucratization and free more
hands for production. At the same time, there is definitely a shortage of
"good" cadres in the Party's sense of the word. The CCP's inability to
turn all of the activists it recruits into model cadres has a very wide
impact since the quality of basic-level cadres is perhaps the single most
important factor in securing "conscious" popular cooperation in the
execution of Party policies.

The basic source of the shortage of good cadres lies in the political
and cultural backwardness of the population as a whole. To some

---

[40] Tseng-Teh-lin, "Improve and Strengthen the Youth League's Political-Ideolog-
ical Work Among University Undergraduates," *Chung-kuo Ch'ing-nien,* 1956,
No. 13, in *SMM,* No. 50 (September 4, 1956).

[41] For examples of this tendency, see Chiang Han and Chang T'ien, "How Does
Niu Han Attempt To Sabotage the Work of the Youth League," *Chung-kuo
Ch'ing-nien,* 1955, No. 14, in *SMM,* No. 5 (September 12, 1955); and Ting Pan-
shih and Yü Kun, "An 'Alarming' Small Clique," *Chung-kuo Ch'ing-nien,* 1956,
No. 15, in *SMM,* No. 52 (September 17, 1956).

extent, the CCP is able to place politically advanced cadres in responsible basic-level positions by bringing in Party members and student
activists from the outside. But local recruitment is the only possible
answer to the demand for leadership at the very lowest level—in the
workshops, villages, and streets—and here the Party sometimes faces an
appalling absence of political and cultural abilities and a general unwillingness to assume the role of political leadership. A report on Hopei in
1960, after great efforts to improve cadre education and to import
outside political leadership for the communes, stated that over half of all
commune cadres had only a "lower middle" cultural level, or less, and
that many of them had had no systematic study of Marxism–Leninism or
the writings of Mao Tse-tung.[42]

When good cadres are not available in quantity, the work load of
those who do serve becomes excessive. Conditions in one district of
Chungking illustrate this point. On the basis of the total number of
posts (for cadres and activists) in this district, about one-sixth to one-
fifth of the total population would have to serve to keep one post to one
man. In fact, however, most activists held four or five posts and one
held fourteen. The tasks handed down to the district by higher levels
forced activists to attend from forty to fifty meetings, of about two hours
each, during the first ten days of the month.[43] In spite of the Party's
desire to maintain good men in office, the demands for cadres at higher
levels, coupled with rectification campaigns, has sometimes caused a
heavy demand for new cadres at the lowest levels. This happened
during the Great Leap when many "new hands" were recruited to
leadership positions at the production team and brigade levels with very
unsatisfactory results.[44]

These comments do not mean that incompetence, illiteracy, apathy,
and corruption are necessarily the primary cadre problems, although
they do occur when the Party has to recruit from an unsatisfactory
base. Judging from Party literature, "commandism" is the greatest
single manifestation of unsuitable cadres. Commandism may be due to
incompetence or bad character but it is more likely to be the result of

[42] Sung Ch'ang-hsing, "Chia-su P'ei-yang ho T'i-kao Nung-ts'un Jen-min Kung-
she ti Kan-pu" (Accelerate the Cultivation and Elevation of Cadres in the Rural
People's Communes), *Tung Feng* (East Wind), 1960, No. 5, p. 21. For some
perceptive and objective comments on the difficulties in recruiting able street
cadres among the housewives, see Shirley Wood, *A Street in China* (London,
1958), *passim;* the author is the American wife of a Chinese professor and resided
in Shanghai in the early years of the regime.

[43] *Hsin-hua Jih-pao* (New China Daily) (Chungking), August 31, 1952. For
similar comments on overworked cadres in rural areas, see Hsiao Tung, "Hsiang-li
ti Wen-t'i" (Problems in the Hsiang), *JMJP*, February 15, 1957.

[44] See *Nan-fang Jih-pao* (Southern Daily), June 12, 1962.

impatience with the mass line on the part of cadres who are overly enthusiastic or who are harassed beyond endurance by demands from above. Commandism is not, as the word might imply, forcing the masses to carry out orders; as noted earlier, the use of force or threats is definitely discouraged and is more likely to brand the cadre who engages in it as a "bad element." Commandism is defined as "issuing orders to the masses," that is, presenting them with a certain task or decision that has not been thoroughly discussed and propagandized before it is executed. The defect of commandism, therefore, is that it *omits* popular participation rather than secures it by force. Another manifestation of improper cadre work style is "tailism," that is, sacrificing Party policies to the immediate demands of the people. One might well question if such a "defect" can emerge in Communist China, but it does occur and was apparently very widespread in rural areas during 1961–1962. This point leads directly to the problem of particularism, which the Party sees as placing loyalties to one's family, clan, village, class, or unit before loyalty to the state, nation, and Party.

The survival of particularism   Basic-level cadre problems provide what is probably the most tangible evidence of the survival of particularism in rural China. The evidence itself is fragmentary but highly suggestive. During the agricultural crisis of recent years, the Party found that some basic-level cadres were encouraging the peasants to withhold grain from the commune and to devote their energies to their private plots.[45] More significantly, the CCP acknowledged the particularistic foundations of successful village leadership by restoring to their posts many longtime village leaders who had been transferred to higher levels when the communes were formed; in some cases, the Party expressly stated that these "veteran" cadres were uniquely qualified for village leadership because they were the "relatives and friends" of the peasants.[46] Do these instances of Party assignment of rural cadres whose authority is based on village and kinship loyalties mean that particularism is still strong in the Chinese village? The answer is by no means conclusive but a qualified affirmative seems justified.

The Party's preference for "veteran" cadres is not, in itself, a sufficient answer as this can be explained by superior experience and competence. What is significant is that the veteran cadres are those who emerged during land reform and early cooperativization, a time when the particular interests of peasants were fully aroused, and that the Party

[45] See the materials in *Union Research Service,* Vol. 27, Nos. 7–9.

[46] John Wilson Lewis, "The Leadership Doctrine of the Chinese Communist Party" (*Asian Survey,* October, 1963). This article is an explicit analysis of traditional influences on rural leadership in Communist China.

admitted the importance of their personal ties within the village in maintaining their authority. The suggestion that some cadres owing primary loyalties to the villages have remained in positions of rural leadership ever since 1949 is not easily reconciled with Party doctrine and practice. Several points suggest this possibility, however, in addition to the evidence mentioned. The first is simply the depth of particularistic patterns of authority that existed in the villages when the Party came to power; no efforts could eradicate this completely in fifteen years. Moreover, in its attempt to make political education meaningful to the peasants, the Party has encouraged the translation of abstract and general policies into terms of village experience. The message of national loyalty has, of course, remained, but it is doubtful if political education, as it has actually been presented to the peasants by village leaders, has been as strongly oriented toward the destruction of particularism as central policy and propaganda suggest.

Finally, the institutional development of Chinese Communism has, in effect, left a wide opening for the survival of particularism in the countryside. By removing the peasants from any significant contact with basic-level government and by confining nearly all their political activities to the village, the CCP has denied the peasants the opportunity to practice the broader political loyalties and interests that Party propaganda stresses. The difference between basic-level government and village government (the production team) is not simply one of size and diffuseness of interests among the population, although that is a significant factor. It is also one of political character—the difference between an administratively defined unit that is part of a national political structure and a functionally defined unit that exists only for its own purposes. How much difference changes in the institutional focus of political participation would make is difficult to say, since the CCP would not grant the people genuine political power even in basic-level government. However, greater popular participation in the state structure, even if ritualistic, would raise the peasants' political horizons above the village and open up more channels for the subversion of particularism than does the present system.

The survival of particularism is a relative concept. It may still be widespread in rural China, but it is not as strong as it was before 1949. The fact that it survives to a greater extent than one would expect from a surface examination of Party goals does not mean that the production team is identical in political character to the traditional village. The peasants participate more formally and consistently in the management of village affairs than they did in the past and they are certainly exposed to a far greater amount of outside political influence than ever before in Chinese history. Moreover, the social composition of village leadership has undergone a major change. The poor and middle peasants have replaced the landlords and scholar-gentry as the main source of village leaders.[47] Therefore, there is no reason to doubt the Party's professed desire to change the political character of rural China. Its toleration of some particularistic features is apparently a matter of necessity. Mobilization of the masses for production has been and is the Party's primary concern. For this purpose, the Party has found it advantageous to rely on old village units and loyalties. In return for the organizational control that this ensures, it has sacrificed, at least temporarily, some of its ambitions for political modernization.

[47] The old type of leadership has not entirely disappeared, as frequent Party statements admit. For example, in Hopei in 1960, there was said to be "a small number of third class communes" in which middle or rich peasants, or even landlords and "evil elements," retained control. The number of such communes was not given, but the Hopei Provincial Party Committee had decided to send 20,000 cadres to this "small number" of communes, for a period of three years, to correct the situation. See Lin T'ieh, "Shen-ju K'ai-chan Nung-ts'un ti She-hui Chu-i, Kung-ch'an Chu-i Chiao-yü Yün-tung" (Deeply Open Up the Socialist and Communist Education Movement in the Villages), *Hung Ch'i,* 1960, No. 15.

EIGHT

Political Participation and
Political Change in Modern China

The nature of Chinese Communist politics inhibits conclusive answers to many of the most important questions about political participation in China. What is the character of popular response to Communist rule? To what extent are the "political" activities of the Chinese citizen truly political, in the sense that they involve conscious commitment to a particular resolution of controversial public issues? Who are the "activists" and "passivists" and what does the pattern of "activism" tell us about the future of Chinese politics? The passage of time, the growth of new generations to adulthood, the relaxation of restrictions on reporting about the Chinese mainland, the systematic interviewing of refugees, and the intensive study of particular groups or units in Chinese society are some of the temporal, political, or methodological developments that will ultimately give us better answers to these questions. However, the materials explored in this study support only the cautious generalizations already offered. The CCP certainly holds considerable popular support, but it is neither as universal nor as "conscious" as the Party claims or would like. Political activities are normally voluntary, but, again, they frequently lack "consciousness" and are hardly ever spontaneous. Most of what the Party defines as political is indeed related to significant public issues, but there are signs of sterility and artificiality in some of the key areas of popular political participation, such as basic-level congresses and small-group discussion. Young people have undoubtedly led in "activism," but today the Party expresses deep suspicion about the revolutionary reliability of China's youth. These are but a few examples of the conflicting strands that appear in the Chinese pattern of participation and make definitive judgments about it extremely difficult.

Against the uncertainty that characterizes such questions stands the certainty of the CCP's accomplishments in organizing the masses for political activity. Whatever the precise degree of political content, consciousness, and voluntarism, the scope and volume of mass participation surely has great significance for the Chinese Communist political system and the political history of modern China. In the Chinese political system, popular political activities constitute one of the primary structures through which the CCP executes its policies. The Party also relies on mass political participation for political education of the people, the recruitment of new Party members and other activists, the creation and maintenance of popular identification with the present regime, and informing the Party about popular moods and demands. Participation also performs what are for the CCP the unintended (though not unnoticed) functions of advancing and protecting personal careers and maintaining a citizen's sense of belonging in his local community. Discussion of participation's complex role in the Chinese political system has, of course, been a recurring theme throughout most of this book.

The second theme of the historical dimension of the Chinese style of political participation has received less explicit attention, but the implications are no less clear. In broadest terms, Communist mobilization of the masses has politicized an apolitical population. It has brought the Chinese people into direct and continuing contact with higher levels of government and organized them for active support of national objectives; it has tried, albeit with mixed success, to replace loyalties to the family and other particularistic units with loyalty to the political community. The result is the fulfillment of one of the most powerful currents in modern Chinese history. The idea that effective state power must be based on the people themselves—an idea that appeared in a superficial way with the nineteenth century reformers and rapidly entrenched itself in the ideology of Chinese nationalism—has come to fruition in Communist China. In the first instance, efforts to rouse the Chinese people to political action added to the weakness of existing governments and the instability of Chinese politics. With the victory of the Chinese Communist movement, however, mass participation became a source of governmental strength and stability and a leading contributor to the rapid resurrection of Chinese power and influence.

The transformation of China into a modern nation-state, which is an abbreviated statement of the changes referred to here, brings with it a change in the life of the people as well as in the fortunes of the polity. For better or worse, the common man in China is now deeply affected by the programs and ambitions of his national government; his response to political pressures from above not only accelerates the rate of change but may also widen his own horizons and ambitions. At the most intimate level, he finds his social relationships extended beyond his family and personal friends to include, in some way, every member of society.[1] While such changes in personal experience and outlook are directly associated with Communist rule, particularly with the present style of political participation, they are not necessarily limited to the results the Party wishes to produce. The CCP hopes that the politicization of the Chinese people will proceed hand in hand with their communization. By and large this may be the case, especially among the activists. Yet we know that the level of "Communist consciousness" has lagged behind the extent of political mobilization, which suggests that many Chinese must be undergoing changes in political attitudes even without developing Communist consciousness. Specifically, the Chinese style of participation, with its emphasis on political education, obligation, and action, definitely encourages the growth of national consciousness and a general awareness of political phenomena. To the extent that this occurs without acceptance of CCP ideology, it is a latent function of participation that is as significant in the long run as the intended consequences.

The Communists' role in the political transformation of modern China should not be overstated. It is worth repeating that changes in Chinese political behavior, attitudes, and institutions were in progress long before the CCP became a significant force in Chinese politics.[2] From the late nineteenth century on, various Chinese leaders of differing political persuasions were to diagnose China's ills, and the steps needed to correct them, in ways that anticipated the Communist movement. Programs for national regeneration, social and economic reform, mass mobilization, and the political education of the people were in no sense Communist monopolies. In the 1920's and 1930's, the KMT and even some of the provincial warlords spoke a language of modernization and mobilization that was in some respects very close to the language of Communist China. On the surface, the political system established by the CCP is a radical innovation in Chinese political history, but it depends heavily on the momentum for change that was building up during the preceding century.

Moreover, as noted many times, the political landscape of Communist China retains many of its old landmarks. No simple explanation can do justice to the intermingling of old and new in contemporary China. Jan Myrdal's record of his interviews with the residents of a village in northern Shensi in 1962 illustrates this point. For example, the Secretary of the local Party committee, a man who had been in the forefront of the Communist movement in the area since the 1930's, told Myrdal that family ties were very important in the revolution, that support of the

---

[1] See Ezra Vogel, "From Friendship to Comradeship: The Change in Personal Relationships in China," *China Quarterly*, No. 21 (January–March, 1965).

[2] For an excellent discussion of this point, see Mary C. Wright, "Modern China in Transition, 1900–1950," *Annals*, Vol. 321 (January, 1959).

revolution from relatives was more influential than propaganda from outside agitators.[3] Is this man's career, then, an example of political innovation (the recruitment of a poor peasant to revolutionary political leadership) or of the persistence of tradition (particularistic influences in all social action)? Again, Myrdal tells the story of a girl who, on her grandmother's authority, stayed out of school for a year before cadres persuaded her to return.[4] Are we to emphasize her grandmother's ability to resist the standards of the new society or the ultimate success of the cadres in implementing the wishes of the national government? Trivial in themselves, such examples demonstrate the need for caution in assessing the character and extent of political change in China. Although new modes of thought and behavior are omnipresent, and usually dominant when put to the test, they have neither replaced nor repressed all of the influences of the old society.

Political change in modern China has, therefore, been gradual and partial, rather than abrupt and total as the CCP and foreign observers sometimes suggest. Nevertheless, the cumulative effects are still immensely important, especially in the realm of popular political action. The Chinese Communist style of participation has its roots and forerunners in the republican period, but in terms of the politics of traditional China it is an unprecedented change. The way in which the CCP has extended the central government's authority down to the lowest levels of society and demanded political participation and commitment from every citizen is perhaps the most striking difference between the political system of Communist China and that of imperial China. For this reason, our study of political participation in Communist China may shed light on the more general question of Chinese political development.

One important point to note is the ease with which the Chinese Communist style of participation fits into its Chinese setting. This is a relative matter, of course, as mass political mobilization in China necessarily clashes with traditional political patterns. Political development in non-Western areas characteristically involves the introduction of new political institutions and relationships, which derive to some extent from foreign sources and which are imposed under the leadership of a foreign trained or foreign influenced elite. As a result, one of the typical problems of development is the "gap" between the urban, intellectual elite, who are at least partially "Westernized" in education and values, and the rural masses, who remain largely bound by tradition.[5] The "gap" between the modernistic culture of the elite and the tradition-

---

[3] Jan Myrdal, *Report from a Chinese Village,* trans. from the Swedish by Maurice Michael (New York, 1965), pp. 340, 348.

[4] *Ibid.,* p. 20.

[5] Edward Shils, *Political Development in the New States* (s'Gravenhage, 1962), especially chap. 2.

alistic culture of the masses creates mutual suspicions, resentments, and misunderstandings that greatly complicate the process of development. Modern China has not escaped this problem. The ideas that stimulated an interest in mass mobilization came from the West, whether through the liberal or Marxist–Leninist channel. New political institutions were imposed somewhat blindly in the republican period in a vain attempt to imitate the practice of the West, and there were certainly major differences between the treaty-port intellectuals and the rural masses. Nevertheless, the CCP has been relatively successful in minimizing the "gap" and its effects.

In soliciting mass political action, the Chinese Communists avoided imitation of Western democratic processes and focused on face-to-face discussion and indoctrination in familiar social settings. Although they established electoral and representative institutions, they never regarded them as the cornerstones of popular political life. Like the KMT's concept of tutelage, the CCP concept of participation placed more emphasis on education and elite leadership than on representative democracy, but, unlike the KMT, the CCP made it work. It worked partly because of the Party's organizational skills and partly because the Party infused it with certain values that had strong traditional appeal, primarily the idea of study as a road to reform and self-improvement and the insistence that political leadership derived its legitimacy from dedication to moral principles.

Moreover, the CCP has kept the elite-mass gap under control either by escaping it in the first instance or resisting it when it has appeared. In a very real sense, most of the older Party cadres are men of the people. They might be classified as intellectuals but they are neither urbanized nor Westernized. Although some studied abroad in their youth, they all spent major portions of their lives in relatively intimate contact with the masses, in most cases in rural areas. After 1949, the top leadership inevitably became more isolated from the people, and large numbers of youths and intellectuals who lacked the popular associations of the older cadres began to move into responsible positions. Still, the Party kept foreign influence to a minimum (it had little choice so far as the non-Communist West was concerned) and initiated techniques such as *hsia-fang* for forcing regular contacts between elites and masses. The mass line may be regarded, in part, as an effort to implant a populistic ethos in the culture of new China. The Chinese style of participation has, therefore, minimized many of the problems of political innovation and elite-mass relations that arise in the course of political development.

Popular political participation has had a much more ambiguous effect on the growth of functional differentiation and specialization in administration that is usually associated with political development. On the surface, the effect is not ambiguous at all but positively destructive. The primacy of politics and the emphasis on "redness" over "expertness" reveal a pronounced CCP desire to control and possibly restrict the growth of specialization. Above all, the mass line—including popular execution of policy and the idea that ideologically inspired mass movements can substitute for skill and training—is directly antithetical to administrative "modernization." If functional differentiation and specialization is a necessary condition of political development, then the Chinese style of participation is an obstacle to development. The relationship is not so simple, however. Some writers have suggested that a key difference between a "transitional" system and a "modernizing" system is precisely the latter's ability to establish the primacy of politics, to bring the bureaucracy under firm political control.[6] Moreover, even when political direction of the bureaucracy has been established, increasing specialization in administration may have a narrowing, divisive effect that reduces the bureaucracy's ability to promote a general political program and increases the possibility of disunity and rivalries within the government.[7]

In the light of these arguments, the CCP's assertion of the primacy of politics is not as antithetical to development as appears at first glance. In China, where the tradition of bureaucratic power is so strong and the need for unified and purposeful action so great, the CCP's hostility toward bureaucratic independence is understandable. It is significant, given the hypotheses just cited, that the CCP frequently equates desires for "expertness" with desires to "escape from politics." The Chinese leadership certainly noted that much of the criticism it received during the "hundred flowers" period (criticism it regarded as narrow and divisive) came from professional and technical circles on grounds that the Party ought not to meddle in matters requiring specialized competence. The fact is that the Party is determined to "meddle" in every sphere of public activity to ensure that its programs and priorities will be universally observed. The mass line and the popular political activities associated with it are, from the Party's point of view, tools for promoting political unanimity and weapons for checking the potentially divisive influence of bureaucrats and specialists. Of course the Chinese leaders are aware of the importance of specialization and technical competence;

[6] See Manfred Halpern, "Toward Further Modernization of the Study of New Nations," *World Politics*, 17:1 (October, 1964), and Fred W. Riggs, "The Theory of Developing Polities," *World Politics*, 16:1 (October, 1963).

[7] Fritz Morstein Marx, "The Higher Civil Service as an Action Group in Western Political Development," in Joseph LaPalombara, ed., *Bureaucracy and Political Development* (Princeton, 1963), pp. 70–75.

in critical fields, such as nuclear research and development, they obviously encourage it. However, the character of political life in China indicates that the leadership currently values the creation of national loyalties, unanimity, and purpose over the growth of functional differentiation and specialization.

If the CCP truly emphasizes nation-building over other aspects of political development, why has it tolerated the "survival of particularism" by structuring political activities around small functional units such as the neighborhood, the workshop, and the village? The commune experiment provides at least a partial answer. The formation of communes was certainly a frontal assault on particularism. Political and economic units were enlarged and assumed greater social functions, local leaders were shifted from one position to another, and the labor force generally became much more mobile. Had the experiment continued, it is doubtful if particularistic loyalties could have maintained their strength for long. Nevertheless, this aspect of the communes apparently had little influence on the decision to form them, a decision in which economic considerations were foremost. By the same token, the decision to retreat from the communes was also motivated mainly by economic difficulties and reinforced by the specter of diminished political control over the countryside. The point is simply this: the Chinese Communist leadership may be a modernizing force in historical perspective, but its immediate objectives and priorities are oriented toward the hard realities of political power. Specifically, the Party has placed, and will continue to place, the preservation of its political control and the development of the Chinese economy above all other objectives. In principle, the CCP has no desire to preserve the Chinese village and the kinship orientations that pervade it. In practice, it will do so if it finds that the population can thereby be organized more effectively for production and other urgent tasks.

A final point to which our analysis of political participation is relevant is the tension in Communist China between revolution and institutionalization. One critic of current theories of political development has argued that mass political mobilization without institutionalization produces political decay and disintegration rather than development; political development ought to be defined as "the institutionalization of political organization and procedures," institutionalization being "the process by which organizations and procedures acquire value and stability." [8] In general terms, the CCP has certainly created a stable political environment, an accomplishment which no other modern Chinese government can claim. It has given the Chinese people a fixed set of

[8] Samuel P. Huntington, "Political Development and Political Decay," *World Politics,* 17:3 (April, 1965), pp. 393–394.

national objectives, a single and apparently unshakable national authority, and a remarkably stable political leadership. Such stability ought to
provide a favorable climate for institutionalization, but it has not necessarily done so in China.

The political organizations and procedures in Communist China that
have acquired most value and stability are the Party itself and the mass
line, including the techniques of study, discussion, criticism, and emulation and the constant encouragement of "activism" in all modes of
conduct. The "institutionalization" of Party organization and leadership and of the mass line, and even of the mass movements as training
grounds for "revolutionary" thought and behavior, injects strong elements of continuity and predictability into Chinese politics. At the
same time, it has kept other political organizations and procedures in
nearly constant flux. Although functional groupings at the lowest level
of Chinese society have remained relatively stable since the early period
of political reconstruction, other basic-level organization has changed
frequently. Peasant associations were organized in the wake of Communist military victory, became the key political organizations in the
countryside, disappeared in 1953–1954, and are now reviving. Rural
production organization has gone through mutual-aid teams, two stages
of cooperativization, the communes, and back to a village-based cooperative within the administrative lines of the commune. Similar, though
less drastic, changes have occurred in the organization of the urban
labor force. Basic-level governmental units, as earlier discussion has
demonstrated, have been altered in 1951–1952, 1956–1957, 1958, and
1961–1962. The democratic parties have survived virtually intact in
name, and have endured longer than might have been anticipated in
1949, but the United Front has in no sense acquired value and stability
by its prolongation. Electoral and representative procedures have become sterile institutions, at least at the governmental level, and may
even have ceased to exist in the sense of a coordinated national system.
The operation of higher levels of government falls outside the scope of
this study, but it might be noted that there have been numerous changes
in the number and composition of the central ministries, that there has
been a great deal of experimentation with administrative centralization
versus decentralization and the character of Party control within individual enterprises, and that the judicial arm of government has been severely curtailed since 1956.

The radical contrast between CCP objectives and the actuality of the
society over which the Party assumed direction in 1949 may explain
much of this flux. A certain degree of institutional experimentation was
no doubt necessary. Nevertheless, our analysis of political participation
shows that the relative weakness of institutionalization in China is not

wholly a matter of necessity but rather to some degree a function of the CCP's political style which places a high value on mass mobilization and revolutionary action and a low value on institutions as such. This revolutionary style has not led to political instability and decay because of the strength of Party leadership and the thoroughness with which it has controlled the political actions of the mobilized population. The CCP's institutionalization of revolution has, therefore, compensated for its failure to promote institutionalization in a more general sense.

Earlier, we concluded that the CCP's hostility to functional differentiation and specialization was understandable in terms of its more compelling desire for the creation of national unanimity and purpose. Can its attempt to perpetuate a revolutionary style of politics also be explained in terms of developmental priorities? The idea of continuing revolution is admittedly a useful instrument for justifying the primacy of politics and the total mobilization of popular energies. When practiced, however, it also tends to depreciate the symbolic benefits that derive from regular participation in elections, representative bodies, and organizations that have a clear and permanent relationship to other parts of the political community. Nation-building in Communist China might profit greatly from more stable institutional arrangements for the demonstration of the new political values. These considerations have little impact on the present leadership, however, for its commitment to the revolutionary style stems from experience and habit, now reinforced by an almost pathological fear of "revisionism" at home and abroad.

So long as Mao and his colleagues survive, their prestige and determination will probably suffice to maintain the current political style. Once they are gone, the difficulty of perpetuating revolutionary enthusiasm in a nonrevolutionary situation will become one of the most critical problems for the second generation of leaders. There is no way to predict, with confidence, the resolution of this problem. In all probability, the mass line will remain in Party dogma—Mao's ideological legacy to the next generation, just as the demand for national regeneration was the legacy to his—but will yield in practice to a less revolutionary, less populistic, more institutionalized, and more bureaucratic political style. This trend will undoubtedly alter the character and extent of popular political participation, but the political awakening of the Chinese people will still stand as one of the most significant political changes in modern China.

BIBLIOGRAPHY

Compilations of Chinese Communist materials by non-Communist writers, except for serial translations, are included in the China section of secondary sources. The bibliography omits Chinese Communist newspaper and periodical articles as many are of minor importance and all are fully identified in the footnotes. However, all mainland newspapers and periodicals from which materials have been used are listed for general reference.

A. Chinese Communist Sources
1. Books and Documents
The Agrarian Reform Law of the People's Republic of China. Peking: FLP, 1950.
"Ch'eng-shih Chü-min Wei-yüan-hui Tsu-chih T'iao-li" (Regulations for the Organization of Urban Residents' Committees), *JMJP*, Jan. 1, 1955.
Chou En-lai. *Report on the Question of the Intellectuals.* Peking: FLP, 1956.
————. *Report on the Work of the Government.* Delivered at the First Session of the Second National People's Congress on April 18, 1959. Peking: FLP, 1959.
————. "Report on the Work of the Government," Delivered at the First Session of the Third National People's Congress on December 21–22, 1964, *Peking Review,* 1965, No. 1, pp. 6–20.
Chou Fang, ed. *Wo-kuo Kuo-chia Chi-kou* (Our State Structure). Rev. Peking: Jen-min Ch'u-pan She, 1957.
Chung-hua Jen-min Kung-ho-kuo Ti-i Chieh Ch'üan-kuo Jen-min Tai-piao Ta-hui Ti-ssu Tz'u Hui-i Wen-chien (Documents of the Fourth Session of the First National People's Congress of the People's Republic of China). Peking: Jen-min Ch'u-pan She, 1957.
"Chung-kung Chung-yang Kuan-yü Tsai Nung-ts'un Chien-li Jen-min Kung-she Wen-t'i ti Chüeh-i" (Resolution of the CCP Central Committee on the Problem of Establishing People's Communes in the Villages), *JMJP,* Sept. 10, 1958.
Chung-kuo Chih-kung Yün-tung ti Tang-ch'ien Jen-wu (Present Tasks of the Chinese Workers' Movement). Ed. by Chieh-fang She (Liberation Press). Shanghai: Hsin-hua Shu-tien, 1949.
Chung-kuo Kung-ch'an-tang Ti-liu Tz'u Ch'üan-kuo Ta-hui I-chüeh-an (Resolutions of the Sixth Congress of the Chinese Communist Party). N.p., n.d. [1928?].
"Chung-yang Hsüan-chü Wei-yüan-hui Kuan-yü Chi-ts'eng Hsüan-chü Kung-tso ti Chih-piao" (Directive of the Central Election Committee on Basic Level Election Work), *Ta Kung Pao,* April 6, 1953.
"Communique of the Ninth Plenum of the Eighth Central Committee of the Communist Party of China," *Peking Review,* 1961, No. 4, pp. 5–7.

"Communique of the Tenth Plenum of the Eighth Central Committee of the Communist Party of China," *Peking Review,* 1962, No. 39, pp. 5–8.

Documents of the First Session of the First National People's Congress of the People's Republic of China. Peking: FLP, 1955.

Eighth National Congress of the Communist Party of China. Peking: FLP, 1956. 3 vols.

The Electoral Law of the People's Republic of China. Peking: FLP, 1953.

The Historical Experience of the Dictatorship of the Proletariat. Peking: FLP, 1959.

Hu Yao-pang. *Revolutionize Our Youth!* Peking: FLP, 1964.

K'ang-Jih Chan-cheng Shih-ch'i Chieh-fang-ch'ü Kai-k'uang (The General Situation in the Liberated Areas During the Anti-Japanese War). Peking: Jen-min Ch'u-pan She, 1953.

"Kao-chi Nung-yeh Sheng-ch'an Ho-tso-she Shih-fan Chang-ch'eng" (Model Regulations for the Higher Agricultural Producers' Cooperatives), *1957 Jen-min Shou-ts'e,* pp. 173–179.

Labour Laws and Regulations of the People's Republic of China. Peking: FLP, 1956.

Laws and Regulations of the Shensi–Kansu–Ninghsia Border Region. [Yenan?]: 1945.

Li Kuang-ts'an. *Wo-kuo Kung-min ti Chi-pen Ch'üan-li ho I-wu* (The Basic Rights and Duties of Our Citizens). Peking: Jen-min Ch'u-pan She, 1956.

Liu Shao-ch'i. *On the Party.* Peking: FLP, 1950.

Lo Ch'iung, ed. *Fu-nü Yün-tung Wen-hsien* (Documents on the Women's Movement). 2d ed. Harbin: Tung-pei Shu-tien, 1948.

Lu Ting-yi. *"Let Flowers of Many Kinds Blossom, Diverse Schools of Thought Contend!"* Peking: FLP, 1950.

Lun Ch'ün-chung Lu-hsien (On the Mass Line). Hong Kong: Hsin Min-chu Ch'u-pan She, 1949.

Lun Jen-min Kung-she yü Kung-ch'an Chu-i (The People's Communes and Communism). Ed. by the Basic Marxism–Leninism Department of the Chinese People's University. Peking: 1958.

Mao Tse-tung. *Mao Tse-tung Hsüan-chi* (Selected Works of Mao Tse-tung). Peking: Jen-min Ch'u-pan She, 1961. 4 vols.

———. *Selected Works.* New York: International Publishers, 1954–1956. 4 vols.

———. *Selected Works of Mao Tse-tung.* Peking: FLP, 1961. Vol. IV.

———. *Let a Hundred Flowers Bloom* ["On the Correct Handling of Contradictions Among the People"]. Notes and intro. by G. F. Hudson. New York: The New Leader, n.d.

Shen-Kan-Ning Pien-ch'ü Hsiang-hsüan Tsung-chieh (A Summary of Village Elections in the Shen-Kan-Ning Border Region). [Yenan]: Shen-Kan-Ning Pien-ch'ü Min-cheng T'ing, 1941.

Shen-Kan-Ning Pien-ch'ü Ts'an-i-hui Wen-hsien Hui-chi (Collected Documents of the Shen-Kan-Ning Border Region Assembly). Ed. by Chung-kuo K'o-hsüeh-yüan Li-shih Yen-chiu-so Ti-san So (Third Office of the Institute of History of the Chinese Academy of Science). Peking: K'o-hsüeh Ch'u-pan She, 1958.

Sixth Plenary Session of the Eighth Central Committee of the Communist Party of China. Peking: FLP, 1958.

Socialist Industrialization and Agricultural Collectivization in China. Peking: FLP, 1964.

Su-wei-ai Chung-kuo (Soviet China). Moscow: Publishing House for Foreign Workers in the Soviet Union, 1933.

Tao Chu. *The People's Communes Forge Ahead.* Peking: FLP, 1964.

Ten Glorious Years. Peking: FLP, 1960.

Teng Hsiao-ping. *Report on the Rectification Campaign.* Peking: FLP, 1957.

Tung Pi-wu. *Memorandum on China's Liberated Areas.* San Francisco: 1945.

2. Newspapers Cited

Chang-chia-k'ou Jih-pao (Kalgan Daily).

Ch'ang-chiang Jih-pao (Yangtze Daily). Hankow.

Ch'ang-chou Jih-pao (Changchow Daily).

Ch'ang-ch'un Jih-pao (Changchun Daily).

Chi-lin Jih-pao (Kirin Daily). Changchun.

Chieh-fang Jih-pao (Liberation Daily). Shanghai.

Chin-pu Jih-pao (Progressive Daily). Tientsin.

Ch'ing-tao Jih-pao (Tsingtao Daily).

Chung-kuo Ch'ing-nien Pao (China Youth News). Peking.

Ch'ung-ch'ing Jih-pao (Chungking Daily).

Ho-nan Jih-pao (Honan Daily). Chengchow.

Hsin-hua Jih-pao (New China Daily). Chungking.

Hsin Wan-pao (New Evening News). Tientsin.

Jen-min Jih-pao (People's Daily). Peking.

Kuang-chou Jih-pao (Canton Daily).

Kuang-ming Jih-pao (Bright Daily). Peking.

Kuei-chou Jih-pao (Kweichow Daily). Kweiyang.

Kung-jen Jih-pao (Workers' Daily). Peking.

Lü-ta Jen-min Jih-pao (Port Arthur–Dairen People's Daily).

Nan-fang Jih-pao (Southern Daily). Canton.

Pei-ching Jih-pao (Peking Daily).

Shan-hsi Jih-pao (Shensi Daily). Sian.

Ssu-ch'uan Jih-pao (Szechwan Daily). Chengtu.

Ta-chung Jih-pao (Masses' Daily). Tsinan.

Ta Kung Pao (Impartial News). Peking. Published in Tientsin until October, 1956.

Ta Kung Pao (Impartial News). Hong Kong.

T'ien-chin Jih-pao (Tientsin Daily).

Wen-hui Pao (Literary News). Shanghai.

3. Periodicals Cited

Cheng-chih Hsüeh-hsi (Political Study). Monthly.

Cheng-fa Yen-chiu (Political and Legal Research). Bimonthly.

Chung-kuo Ch'ing-nien (China Youth). Semimonthly.

Chung-kuo Kung-jen (China Worker). Semimonthly.

Hsi-pei Ta-hsüeh Hsüeh-pao (Jen-wen K'o-hsüeh) [Journal of Northwestern University (Humanities)]. Quarterly.

Hsin Chien-she (New Construction). Monthly.

Hsin-hua Pan-yüeh K'an (New China Semimonthly). Replaced *Hsin-hua Yüeh-pao* in 1956.

Hsin-hua Yüeh-pao (New China Monthly).
Hsüeh-hsi (Study). Semimonthly. Discontinued in 1958.
Hung Ch'i (Red Flag). Semimonthly.
Jen-min Chiao-yü (People's Education). Monthly.
Jen-min Shou-ts'e (People's Handbook). Annual.
Peking Review. Weekly.
People's China. Semimonthly.
Shih-shih Shou-ts'e (Current Events). Semimonthly.
Tung Feng (East Wind). Semimonthly.
Wen-yi Pao (Literary Gazette). Semimonthly.

4. Serial Translations
American Consulate General. Hong Kong. *Current Background*. Irregular.
———. *Selections from China Mainland Magazines*. Weekly. Issues No. 1
    (August 15, 1955) through No. 213 (June 7, 1960) were titled *Extracts
    from China Mainland Magazines*.
———. *Survey of China Mainland Press*. Several times a week.
Union Research Institute. Hong Kong. *Union Research Service*. Approxi-
    mately twice weekly.

B. A Selected List of Secondary Sources
1. General
Almond, Gabriel A., and Sydney Verba. *The Civic Culture: Political Atti-
    tudes and Democracy in Five Nations*. Princeton: Princeton University
    Press, 1963.
Bendix, Reinhard. *Nation-Building and Citizenship: Studies of Our Changing
    Social Order*. New York: Wiley, 1964.
Binder, Leonard. "National Integration and Political Development," *Ameri-
    can Political Science Review*, 58:3 (September, 1964), pp. 622–631.
Fainsod, Merle. *How Russia is Ruled*. Cambridge, Mass.: Harvard Univer-
    sity Press, 1957.
Halpern, Manfred. "Toward Further Modernization of the Study of New
    Nations," *World Politics*, 17:1 (October, 1964), pp. 157–181.
Huntington, Samuel P. "Political Development and Political Decay," *World
    Politics*, 17:3 (April, 1965), pp. 386–430.
LaPalombara, Joseph, ed. *Bureaucracy and Political Development*. Prince-
    ton: Princeton University Press, 1963.
Lasswell, Harold D. *Psychopathology and Politics*. New ed. New York:
    Viking Press, 1960.
Lenin, V. I. *Selected Works*. New York: International Publishers 1943. 12
    vols.
Marx, Karl, and Frederich Engels. *Basic Writings in Politics and Philosophy*.
    Ed. by Lewis S. Feuer. Garden City: Doubleday Anchor Books, 1959.
Merriam, Charles E. *Systematic Politics*. Chicago: University of Chicago
    Press, 1945.
Merton, Robert K. *Social Theory and Social Structure*. Rev. and enl. ed.
    Glencoe: The Free Press, 1957.
Riggs, Fred W. "The Theory of Developing Polities," *World Politics*, 16:1
    (October, 1963), pp. 147–171.
Ritvo, Herbert, intro. and annotator. *The New Soviet Society: Final Text of
    the Program of the Communist Party of the Soviet Union*. New York: The
    New Leader, 1962.

Shils, Edward. *Political Development in the New States.* s'Gravenhage: Mouton, 1962.

Stalin, J. *Problems of Leninism.* Moscow: Foreign Languages Publishing House, 1953.

Venable, Vernon. *Human Nature: The Marxian View.* New York: Knopf, 1945.

Wolin, Sheldon S. *Politics and Vision.* Boston: Little, Brown, 1960.

2. China

Belden, Jack. *China Shakes the World.* New York: Harper, 1949.

Bisson, T. A. *Japan in China.* New York: Macmillan, 1938.

Bodde, Derk. *China's Cultural Tradition.* New York: Rinehart, 1957.

Boorman, Howard L. *"How To Be A Good Communist:* The Political Ethics of Liu Shao-ch'i," *Asian Survey,* 3:8 (August, 1963), pp. 372–383.

Brandt, Conrad. *The French-Returned Elite in the Chinese Communist Party.* Hong Kong: Hong Kong University Press, 1961. University of California, Center for Chinese Studies, reprint No. 13.

———. *Stalin's Failure in China.* Cambridge, Mass.: Harvard University Press, 1958.

Brandt, Conrad, Benjamin Schwartz, and John K. Fairbanks. *A Documentary History of Chinese Communism.* Cambridge, Mass.: Harvard University Press, 1952.

Burgess, John Stewart. *The Guilds of Peking.* New York: Columbia University Press, 1928.

Chao Kuo-chün. *Agrarian Policy of the Chinese Communist Party, 1921– 1959.* London: Asia Publishing House, 1960.

———. *The Mass Organizations in Communist China.* Cambridge, Mass.: Massachusetts Institute of Technology, Center for International Studies, 1953.

Ch'en Ch'üan, ed. *"Ming-fang" Hsüan-ts'ui* (Selections from the Blooming and Contending Campaign). Hong Kong: Tzu-yu Ch'u-pan She, 1958. 2 vols.

Cheng, J. Chester. "Problems of Chinese Communist Leadership as Seen in the Secret Military Papers," *Asian Survey,* 4:6 (June, 1964), pp. 861–872.

Chiang Kai-shek. *China's Destiny and Chinese Economic Theory.* With notes and commentary by Philip Jaffe. New York: Roy Publishers, 1947.

Ch'ien Tuan-sheng. *The Government and Politics of China.* Cambridge, Mass.: Harvard University Press, 1950.

China News Analysis. Hong Kong. Nos. 422 (May 25, 1962), 429 (July 20, 1962), and 432 (August 10, 1962).

Chinese Ministry of Information. *China Handbook, 1937–45.* Rev. and enl. with 1946 Supplement. New York: Macmillan, 1947.

Chow Tse-tsung. *The May Fourth Movement: Intellectual Revolution in Modern China.* Cambridge, Mass.: Harvard University Press, 1960.

Ch'ü T'ung-tsu. *Local Government in China Under the Ch'ing.* Cambridge, Mass.: Harvard University Press, 1962.

Cohen, Arthur A. *The Communism of Mao Tse-tung.* Chicago: University of Chicago Press, 1964.

"Comment" [On China's Descending Spiral], *China Quarterly,* No. 12 (October–December, 1962), pp. 140–159.

Communist China: The Politics of Student Opposition. Trans. with intro. by Dennis J. Doolin. Stanford University, The Hoover Institution, 1964.

Crook, David and Ysabel. *Revolution in a Chinese Village, Ten Mile Inn.* London: Routledge and Kegan Paul, 1959.

De Bary, William Theodore, Wing-tsit Chan, and Burton Watson, compilers. *Sources of Chinese Tradition.* New York: Columbia University Press, 1960.

Fairbank, John K., ed. *Chinese Thought and Institutions.* Chicago: University of Chicago Press, 1957.

————. *The United States and China.* Rev. and enl. Cambridge, Mass.: Harvard University Press, 1958.

Favre, B. *Les Sociétés Secrètes en Chine.* Paris: Maisonneuve, 1933.

Fei Hsiao-tung. *China's Gentry: Essays in Rural-Urban Relations.* Rev. and ed. by Margaret Park Redfield. Chicago: University of Chicago Press, 1953.

————. *Peasant Life in China.* London: Kegan Paul, Trench, Trubner, 1939.

Freedman, Maurice. *Lineage Organization in Southeastern China.* University of London, Athlone Press, 1958.

Gamble, Sidney D. *Ting Hsien: A North China Rural Community.* New York: Institute of Pacific Relations, 1954.

Gamble, Sidney D., and John Stewart Burgess. *Peking: A Social Survey.* New York: Doran, 1921.

Hofheinz, Roy. "Rural Administration in Communist China," *China Quarterly,* No. 11 (July–September, 1962), pp. 140–159.

Holcombe, Arthur N. *The Chinese Revolution.* Cambridge, Mass.: Harvard University Press, 1930.

Hsiao Kung-chuan. *Rural China: Imperial Control in the Nineteenth Century.* Seattle: University of Washington Press, 1961.

Hsieh Pao-chao. *The Government of China (1644–1911).* Baltimore: Johns Hopkins Press, 1925.

Hsu Yung Ying. *A Survey of the Shensi–Kiangsu [Kansu]–Ninghsia Border-Region.* New York: International Secretariat, Institute of Pacific Relations, 1945. Part I.

Isaacs, Harold R. *The Tragedy of the Chinese Revolution.* 2d rev. ed. Stanford: Stanford University Press, 1961.

Johnson, Chalmers A. *Peasant Nationalism and Communist Power.* Stanford: Stanford University Press, 1962.

Kiang Wen-han. *The Chinese Student Movement.* New York: King's Crown Press, 1948.

Kulp, Daniel Harrison. *Country Life in South China: The Sociology of Familism.* New York: Teachers College, Columbia University, 1925.

Leong, Y. K., and L. K. Tao. *Village and Town Life in China.* London: Allen and Unwin, 1915.

Lethbridge, Henry J. *China's Urban Communes.* Hong Kong: Dragon Fly Books, 1961.

Levenson, Joseph R. *Confucian China and Its Modern Fate: The Problem of Intellectual Continuity.* Berkeley and Los Angeles: University of California Press, 1958.

————. *Liang Ch'i-ch'ao and the Mind of Modern China.* Cambridge, Mass.: Harvard University Press, 1953.

Levy, Marion J. *The Family Revolution in Modern China.* Cambridge, Mass.: Harvard University Press, 1949.

Lewis, John Wilson. "The Leadership Doctrine of the Chinese Communist Party: The Lesson of the People's Commune," *Asian Survey*, 3:10 (October, 1963), pp. 457–464.

———. *Leadership in Communist China*. Ithaca: Cornell University Press, 1963.

Li Chien-nung. *The Political History of China, 1840–1928*. Trans. and ed. by Ssu-yu Teng and Jeremy Ingalls. Princeton: Van Nostrand, 1956.

Liang Ch'i-ch'ao. *History of Chinese Political Thought During the Early Tsin Period*. Trans. by L. T. Chen. New York: Harcourt, Brace, 1930.

Lifton, Robert J. *Thought Reform and the Psychology of Totalism: A Study of "Brainwashing" in China*. New York: Norton, 1961.

Linebarger, Paul M. A. *The China of Chiang K'ai-shek*. Boston: World Peace Foundation, 1941.

MacFarquhar, Roderick. *The Hundred Flowers Campaign and the Chinese Intellectuals*. New York: Praeger, 1960.

Mao's China: Party Reform Documents, 1942–1944. Trans. with intro. by Boyd Compton. Seattle: University of Washington Press, 1952.

Morse, Hosea Ballou. *The Gilds of China*. London: Longmans, Green, 1909.

Mu Fu-sheng. *The Wilting of the Hundred Flowers: The Chinese Intelligentsia Under Mao*. New York: Praeger, 1963.

Myrdal, Jan. *Report from a Chinese Village*. Trans. from the Swedish by Maurice Michael. New York: Random House, 1965.

Orleans, Leo. *Professional Manpower and Education in Communist China*. Washington: GPO, 1961.

Rickett, Allyn and Adele. *Prisoners of Liberation*. New York: Cameron, 1957.

Robertson, Frank. "Refugees and Troop Moves—A Report from Hong Kong," *China Quarterly*, No. 11 (July–September, 1962), pp. 111–115.

Rosinger, Lawrence K. *China's Wartime Politics, 1937–44*. Princeton: Princeton University Press, 1944.

Scalapino, Robert A., and George T. Yu. *The Chinese Anarchist Movement*. Berkeley: University of California, Institute of International Studies, Center for Chinese Studies, 1961.

Schram, Stuart R. *The Political Thought of Mao Tse-tung*. New York: Praeger, 1963.

Schurmann, H. Franz. "China's 'New Economic Policy'—Transition or Beginning," *China Quarterly*, No. 17 (January–March, 1964), pp. 65–91.

———. "Organization and Response in Communist China," *Annals*, Vol. 321 (January, 1959), pp. 51–61.

———. "Organizational Principles of the Chinese Communists," *China Quarterly*, No. 2 (April–June, 1960), pp. 47–58.

Schwartz, Benjamin I. *Chinese Communism and the Rise of Mao*. Cambridge, Mass.: Harvard University Press, 1958.

Skinner, G. William. "Marketing and Social Structure in Rural China," Part III, *Journal of Asian Studies*, 24:3 (May, 1965), pp. 363–399.

Smith, Arthur H. *Village Life in China: A Study in Sociology*. New York: Revell, 1899.

Snow, Edgar. *Red Star Over China*. Rev. ed. New York: Garden City Publishing Co., 1939.

Sun Yat-sen. *San Min Chu I*. Trans. by Frank W. Price. Shanghai: Commercial Press, 1928.

Teng Ssu-yü and John K. Fairbank. *China's Response to the West: A Documentary Survey, 1839–1923*. Cambridge, Mass.: Harvard University Press, 1954.

Vogel, Ezra. "From Friendship to Comradeship: The Change in Personal Relationships in China," *China Quarterly,* No. 21 (January–March, 1965), pp. 45–60.

W. K. "Communist China's Agricultural Calamities," *China Quarterly,* No. 6 (April–June, 1961), pp. 64–75.

Whiting, Allen S. *Soviet Policies in China, 1917–1924*. New York: Columbia University Press, 1954.

Wilbur, C. Martin, and Julie Lien-ying How, eds. *Documents on Communism, Nationalism, and Soviet Advisers in China, 1918–1927*. New York: Columbia University Press, 1956.

Wood, Shirley. *A Street in China*. London: Michael Joseph, 1958.

Wright, Mary C. "From Revolution to Restoration: The Transformation of Kuomintang Ideology," *Far Eastern Quarterly,* 14:4 (August, 1955), pp. 515–532.

———. "Modern China in Transition, 1900–1950," *Annals,* Vol. 321 (January, 1959), pp. 1–8.

Yang, C. K. *A Chinese Village in Early Communist Transition*. Cambridge, Mass.: Technology Press, Massachusetts Institute of Technology, 1959.

Yang, Martin C. *A Chinese Village: Taitou, Shantung Province*. New York: Columbia University Press, 1945.